Virtual Reality: The Last Human Narrative?

# Critical Posthumanisms

*Edited by*

Ivan Callus (*University of Malta*)
Stefan Herbrechter (*Coventry University*)

VOLUME 1

The titles published in this series are listed at *brill.com/cph*

# Virtual Reality: The Last Human Narrative?

*By*

Thorsten Botz-Bornstein

BRILL
RODOPI

LEIDEN | BOSTON

Cover illustration: Blend Images – Colin Anderson, Getty Images

Library of Congress Control Number: 2015944604

ISSN 1872-0943
ISBN 978-90-42-02109-9 (hardback)
ISBN 978-90-04-30230-3 (e-book)



This book is printed on acid-free paper.

# Contents

## Acknowledgements

I would like to thank the following journals for having granted the permission to reprint revised versions of their articles: *Philosophy in the Contemporary World, which* published 'Virtual Reality and Dream: Towards the Autistic Condition?' (now Chapter 2) in its 11:2, 2004 issue; *Cinemascope*, which published 'Would You Accept a Politics of "Multi-Realism?" Comparing *The Matrix* with Tarkovsky's *Stalker* and *Solaris*' (now Chapter 3) in its 10, 2008 issue. *Angelaki*, which published 'Genes and Pixels: Popular Bio-Genetics Virtual Aesthetics' (now Chapter 5) in its 11:2, 2006 issue; *Seeking Wisdom*, which published 'All-Unity Seen Through Perspective or the Narrative of Virtual Cosmology' (now Chapter 7) in its 2, 2005 issue; *Continuum: Journal of Media and Cultural Studies*, which published 'What Would Nietzsche Have Said About Virtual Reality? Dionysus and Cyberpunk' (now Chapter 8) in its 25:1, 2011 issue; *CTheory*: *An International Journal of Theory, Technology and Culture*, which published 'The Clony-Virtual Dreamsphere' (now Feature Scene 1) in its November 2003 issue and 'Liquid Grammar, Liquid Style: On the East-Asian Way of Using English or Reflections on the Linguistic Air-Guitar' (now Feature Scene III) in its April 2006 issue; *Janus Head: Journal of Interdisciplinary Study in Literature and Continental Philosophy*, which published 'The New Surrealism: Loft Stories, Reality Television, and Amateur Dream-Censors' (now Feature Scene IV) in its Summer 2006 issue; *Kritikos, which* published 'Overcoming the Logos, Overcoming Lego: From Imagined Space to the Spatial Imagination of the Bionicle World' (now Feature Scene VI) in its 2: 2006 issue; I also thank Sura P. Rath who published 'From Civilization to Culture: About the Dreamlike Character of Global Civilization' (now Chapter 4) in her *Dialogics of Cultural Encounters: New Conversation Among Nations and Nationalities* (Delhi: Pencraft International, 2005).

# Introduction

## 1. Uncritical Posthumanism

This book on virtual reality appears in the book series "Critical Posthumanisms", a series that attempts to foster a critical attitude towards posthuman phenomena.[1] Critical posthumanism exists already in various forms, reaching from straightforward anti-cloning campaigns to sophisticated studies informed by disciplines such as structuralism, postcolonial studies, and feminism. Even if one is tempted to ridicule an elastic concept such as "postmodernism" because of its largely unspecified character one has to admit that during the last thirty years or so, together with the rejection of totalizing concepts such as "progress", "race", "rigor", etc., also the idea of the "human" has suffered and will most probably continue to do so. "Uncritical posthumanism" (I avoid calling it "popular posthumanism" or "transhumanism") celebrates the continuation of the human by non-human means (for example, a new techno-bio body) as well as the creation of a reality by "unreal" means. Futurist ideologies of posthumanism suppose that human beings may eventually expand their abilities through different forms of enhancement that merit the label posthuman. One day the constraints of the human condition will have been abolished; humans will be freed of their bodies, united with a computer, and reach immortality. In Wally Pfister's film *Transcendence* (2014), human consciousness is uploaded into a quantum computer enabling the protagonist to not only live in a virtual form but also to use the vast amount of intelligence that has become available to build a technological utopia in a remote desert town.

Originally, posthumanism developed around an appeal for the cyborg in the 1980s and 1990s and fostered an intellectual attitude that sees the body as a commodity malleable in the hands of modern technology predicting a prosthetic "biocultural" future. This attitude is often sparked off by "weariness with the human condition itself" (Baillie & Casey 2005: 31). In 1991 the artist Stelarc announced that it is "time to question whether a bipedal, breathing body with binocular vision and a 1,400cc brain is an adequate biological form" (Stelarc 1991: 591). Equally in the early nineties, the "World Transhumanist

Association" declared that "humanity will be radically changed by technology in the future. We foresee the feasibility of redesigning the human condition" (quoted in Winner 2005: 392). Closely linked to this adventure are ambitions to make life eternal, as they were pronounced by Human Genome Science CEO William Haseltine who said that "as we understand the body's repair process at the genetic level [...] we will be able to advance the goal of maintaining our bodies in normal function perhaps perpetually" (quoted in Fukuyama 2002: 18).

All these statements concern the body which posthumanists attempt to make "more self-contained [and] energy-efficient" (Stelarc 1991: 592). The brain represents a similar challenge. Strictly speaking, it is not the brain as a self-contained machine that fascinates posthumanism; such an entity is rather an object of interest for more technical branches of cognitive science. The item that has received a good deal of interest in posthuman theory is *consciousness* as a mixture of intellectual, bodily, and spatial awareness. While bioengineering and nanotechnology (which develops molecular-scale self-replicating machines) establish a posthuman body, digitality establishes a consciousness able to function posthumanly. Katherine Hayles thinks that the coupling of human cognition to digital machinery makes the construction of posthuman beings possible (Hayles 1999: 3). Things become compelling and much more dynamic at the moment the cognitive-digital domain and the prosthetic-bodily domain begin to overlap. "Merging with computerized entities requires an extension of our humanity", writes Michael Heim (Heim 1998: 62). While a first phase of posthumanism came of age simply through the coupling of the natural and the technological, a second phase announced itself through the interaction of body-technology and consciousness-digitality, biotechnology or bioinformatics, as mergers of biology and information technology let computers interpret and build models provided by biological sciences, especially genomics. "Biological and digital domains are no longer rendered ontologically distinct", writes Eugene Thacker (2004: 7), which means that the posthuman reality is no longer a reality "out there" but a realm established in relationship with both consciousness and the body. "The biological 'informs' the digital just as the digital 'corporealizes' the biological", continues Thacker (7). The body is no longer, as Hans Moravec still postulated, a container of consciousness that can one day be cast away because "consciousness" can be unloaded into some sort of brain vat.[2] On the contrary, the body itself is both biomolecular and "'compiled' through modes of visualization, modeling, data extraction, and *in siclo* simulation" (Thacker: 13). To this must be added the fact that biotechnology is more and more web-based and takes place in a web-lab.

The Copernican revolution led humanity to recognize that it did not stand at the center of the universe; the genomic revolution showed us that we are "the most undistinguished spot at the periphery of evolution" (Sagoff 2005: 68); finally, the digital revolution shows us that reality itself is not a stable platform on which we can stand but that it is manipulable, prone to all sorts of combinations and hybridizations dependent on consciousness and the body.

## 2. Critical Posthumanism and Critical Humanism

The present book does not embrace the posthuman as an exciting adventure nor does it attempt to reinstall "humanism". It steers a middle course able to locate the *human in the posthuman*. This is what I see as the task of critical posthumanism. Criticism of nature-transcending technology has a long tradition in Western culture, beginning with the Greek myth of Prometheus who stole fire from Zeus, gave it to humans and was punished for it. Critics who find optimistic utopian posthuman visions simplistic and dangerous can be called "humanists." However, "humanism" is also the name of the Renaissance movement trying to revive classical learning and basing universal standards on what it believed to be human. Inscribing my reflections on the posthuman into a poststructuralist critique of universal values, "humanism" is certainly not the point to which I want to recede, be it only for the reason that uncritical posthumanists (or transhumanists) often base their approach on precisely this humanism. Nick Bostrom states that "transhumanism has roots in rational humanism" of the enlightenment because "in the 18th and 19th centuries we catch glimpses of the idea that humans themselves can be developed through the application of science" (Bostrom 2005: 3). In other words, uncritical posthumanism cannot and does not even attempt to escape humanist metaphysics or anthropocentrism (see Herbrechter 2013: 15). Cary Wolfe very aptly calls transhumanism or uncritical posthumanism an "intensification of humanism" (Wolfe 2010: xv).

Critical posthumanism reevaluates the meanings of both the human and the posthuman. I thus share the basic convictions of Rosi Braidotti and Stefan Herbrechter who find that the existence of posthuman technology is also due to a "crisis and end of a certain conception of the human, namely the humanist notion of the human" (Herbrechter 2013: 3). In her philosophy of the posthuman, Braidotti criticizes the erasing of categorical distinctions between the human and other species from which contemporary market economies profit and concludes that "advanced capitalism and its bio-genetic technologies engender a perverse form of the posthuman" (Braidotti 2013: 7). Braidotti is very much aware that "the fluid workings of power in advanced or cognitive capitalism, also known as information or network society" (159) in combination with the above mentioned movements can create a dangerous situation. Still she does not want to reestablish the human as a self-enclosed notion. In critical posthumanism, the human needs to be deconstructed while uncritical posthumanism *constructs* a posthuman utopia that remains dependent on humanism's premises.

Finally, this kind of critique of the posthuman also differs from that of the Future of Life Institute (founded in 2014), which points out the risks of technical development by explaining that while this kind of "'intelligence' is related to statistical and economic notions of rationality", researchers need to be urged to "maximize the societal benefit of AI" (FLI Open Letter). For critical posthumanists, this kind of criticism is insufficient.

### 3. The Last Human Narrative

In posthumanism, the human is combined with non-human elements, which can lead to a post-anthropocentric situation in which the world develops without humans. Already today, non-human action is sufficient, for example, to lead wars. Does virtual reality represent such a posthuman world? Or is it a world at all? And if it is merely a narrative, is it narrated by humans or by non-humans? This book continues earlier metaphysical discussions about the status of the virtual as a reality, a half-reality, or a special kind of being (see Heim 1993, 1998; Ryan 2001). More precisely, my critical posthumanist agenda consists in characterizing the posthuman world as the latest grand narrative produced by humanity: the narrative of VR. "Narrative" is defined as "the representation of an event or a series of events" (Abbot 2002: 12). Lyotard's statement that "the grand narrative [progress, Marxism, etc.] has lost its credibility" (Lyotard 1984: 37) has generally been accepted but I believe that it is still possible to describe the whole process of civilization as a process that transforms reality into a mediated, narrated reality. In this sense, VR represents the last stage of a continuous development.

Critical posthumanism must be concerned with paradoxes. The first paradox is that, on the one hand, VR, which is "only" a narrative, is de-centered, playful, godless, and disenchanted because all truths it contains have been *made* and not *found*.[3] On the other hand, for reasons of this reality's synthetic power of identification and expansion or simply because of its all-inclusiveness, it can also be seen as *transcendental*. When Robert Pepperell writes that "recent theories of quantum physics have suggested that the traditional division between mind and reality is in doubt" (Pepperell 2003: 6), what he means is *not* that reality will be submitted to a Humeian sort of Matrix-like subjectivism in which "embodiment has become irrelevant" (Jenny Wolmark 2002: 83). His point is rather that in posthuman reality the relation between consciousness (traditionally defined as feelings, emotions, memories, and other mental states) and the world is no longer limited to subjectivism or objectivism but that from now on consciousness is not in the brain alone but "distributed throughout the whole body" (Pepperell: 4). This means that what Pepperell and Winner (2005) call the "posthuman condition" is not limited to the replacement of body parts with technological items but that it concerns a change of consciousness. In contemporary biosciences, the combination of neural and cognitive sciences with the informatics sector makes the technological mediation of human subjects complex and unprecedented.

The "posthuman condition" concerns all mental states including that of eroticism, which becomes a sort of "techno-eroticism" (Springer 1996) directed, for example, towards the Japanese *Mecha Shôjo* (*Mecha Musume* in the West) who is a combination of a beautiful girl and a (weapon like) machine. This imaginary is not typically Japanese but has its own tradition in European fiction. It can be seen as a continuation of Villiers de l'Isle-Adam's Symbolist science fiction imaginary produced in the novel *Future Eve* (1886); or of the demonical robot Maria in Fritz Lang's *Metropolis* (1927). A statement by the British writer J.G. Ballard illustrates in a particularly graphic way the consequences that this will have for the life of humans: "I believe that organic sex, body against body, skin area against skin area, is becoming no longer possible […]. The whole overlay of new technologies are beginning […] to reach into our lives and change the interior design of our sexual fantasies" (Ballard 1984: 157; quoted in Shigematsu 1999: 127). A. Newitz has an original explanation for the "naturalness" of the Mecha Shôjo: "female bodies are (…) best suited to mecha (…) precisely because it is related to reproduction and giving birth" (Newitz 1995: 9).

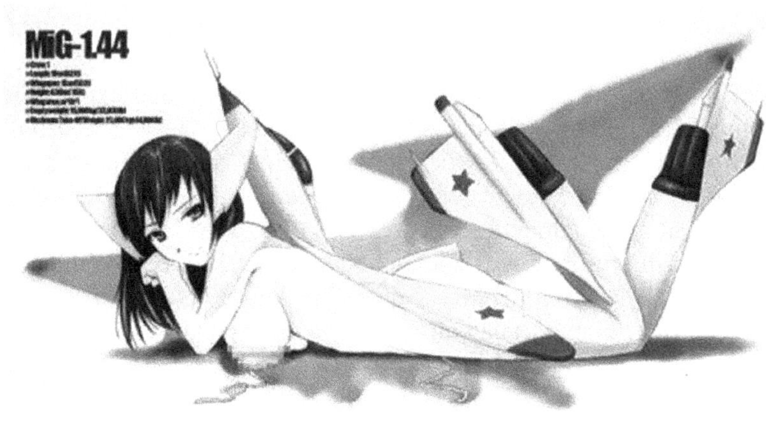


Fig. 1: Mecha Musume

This shows that VR as well as the posthuman world of bioengineered beings is not a utopian, "second world" that can be enthusiastically embraced or refused. On the contrary, in this new world "reality" as much as the body with all its traditional quests continue to exist. It is rather through the mutual interference of body, consciousness and reality that a new space of VR is created. And since consciousness is located in the body as much as in the space within which this body acts, space requires an entirely new dimension as we can guess by simply reading the title of Gregory Stock's book *Metaman: The Merging of Humans and Machines into a Global Superorganism*. In this book the author claims that the "progressively deepening union between humans and machines is symbiotic" (Stock 1993: 60) and will eventually develop into a "planetary creature" (53).

The role of VR in a posthuman world can only be understood within the network of these links that exist between consciousness, reality, and the body. VR is not just a new kind of space but has replaced a certain spontaneity of direct perception – that could traditionally be defined as a straightforward relationship between the subject and the object – with a sort of commodified "second world" that it constantly reproduces.

Francis Fukuyama discusses in his *Our Posthuman Future* Aldous Huxley's *Brave New World* and common reactions to his world as a realm in which people "may be healthy and happy, but [...] have ceased to be *human*" because Huxley's system is "against human nature" (Fukuyama 2002: 6). Fukuyama ridicules these reactions because neither "being human" nor its importance can be defined in an absolute manner (Fukuyama largely follows Leon Kass's interpretation of Huxley, Kass 2001). Any arguments reproaching the *Brave New World* and its intrinsic inhumanism (or posthumanism) establish, so Fukuyama finds, "the human" in a circular fashion as an ethical ground and at the same time as a value dependent on this ground.

Fukuyama's discussions of Huxley does not lead towards a defense of *Brave New World* schemes but rather towards the recommendation of tough government checks in order to prevent the breeding of "people with saddles on their backs" (9). This is Fukuyama's version of "critical posthumanism". However, his almost hysterical focus on *inhuman* bioengineering but simultaneous lax dismissal of anything intrinsically *inhuman* in the *Brave New World* is alarming. In my opinion, what the people in *The Brave New World* loose is not an objectified version of "human" characteristics but simply *reality*. At the moment they "no longer struggle, aspire, love, [and] feel pain" (Fukuyama) they live in a dreamworld in which nothing ever signals that things do really exist. This concept of "reality as resistance" (which follows from the philosophy of Friedrich Bouterwek who coined the concept of "virtual reality" at the end of the eighteenth century), helps to understand what is at stake in discussion on VR and bioengineering. Huxley is not at all recommending to "continue to feel pain, be depressed or lonely", as Fukuyama tries to make us believe, but points to the importance of clinging to *reality* as "the true, yet ephemeral fruit of human life" which is "the surprise [and] the beauty…" (Baillie 2005: 231) and which some kind of VR attempts to undermine, but which remains the only world that it is worth living in.

Critical posthumanism, far from diabolizing VR and bioengineering, settles somewhere between extreme idealism and naïve realism. It attempts to disentangle the common characteristics of human reality and posthuman VR and to establish communicative links between both by firmly sticking to the Baudrillardian conviction that simulation should never win over reality. This is how it will be able to locate the *human in the posthuman*.

As mentioned, the de-centered, playful narrative of VR that is at the same time universal or even transcendental asks for an approach able to take into consideration paradoxes. As a matter of fact, in terms of methodology, critical posthumanism enters a ground that is not well trodden because such curious conceptual combinations of subjectivity and pretensions towards something absolute remain rare in the history of Western thought. Kant's *sensus communis* comes to mind because, just like Kant's construct, the narrative of VR is simultaneously intimate and universal. Kant introduced the term *sensus communis* as a theoretical tool able to grasp the intrinsic character of aesthetic expressions. To Kant it was obvious that aesthetic judgments are subjective, that they are *made* and not *found* by reason in the form of rational rules. However, at the same time he saw that these subjective judgments need to be also universal: what *one* person judges to be beautiful must also be found beautiful at least by many others, otherwise the idea of the beautiful does not make sense. Therefore Kant introduces, in Section 20 of the *Critique of Judgment*, the *sensus communis* (*Gemeinsinn*) as the human ability to judge according to the same "feeling" (*sensus*, *Gefühl*), which is subjective though at the same time universal and transcendental. Aesthetic judgments are declared to be transcendentally valid through a paradoxical *sensus communis*.[4] As shown above, VR is based on a similarly paradoxical constellation and critical posthumanism must take this into consideration. The playful and subjective narrative of VR is at the same time an "All-Unity", if we use the term commonly used in English translations of the works of Russian philosopher Berdyaev whose ideas will be the subject of Chapter 7.

Critical posthumanism approaches VR through still two other paradoxes. One is represented by the fact that, in principle, there is no reason to call the posthuman reality "posthuman" because, after all, it is a project led *by humans*. Still another paradox has to do with the peculiar status of immediacy in VR. On the one hand, our postmodern civilization is dominated by the desire to elude narratives and to experience reality "immediately", that is in an "unmediated" way and in "life" time. On the other hand, the methods that are pursued in order to enable this experience are *technological* and create a second hand reality that, in return, closely resembles a narrative.

## 5. Psychoanalysis, Gene-Technology, Virtual Reality

In this sense, the different chapters of the present book address various aspects of contemporary civilization that are determined by a shift from an "original event" to a virtual "narrative": VR (first of all), but also psychoanalysis, gene-technology, and globalization. Psychoanalysis transformed the dream into a narrative, and, consequently, was able to spell out the dream's symbols. Similarly, gene-technology narrates dynamic, self-evolving evolution as a "gene code". This means that what has first been "nothing" but an undeterminable *process* of "generation" is now spelled out in the form of a code that contains "genes" as elements constituting "generation". Finally reality itself (with all its dreamlike and perhaps virtual components) also has come to be narrated in the form of a second reality that is called "virtual". One might say that the only phenomenon that has not yet been fully "narratized" is "the world", though the discourse on "globalization" (in French "mondialisation", which means "worldization") does its best to let the *globe* appear as once more *globalized* because reproduced through narrative.

In spite of its consistency, a decisive aspect needs to be considered within this version of a history of civilization, an aspect which flows out of the very nature of the new element called "the virtual". The model of "the world as a narrative" makes most sense with regard to Freud when he tried to transform dreams into narratives in order to evaluate them scientifically. It still makes sense with regard to television or the media in general. The particular point about the above-mentioned, more recent, phenomena succeeding psychoanalysis is, however, that these phenomena attempt to reach back to an "originality" that is not simply an "event". In other words, what is at stake in VR, gene-technology, and globalization is much more than the desire to "narrate the world". The striking point about VR, the gene-code, and globalization is that even *if* these phenomena end up as nothing more than as a narrative of something that exists "out there", their existence itself is due to the desire to *elude* any narrative and to express reality "directly". Gene technology tries to grasp not a certain – temporally definable – stage of the entire process of *generation*, but the *gene* itself, as the essential quantity of generation that has no *real* place in generation itself. Globalization "globalizes" the globe and represents it as something that is neither the "real world" nor its narration but a new sphere that we have to accept as such.

In order to examine the paradoxical approach of VR, gene-technology, and globalization, it will first be necessary to establish also the "other" understanding of the virtual that diverges strikingly from the common use of the term "virtual". This is the virtual understood as something dreamlike, unstable and fleeting that can never be transformed into a narrative. I try to establish *this* sense of VR in Chapter 2, by untangling the relationships between the virtual, the dream, the imaginary, and reality, and by analyzing them on the utmost abstract, linguistic level. The "virtual" is reflected against that aspect of life which French philosophers of the 1950s used to call the "existential" one and which, eighty years before them, Nietzsche had called "the tragic". My own terminology is established here. Most of the time I am inclined to call this virtual aspect of life the "dreamlike" one, though I also decided to call it, provocatively, simply "the virtual". I make clear in which way a narrated reality functions as a substitute reality. Such a narrated reality is represented by VR, by eternal life obtained through cloning, as well as by a globalized world (as it designs itself as a repository of the end of history, or as a state of world civilization hardened through opposing core civilizations).

In Chapter 3, I criticize the material concept of civilization by pointing to the fundamental "unrealness" of culture as such. Culture *is* global, and in this sense, it is also always virtual. Culture is a non-materialized, virtual entity, whereas so-called "real" societies like those empirically crystallized by anthropologists through customs, rules or habits, are only objects. Therefore, instead of attempting to establish a world order according to civilizational laws, we should make an effort to recognize the dreamlike state of reality, that is, try to grasp intersubjective cultural experiences that are always linked to the perception of the other.

In Chapter 4, I attempt to apply a similar analysis to the world of bio-genetics by revealing the virtual character of genes in popular bio-genetics. Though Baillie and Casey believe that "genetic mapping and sequencing have [not] yielded the meaning of life" (Baillie & Casey 2005: 10), it is clear that the map of genes *is* a certain kind of narrative. The point is that genes never tell a story about reality but that they generate a "virtual reality" of their own. I claim that a large part of the popular fascination with genes is derived from this "virtual character" of genes. "Reality" tells us that the logic underlying historical processes as well as biological formation (a logic by which philosophers have often been fascinated) cannot be grasped because, "in reality", this logic is nothing. Through genetics however, a part of this logic can suddenly be crystallized within a kind of "narrative" presented in the form of the "genetic map". Along these lines, genes are telling a posthuman narrative that, as Halberstam and Livingston have said, has "replaced previous masternarratives about humanity" (Halberstam & Livingston 1995: 4).

Such a posthuman narrative is also *The Matrix*, as I show in Chapter 5, where I compare three different science fiction films. The "cognitive manipulations" thesis in *The Matrix* employs a one-dimensional model of reality while in Tarkovsky's *Solaris* and in *Stalker* the establishment of a posthuman reality is more ambiguous. In *The Matrix* the shift from human "real" reality to a posthuman VR produces a simplistic idea of "humanity" while in *Solaris* and *Stalker* it remains undefined what it actually means to be human.

In Chapter 6 I examine the aesthetic notion of kitsch and contrast it with traditional values of Japanese aesthetics. Kitsch is linked to the virtual because of its insistence on immediacy of perception as well as its potential of cultural condensation. Japanese traditional art, on the other hand, (just like the art of Jeff Koons, Marcel Duchamp and Andy Warhol) cannot be "kitschified" because these aesthetics suggest a paradoxical and tautological re-articulation of reality, that is, a kind of non-articulated nothingness that necessarily remains beyond all expression. Because they are represented by such a self-regulatory system, they can also appear as posthuman and are clearly linked to the realm of the virtual.

VR represents the idea of a non-physical space enabling humans to grasp the world as a whole. By examining the history of spatial presentation, I show that VR appears as an "All-Unity" seen from one single perspective (Chapter 7). Originally, in the history of philosophy, the religious idea of All-Unity contained a "tragic" and existential moment. However, this tragic moment was stifled in the Renaissance through the invention of "perspective". In Renaissance, according to the Russian philosopher Berdyaev, "the inner drama and dynamic stirring related to religious experience were replaced by a single, static, idolizing gaze dependent only on one single perspective" (Berdyaev 1930: 50). VR offers a new aperspectival consciousness of the whole. I examine whether the current spreading of VR and of "cyberspace" cannot be linked to visions of an all-unifying end of history.

All this leads to provocative questions about ontological parallels between the world of the virtual and the world of autists. Characteristic for autists is an obvious lack of abstraction with regard to space and time, which makes one inclined to define autism as "Hyper-Bergsonism". For autists, everything, including space and time is concrete. But this absolute concreteness becomes an abstraction, precisely because it is absolute. Also here, the "tragic" can be avoided, but, in the end, efforts to live in an eternal present will not succeed. The autistic child substitutes "reality" with an empty game in which reality has no ludic or dreamlike quality.

First of all, the autism-virtual link is provided by the fact that autistic children prefer to play (certain types) of video games. Micah Mazurek and his team at the University of Missouri discovered that 64.2% of youths with ASD spent most of their free time using non-social media (television or video games) (Mazurek et al. 2011).

Whether the connection works the other way round is a different question: does playing video games create autism? Some serious research does suggest this even with regard to television though with many restrictions. Waldman, Nicholson and Adilov (2006) explore in their paper "Does Television Cause Autism?" the hypothesis that "a small segment of the population is vulnerable to developing autism because of their underlying biology and that either too much or certain types of early childhood television watching serves as a trigger for the condition." It does not cause autism, but might "trigger" it. It has also been found that video games can reduce empathy because of the realistic killing (as opposed to the killing of cartoon characters) that is depicted. Douglas Gentile concludes in a quantitative survey of scientific studies that 136 scientific papers on violent video games put forward the concept that playing those games leads to desensitization and aggressive behavior (Bavelier et al. 2011). Again this does not concern all video games. Over the last few years, several researchers have also developed video games that are supposed to teach children with autism to make eye contact or recognize others' emotions. Recent studies by game specialists like David Golumbia ("Games without Play", 2009) explore this line of thought. I will deal with this phenomenon in the conclusion.

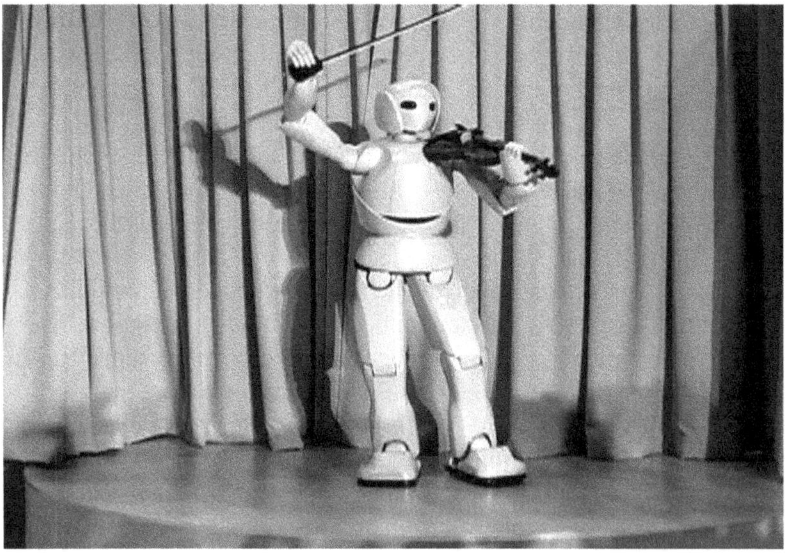

Fig. 2: Toyota's Morobo robot

In several chapters throughout the book I point to the fact that posthumanism has a different face in Far Eastern traditions. It has often been remarked that the distinction between *humans* that have a soul and animals that have no soul does not exist in non-Christian cultures. As a consequence, posthumanism is received in these cultures with less concern. In Japan, this attitude can partly be traced to Buddhism and Shintoism, which holds that all objects possess a spirit (see Bartneck et al. 2007). The Japanese distinguish less strictly the artificial from the natural, and Frédéric Kaplan finds that for the Japanese, "building machines is a positive activity in search of the natural laws that govern [the world]" (Kaplan 2004: 9; see also Gilson 1998). In Japan, which is, according to Ian Buruma, "at once one of the most natural and the most artificial of places" (Buruma 1984: 110), the distance between humans and machines is less large and robots are judged from a more aesthetic point of view. Japanese robots can even contain a considerable amount of cuteness. This does not mean that Japanese would be uncritical towards artificial life; especially hybridizations of humans and machines (cyborgs) are not met with much enthusiasm (Kaplan 2004: 3). Polls have shown that Japanese are most worried about the *emotional* impact of robots, a concern less frequently expressed by Americans (Bartneck et al.).

On the other hand, curiously, real human beings can adopt in Japan a robot like existence as is often the case with doll-like television *talantos*, who are teen stars artificially created through choreographed movements and mechanical smiles, who seem to be appreciated by the public *because* of their flagrant lack of humanity (cf. Buruma 68).

For this reason also the aforementioned posthuman indistinction between the subject and "reality" obtains a new status in the context of East-Asian cultures. David Peat writes about the East-Asian concept of "reality":

> This holistic notion of the atomic world was the key to Bohr's Copenhagen interpretation. It was something totally new in physics, although similar ideas had long been taught in the East. For more than 2000 years, Eastern philosophers have talked about the unity between the observer and that which is observed. They had pointed to the illusion of breaking apart a thought from the mind that thinks the thought.[5]

Peculiar concepts of "virtual reality" will flow out of these constellations; and they become most obvious in the domain of aesthetics. Specialists of Far Eastern art explain that in the East, art is always *necessarily* virtual. For Ryôsuke Ohashi, for example, Japanese culture attempts to attain a vision of the *real world* as something virtual *by means of an aesthetics of the virtual*. According to him, in Japanese culture the paradox which makes the imagined "non-real" more existential than the "virtual real" disappears. Art is a VR as it exists not only for itself but also permits us to recognize the virtual character of *all* reality.[6]

In the "West", on the other hand, the virtual has another status. When, quite unexpectedly, the term VR was introduced to the public in the late 1980s and consequently examined by Western philosophers, it appeared, curiously, not as a component of art but in the form of a quality sticking to a kind of non-existent space created by computers and through electronic communication. For reasons that would never really be examined, it seemed to be predestined to function as an integral element of a posthuman type of new reality. Philosophers tried to disentangle some of these concepts, which was, of course, no easy task, first of all because there was almost nowhere to look for philosophical approaches systematically explaining the nature of the virtual. The only thing that was clear from the beginning was that VR was not simply a matter of illusion (similar to postmodern simulation) created by sophisticated technology. Though formally, VR appeared to be very much like television, it also included a psychologically and ontologically disconcerting quality. Terms like "transcendentality" or "Absolute Spirit" quickly occurred and could not be eradicated. To many, virtual space spontaneously appeared as something "spiritual". At the same time, paradoxically, a human or aesthetic quality of the virtual would never gain over the posthuman, technological one.

My claim is that the phenomenon commonly known as VR should be opposed to a more intimate type of VR that does not aspire to create, as does the latter, a *second reality*, but that creates an *irreality*.[7] VR lacks the existential component that Virtual *Irreality* considers as its main purpose of existence. The shift from posthumanism to "critical posthumanism" is effectuated through this distinction. What distinguishes the Virtual Irreality from common, technological VR is that the latter follows the principal lines of Western aesthetics and attempts to establish an alternative kind of "virtual realism" by means of logic and reason. Zola's approach of capturing "life itself" is based on the "reasonable" approach of attempting to reproduce reality. It is opposed to "Romantic" ways of grasping the world based on personal feelings and other subjective components. However, even when reality is perfectly "represented" to the point that it appears as absolutely real, the fact of re-presenting "something" cannot escape subjectivism.

What Zola can be reproached with represents also the weakest point of computerized VR. Critical posthumanism has to define the subtle differences between a VR in the sense of a technological narrative and an existential Virtual Irreality that interprets the virtual in a more "human" fashion.

The present book develops *philosophical* ideas about the virtual as an abstract notion. It also attempts to spell out in which way precisely VR affects contemporary culture. In a way, it combines philosophy with cultural studies. In brief "Feature Scenes" that appear between the chapters, the practice of VR and posthumanism is demonstrated in the form of sometimes ironical presentations.

## Notes

1. On the definition of critical posthumanism see Callus & Herbrechter 2015 (forthcoming).
2. Moravec, *Une vie après la vie* (Paris: Odile Jacob, 1992). See also "Simulation, Consciousness, Existence" available from Moravec's website.
3. The distinction between made and found truth comes from Rorty 1989, 53.
4. The *sensus communis* has nothing to do with "common sense". As an aesthetic notion it maintains a very indirect relationship with the social phenomenon of the community. Cf. § 20 of Kant's *Critique of Judgment* (entitled: "The Condition for the Alleged Necessity by a Judgment of Taste is the Idea of a Common Sense"): "If judgments of taste had (as cognitive judgments [Erkenntnisurteile] do) a determinate objective principle, then anyone making them in accordance with that principle would claim that his judgment is unconditionally necessary. If they had no principle at all, like judgments of the mere taste of sense [des bloßen Sinnengeschmacks], then the thought that they have a necessity would not occur to us at all. So they must have a subjective principle, which determines only by feeling rather than by concepts, though nonetheless with universal validity [allgemeingültig], what is liked or disliked. Such a principle, however, could only be regarded as common sense [Gemeinsinn]; for the latter judges not by feeling [Gefühl] but always by concepts [Begriffe], even though these concepts are usually only principles conceived obscurely" (trans. Werner Pluhar, Indianapolis: Hackett, 1987) (Original: p. 237-38). See also Kimmerle 2000.
5. David Peat: *Einstein's Moon* quoted in Pepperell 6.
6. Ohashi 1999, 91ff. For further developments of this topic see the Chapter on Noh-plays and icons in Botz-Bornstein 2008.
7. I introduce and explain the term Virtual Irreality in Chapter 2 of Botz-Bornstein 2008. It is in agreement with Michael Heim's definition of "Irrealism" (Heim 1998: 216). See Chapter 5 note 4.

> One comes across cultural difference as an unobjectifiable "feeling" of anxiety or of the uncanny that cannot be contained within the economy of spatialized time governed by the pleasure principle. For this reason, it must be *articulated* in enunciation and be repressed so as to be perceived as *determined* cultural difference, as an identifiable difference between entities.
>
> Naoki Sakai: *Translation and Subjectivity*, p. 117.

# Prelude

## Narrated Time and Non-Narrated Time or Why We Are All Dreaming of the Japanese Clock

Who knows the Japanese clock? This mechanical clock (*wadokei* 和時計) existed until the end of the Edo period and was engineered to measure what was called "seasonal time" or "uneven time". From a technological point of view, this clock was entirely "European". Still, its concept of time was unusual because it was based on a traditional Japanese method of measuring time. It can, as I will explain, serve as a point of departure for reflections on VR.

Traditionally, the Japanese thought that all year both day and night covered periods of "exactly" twelve hours. Each of these two periods supposedly stretched between six o'clock in the morning and six o'clock in the evening. It was of course clear that, apart from two days per year, the respective lengths of day and night were unequal; were one hour really to cover a standard length of 60 minutes, the twelve-hour model for both day and night would not make sense. However, for the Japanese clock this problem did not arise because in winter it automatically shortened the daytime hours and prolonged them during the nighttime; in summer it would do the opposite. In this way, days and nights still stretched over "exactly" twelve hours each – and this all year round – but the length of the hours differred from day to day. Technically this was achieved through the use of two balances called "temps" whose weights and dials were constantly adjusted. The first clock able to measure seasonal time was accomplished around 1780.[1]

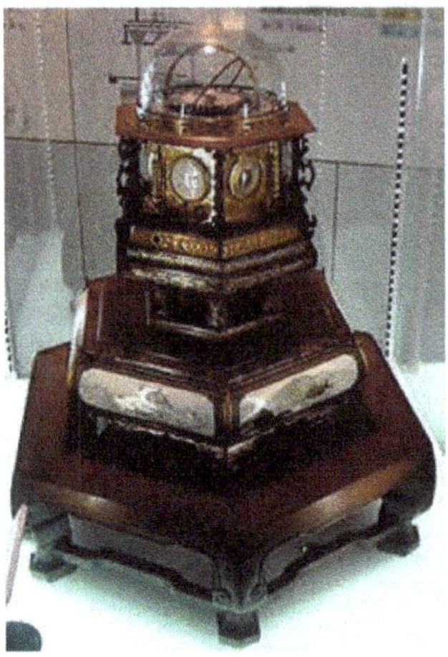

Fig. 3: Hisashige Tanaka's extremely complex Man-nen dokei, which also contains a day of the week indicator. It was completed in 1851.

Seasonal time as such is not a particularly Japanese or a particularly unusual phenomenon; it is even highly likely that, during an age when clocks were not yet available, time was perceived or *felt* like this all over the world. Even today, though practically everyone uses a watch, nobody would be suspected of insanity if he declared that for him in summer the hours seem longer, and in winter shorter. For Bergson, as we will see in Chapter 2, such a time could not be measured by clocks but only by conscious beings because for him, this time was "the very stuff of which life and consciousness are made" (Bergson: 1888: 76). The fascinating point about the Japanese clock is that, instead of converting felt time into measurable units derived from an abstract system, it aspired to *measure* this felt time, and to subsequently build a system out of these "felt" units. The hours appear as less static units but develop according to a dynamic scheme.

First this is surprising because this concept represents the opposite of what we normally expect from a machine. Time feeling is primarily a personal matter and the direct transmission of such a feeling from an intimate level to the abstract level of a mechanical system is unusual. In technical terms, the Japanese clock is a machine. Still, at least to some extent, it gives us the impression that it expresses time "as it is experienced", and not as a mathematical quantity. As opposed to the Western style clock, its way of measuring time contains a moment of immediacy, because it avoids depicting time through a purely representational, symbolic, "second hand" language.

The use of Western-style clocks in modern life has become unavoidable in almost all parts of the globe. Even in Japan the Japanese-style mechanical clock never really came into use because soon after its invention the country witnessed the rapid development of railroad networks whose timetables could only be issued with the help of a Western-style time system. Of course, everybody still had the right to retain his own, intimate feeling of time in his mind or body, which could still be in agreement with the "old" traditional way of measuring time. However, something had changed. Suddenly it had become impossible to communicate indications of time from one person to another without converting it into the mathematical timetable language that had now become standard. It was still possible to say 'today I spent *two hours* in the field,' but the indication 'two hours' now functioned as a mathematical narrative because *seasonal time* was now expressed through "clock-time". The interlocutor would recognize the meaning of "two hours" *primarily* in timetable language, though it was also possible, if he had the desire to do so, to convert the measurement into the temporal span that these "two hours" might have had for the person in the field. In any case, time became the narrative of an event: it was no more than the signifier of a presence.

The two different ways of measuring time are actually two different ways of relating time. Time experience can be related as measured time, and it can be related more immediately without being measured. The first kind of time I call "narrated time". "Narrative" is not only concerned here with the retelling of a past event (in the sense of the German *Erzählung*), but also includes the temporal interpretation of the present. The person who says "this hour" (meaning the present hour that he is experiencing at the moment) refers to different temporal phenomena depending on whether the experience of this "hour" is suggested as a time-experience, or whether it is rendered through a mathematical system.

For the reasons described above, I believe that the Japanese clock can serve as a metaphorical point of departure for reflections on VR. Of course, also for the Japanese who were living with the Japanese clock, clock-time is *mathematically* calculated. However, because the outcome of this calculation seems to overlap much more with time-experience, it gives us a feeling of directness, simultaneity, and immediacy because time feeling and time measurement are not separated by a gap of mediation. In other words, time is not a narrated "second-hand" phenomenon but time-experience and its linguistic expression overlap up to a point that any narrative effect appears to be absorbed in a present.

I said "appears". Of course, time experience and its linguistic expression, or "life time" and "clock time" cannot *completely* overlap, unless one supports the absurd thesis that the Japanese clock produces a time of its own, that this clock "contains" time. All we can say is that the Japanese clock also narrates time, but that the narrative character of this time-narrative is much less evident than in the Western time system because the clock expresses – or simply "shows" – time experience more immediately without going through the distancing stances of a narration. The Western time system divides hours into equal units, and *clearly* narrates time.

I would argue that just because of this difference with regard to the degree of narrativity, the traditional Japanese system appears to have preserved some of the virtual, momentary power of time as a lived phenomenon. Time is not "really" contained in this machine – this would be impossible – but it is not *entirely* mediated through a narrative either; it is not simply an "unreal" narrative. In this sense, the Japanese clock has a virtual character as it permits time to develop independently of possibilities or impossibilities that can be measured with the help of a mathematical time-measuring machine. In some way, it recognizes only "time itself". The scientific, measurable reality in which time "happens" is not considered to be the real yardstick for temporal evolution. What is considered is its experience.

Through this "anti-realism" (which, paradoxically, retrieves something of "real time"), time as it is measured by the Japanese clock also acquires a dreamlike character. I understand here the phenomenon of the "dream" as a mode of being whose most fundamental experience cannot be calculated with the help of a logic derived from a reality existing outside of the dream. For the Japanese clock, as for the dream, the flow of time has no exact measures that could or would be measured from without. Time appears as dynamic and self-evolving and accepts no measurements other than those that it obtains through itself. In still other terms: time is here a self-enclosed phenomenon.

One essential point is still missing. This time, as virtual and dreamlike as it may appear, is not only the time of the virtual and the time of the dream but also time as it should appear in life. "Experiential time" unfolds itself from moment to moment, it is not measured from an outside point of view. Thinking about this more closely, we recognize a problem. One of the reasons why the Japanese clock fascinates us today is that the time-feeling of this machine appears to be *more* dynamic and *more* "lived" than the time that most of us are able to experience in our contemporary lives. The reason is probably that in our "real" lives we consult wristwatches every fifteen minutes. From there comes the paradoxical result of our observation. The time of the Japanese clock appears, at the moment when "real time" becomes entirely regulated by the "Western" time system, as more real than the time that we experience in our lives.

All this confirms the fact that what the Japanese clock produces is VR. Without doubt it is the first man-made machine to do so. And though the machine itself has been far from successful, today it gives us a chance to look at VR from a privileged angle. Because of the simplicity of its mechanism (at least compared to that of the computer), the machine illustrates what VR *does not* mean (what it actually *could mean* will be explored at length in this book). The VR of the Japanese clock is not an imaginary, excitingly new reality invented by an extremely sophisticated machine, but a reality that contains those dreamlike and immediate time experiences that our "real time" is often lacking. If the Japanese clock is a precursor of the home computer, "virtual" signifies here "non-mediated" or "non-narrated" because being *present as such*. This present contains in itself possibilities that are never spelled out because the virtual remains entirely in the domain of the non-material.

## Note

Source: Japanese clock and watch association http://www.jcwa.or.jp/eng/ historyindustry/history01.html#h2

## Feature Scene I

## Cloned Realities: Eat Your Cake and Dream it

The advertisement brochure of the fashion brand Diesel called "Save Yourself" plunges one into the mental world of young people with cultural ambitions and the hope of floating above the waves of dull consumerism. By inverting the sentence "live fast, die young" not into its logical opposite "live slowly, die old", but into a more absolutist, pseudo-elitist "don't live at all, so you'll never die", the posthuman manifesto delivered by the brochure represents a masterpiece of dispersive irony, leaving unclear the limits between sincere / superficial, intelligent / dull, healthy / decadent, and, especially, between reality and the virtual.

The booklet contains photos of young people wearing mostly Diesel Jeanswear accompanied by short paragraphs containing highly elaborated advice on how to "save yourself". This means, in principle, how to "escape death" and to live posthumanly, which turns out to be no problem at the time of cloning and VR.

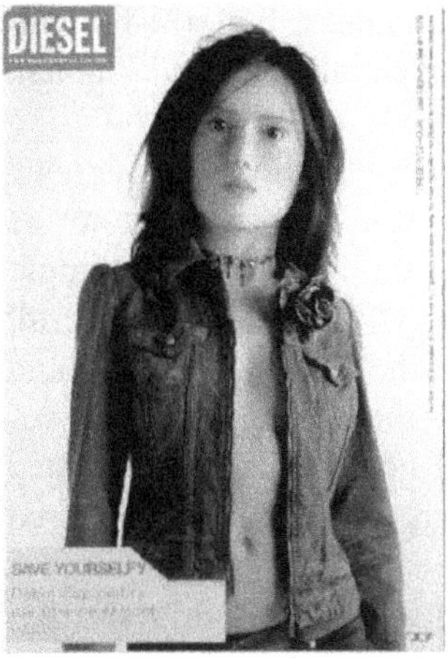


Fig. 4: Diesel "Save Yourself" campaign

On these photos, the young people's faces are expressionless and empty and look as if made up with wax. Their eyes are staring into emptiness, their postures are frozen though not uncomfortable. At first sight, one very much doubts the "realness" of these persons. At the same time, there is nothing "surrealist" in these pictures, nor do we encounter the kind of cold stylization that so often, in magazines, objectifies bodies beyond any attitude. These people do have an attitude; however, this seems to be all they have. What we see are self-contented beings radiating a disconcerting lack of sense, humans transformed not really into posthuman objects but into these lukewarm intermediary beings, kinds of *unheimliche* puppets, sufficiently different from us to dissuade us from any engagement, but still not leaving us entirely indifferent. The ambiguity they radiate is similar to that of autists who will be explored in Chapter 2. Though the faces look "unreal", the hands' skin and positions are natural and relaxed in order to avoid the effect of dummies. A refined ambiguity lets us suspect that the images of these "people" are perhaps not destined for consumption because their symbolizing power is strangely broken. We might suspect that their message is perhaps to be looked for outside the pragmatic values and anti-values of our image loaded consumer world.

When there are two persons on the same picture, their relationship appears mechanic and sterile. Males and females look rather alike. First of all, it is remarkable how a posthuman status is here achieved without the involvement of any technology. Through an evident lack of individual life force, these "persons" appear as manifestations of a strange kind of "lifeless health" lacking humanness, but still remaining in a strange way integrable into a most generally defined "human condition".

"Health" is then also the main subject of the texts. You need "health" to "save yourself", but since the "sense" of health cannot be established as a virtue to be located outside the flat and simple "healthy condition", health becomes, like everything else in the world, an end in itself. The result is not really an aesthetization of people and everything around them but, more radically, the declaration that everything is aesthetic from the beginning, as if nothing had ever existed before the aesthetic state of the world that has come to be engendered in these photos.

The most striking idea in these sophisticated and highly stylized elaborations is that "youth", "health", and "beauty" are best to be obtained through an efficient combination of bio- and computer technology. The parallel treatment of these two branches of modern science, and their squeezing out of a combined clony-virtual dreamsphere, appears in this advertisement for the young as almost naturally established. In the end, a cyborg is a self-regulating organism that does not need to be seen as artificial but can be perfectly natural in its own terms. What makes you posthuman is the virtual detachment from "real" reality and your unconditional melting into a virtual mass. And once you are there, the distinction between nature and the artificial ceases to make sense.

Eternity can be attained in two ways: through cloning and through the consistent integration of VR into one's life. Both, cloning and VR serve to stop time in order to transform it into something aesthetic. However, this is not simply an aesthetization or a stylization, but, in a way more efficient than it has been possible for preceding generations, it represents the creation of a "life style" as something absolute. In the end, everything becomes a matter of style: we do not even need a techno-body (as first-generation posthumanists told us) but all we have to do is wait that simulation wins over reality. Then, once our life has been entirely detached from human needs, it will be purely aesthetical.

The texts and images of the "save-yourself" campaign demonstrate the proximity of the idea of cloning and the realm of dream as well as of the virtual. How dreamlike must be a world peopled with clones, and how consistently is VR working towards the "realization" of this aim.

"Aesthetic" signifies henceforth rather the ironic version of the "spiritual" (for example mockery versions of the theme of "reincarnation" in various sects, or the advice to avoid sex in order to "give your body to the goddess of beauty"), and at the same time of the biological. For the "save-yourself" aesthetician, biological approaches to life are at the same time "spiritual" approaches. Both serve the same objective, which is spirito-biological reincarnation: drink your own urine, clone yourself, eat algae, sleep…

However, the safety obtained through the displacement of the aesthetic project into the sphere of the virtual makes "save-yourself" different from the mere dream world of, say, the nineteenth century dandy. In this world you could really get lost. The adoption of VR as a "life-saving" device flows out of technical spirito-biological approaches that are absolutely safe: don't think, sleep, and be a computer. In other words, create your own clone by dispersing yourself in data.

The wish to stay forever young is certainly not new; even less new is the idea to demonstrate this wish through photos of young people who, though obviously possessing all "aesthetic" attributes of youth, are stiff, quiet, and lack any vital energy. The ironical message is: if you behave like an old person while being young, you will never become old in reality. The old are old because they couldn't stop time. The dead are even worse off. The audacity of the young is to *pretend* to be old or even dead and to enter, in this way, the realm of the timeless Virtual. From now on, living death replaces life. And technology will help you to swap the hard and thorny path of asceticism for that of the soft aestheticism of Virtual Culture. What has formerly been preached by popular Schopenhauerian Buddhism and what could still appear as rather painful is now simply "done" by science. All you have to do is to say yes. By letting science enclose your self in yourself, your self will re-emerge like a clone within a dreamlike sphere of virtual self-sufficiency. If you only recognize that, as a potential clone, you are bound to be the incarnation of a "virtual person", you can immediately be reincarnated as a posthuman dandy. Then you will grow posthuman wings through the lightness of "style". And it's absolutely safe. The virtual clone can live in reality without touching it, she can dwell on a playground without ever playing, be the best simply because she is alone, eat her cake and have it, too, and be somebody simply by being nobody.

We could have noticed this earlier: aestheticism is safe, especially when it is virtual. Already in the late 1970s Pierre Bourdieu noted in his work on social distinction and taste that the "new petty bourgeoisie" does not strive, like their parents, for conservative, bourgeois, "real" values, but tends to externally imitate the adventurous, progressive, unconventional, daring, emancipated, "intellectual" without, of course, putting at risk their own social or physical security (Bourdieu 1984). The Diesel advertisement brochure "Save Yourself" shows that these postmodern ideals no longer represent only an external, imitable side of a lifestyle but that "petty-intellectual" dandyism is now re-edited as a virtual dream in the form of posthuman, cloned realities. Computer technology and biotechnology combined have found the possibility to make them "absolutely real", that is: absolutely safe.

# 1. Eighteenth-Century Rationalism and the Search for the Absolutely Real: When Friedrich Bouterwek Invented Virtual Reality

At the beginning of the twenty-first century, the term VR has entered the consciousness of almost all inhabitants of industrialized countries. However, though used frequently and in different contexts, *philosophically* "virtual reality" has not been very well established. Still, since the day it was introduced to the public in the late 1980s and immediately popularized by Jaron Lanier (cf. Ryan 2001, Aunger 2000: 2) in the form of a computerized "dream reality", some sought for concrete indicators able to conceptually link VR to various traditional metaphysical concepts such as "the transcendental" or "Absolute Spirit" (see Chapter 2). In some cases their attempts to approach VR philosophically have been successful. Still, these attempts remain far from establishing the virtual as a phenomenon occupying a definite position within the Western philosophical tradition. It is surprising that, so far, few people are aware of the existence of an outspokenly "virtual" branch of idealist philosophy that was well known in Germany and in France in the late eighteenth century. It is useful to let the present book, which analyzes the meaning of the virtual for posthuman culture, start with an analysis of the original meaning of VR.

The term "Absolute Virtualism" was actually coined by the German Kantian philosopher Friedrich Bouterwek (1766-1828), a professor of philosophy at the University of Göttingen and a contemporary of Hegel. "Absolute Virtualism" suggested a kind of absolute intensification of the Kantian rationalist critique of idealism. Though it never existed in the form of an established philosophical school or branch, it left traces in Schopenhauer's philosophy as well as in the French tradition of "spiritualist positivism" that would pave the way for Bergson.[1]

## 1. Bouterwek and Virtual Reality

Though, at his time, the period of authentic Kantianism was almost finished, Bouterwek made himself a reputation as an interesting developer of "critical idealism". Kant had introduced this discipline in

1781 in his *Critique of Pure Reason*. By formulating the necessity of a critique of reason to be undertaken by reason itself, Kant drew philosophical attention to the limits of human knowledge. The real world as it exists "in reality" cannot be simply an empirical quantity existing "out there". At the same time, it cannot be based only on human reason. Kant inaugurated a "transcendental" or "critical" procedure that would establish reason, at the moment it comes to terms with reality, as a phenomenon able of self-control.

The Kantian procedure was immediately recognized by most German universities as a valid philosophical approach.[2] Younger thinkers like Schiller, Reinhold,[3] and Fichte welcomed the new philosophy and developed independent and original approaches; still younger philosophers, like Krug, Fries,[4] and Bouterwek did the same.

It is possible that the contradictory historical situation of a generation born into the transitory phase between Enlightenment and Idealism is responsible for creative outputs like Bouterwek's. Already "idealists" like Schiller found the Kantian procedure far too intellectual. Schiller, though fascinated by Kant in general, disliked Kant's apparently unbridgeable separation of reason and nature; he tried to unite both through the idea of an "aesthetic impulse" or aesthetic "play" able to create a middle-ground between reason and nature. In general – though the elderly Kant could only be bewildered by these developments – it has probably been unavoidable that the three *Critiques* would be adopted as a solid ground for German idealist philosophy of the nineteenth century.

Also Bouterwek criticized Kant. Influenced by German and Italian idealism, Bouterwek disliked, like Schiller, a certain strain of Kant's rationalism. At the same time he was, like Reinhold and Fichte, interested in "first principles". Instead of suggesting, like Schiller, a new ontological sphere of "play", he decided to define "reality" as the last foundation of philosophical thought. This "reality" was not the empirical one suspicious to Kantians but a VR whose existence Bouterwek saw as entirely compatible with Kantianism.

Bouterwek developed his ideas on Virtualism in three consecutively written books, *Idee einer Apodiktik* (1799), *Anfangsgründe der spekulativen Philosophie* (1800), and *Epochen der Vernunft nach der Idee der Apodiktik* (1802).[5] Though "Kantian" in essence, Bouterwek used, in these three books, elements of skepticism and of Spinozism, Fichte's "principle of intelligence",[6] and Jacobi's *Lebensphilosophie* as well.

While idealism holds that reality is only the embodiment of ideas, Bouterwek is convinced that reality exists in the form of a Being that is independent of human reason. However, also the existence of this reality must be justified through reason. Just like Kant, Bouterwek affirms that purely abstract thinking (like formal logic) that does not take into account the elements provided by experience will never be able to provide knowledge (*Wissen*). This thought inspires in Bouterwek a *virtual turn* within Kantian thinking. Should it ever be possible to have knowledge about reality, then only if thinking is itself part of this reality. Furthermore, only if both thinking *and* Being are "real", can knowledge be immediate. Only if thinking and Being are real can knowledge be truly a *knowledge of reality*.

Bouterwek calls his requirement an "absolute reality principle" (*absolutes Realitätsprinzip*) and he wants it to be valid for thinking as well as for feeling. What follows is a conception of an "Absolute Virtualism" holding that "the subject is known by the fact of will, and the object by that of resistance" (*Apodiktik* II: 62ff).[7]

## 2. Bouterwek's System

Bouterwek constructs his thoughts about VR with the help of what he calls "apodictics". Apodictics is a fundamental philosophy (*Elementarphilosophie*) able to locate the foundation of experience (I, xvii) and to subsequently justify this experience in terms of reason. Its name comes from the Greek *apodeisis*, the "last foundation of all proofs". As the science of the ultimate foundations of truth and knowledge, apodictics is supposed to provide a ground not only for Kantian philosophy but for all philosophy (I, 7ff).

Bouterwek divides his apodictics in three parts: logical, transcendental, and practical apodictics. Logic is unable to reach into the domain of experience and knowledge. Transcendental philosophy, though able to develop theories about reality, has no access to reality as such. In order to avoid skepticism, philosophers are asked to rise to the highest level of apodictics, that is to *practical* apodictics. Through it they will recognize the last ground of reality as constituted by nothing other than by absolute virtuality.

### 2.1. Logical Apodictics

The main objective of the *Logical Apodictics* is to demonstrate the impossibility of grounding philosophy on general logical principles. Logical procedures end up in circular attempts of grounding one principle upon another, inviting the kind of criticism that is usually led by the skeptics (I, 30). Bouterwek accuses Reinhold and Fichte of such circular procedures (I, 44). Though Bouterwek's own positions turn out to be skeptical in many respects (he even subsumes his own thoughts on logic under the label "Pyrrhonism") (I, 134), his aim remains to provide a "practical" foundation for philosophy that transcends empty formalism and is therefore able to save philosophy (and especially Kantianism) from skepticism.

**2.2. Transcendental Apodictics: The First Definition of the Virtual**
In his second apodictics Bouterwek attempts to think in more "positive" terms. His guideline is Kant's fundamental insight that there is no way to develop knowledge (*Wissen*) out of thinking alone. The problem with Kant is, however, that he accepted the existence of a "thing as such" as the direct foundation of his system, that is, that he defined, within the domain of transcendental philosophy, a sphere of stable reality. This is a major mistake because, by definition, transcendental philosophy has nothing to say about reality (I, 166). Kant's "thing as such" can be a subject of interest only for metaphysics (I, 172).

Bouterwek's "transcendental philosophy" is radical because it is *only* interested in principles. What is the most original principle (the highest transcendental idea) through which knowledge becomes possible? For Bouterwek it is the idea of the *Absolute* (I, 175). The *Absolute* manifests itself in the satisfaction that we feel when a judgment is both true and necessary. Even the skeptic cannot deny this satisfaction because, if she would, she would have to base her assertions on the same kind of satisfaction.

At the same time this *Absolute* maintains no link with logic. The *Absolute* is not simply a notion [*Begriff*] (otherwise all reality could be reduced to a notion). Further, it remains indefinable because all definitions, like everything that is thought, are based on this idea.

Finally, since even empathy or feeling are based on it, the *Absolute* cannot be empathized either. Any explanation of the *Absolute* through empathy or feeling is circular because one would have to use the *Absolute* as an explanation for the very thing one wants to explain (I, 194-96). The conclusion of all this is that the *Absolute* exists in a virtual manner: it is absolutely real though irreducible to any definition and not traceable to any scientific ground. Even the skeptic has to recognize the existence of this reality because *Absolute Reality* or *virtual reality* is not a matter of theoretical but of practical philosophy.

It cannot be demonstrated or felt, but only located in an indirect manner (I, 60) through everyday life practice.

However, empiricists who believe that Absolute Reality is represented by not more than the plurality of data are also mistaken (I, 267). In Absolute Reality, the reality of the senses and the reality as conceived by human reason overlap. Absolute Reality deals with a form of being that is sensible and reasonable at the same time. It is a reality that has been established by knowledge and is therefore a matter for the *absolute faculty of knowledge* (*absolutes Erkenntnisvermögen*).

In a way Bouterwek develops a highly skeptical approach towards reality. He cannot and does not want to prove the existence of Absolute Reality (at least not in the way in which Kant attempted to prove the existence of the "thing as such"). All Bouterwek does is point out the impossibility of the non-existence of Absolute Reality, a strategy he calls "negative Spinozism" (I, 392). Just for this reason it might look as if Bouterwek's unknowable VR is just another name for Kant's *Ding an sich*: Kant's notion characterizes a being that can never become an "object" because it exists independently of the fact whether it is perceived by a subject or not. In reality, negative Spinozism attempts to avoid this as it "can teach only that to the 'consciousness in general' a 'something in general' corresponds, concerning which nothing whatever is to be affirmed in absolute knowledge" (Windelband 1901: 587). Bouterwek was aware of this, and this is why he adds another approach to the theoretical one that he names "practical apodictics".

### 2.3. Practical Apodictics: The Second Definition of the Virtual

In spite of Bouterwek's detailed analysis of the character of VR, some of its regions must remain obscure because, as he admits, "theory" has simply nothing to say about them. Within the third apodictics those things that had to remain undefined (or defined negatively as "negative Spinozism"), are developed into a sub-system that has entered the history of philosophy under the name of "Virtualism" (II, 207).

Here Bouterwek presents a positive theory of VR that he understands as a concentration of psychic and natural energy. VR is established through "individuality" which is a "vital force" (*lebendige Kraft*, II, 67) and the force of nature that resists reality (*Naturkraft*). "Force within or outside of us is relative reality" (ibid.) Also resistance is such a relative reality, but both together are virtuality: "We are through virtuality" and "absolute reality is nothing other than the virtuality in us" (68). Natural force in itself is nothing, it is no fundamental force or *Urkraft* (as metaphysics likes to think). Reality comes about only through force and resistance. VR is an "absolute unity of opposed forces that comes into being as something absolute only through this interchange" (69).

We know that *we* are real only because we feel a *will* in us; and we know about the existence of *practical reality* only because we can feel the *resistance* of this reality. Apart from *will* (with regard to the existence of ourselves) and *resistance* (with regard to the existence of the outside world) there is nothing that would indicate for us the existence of reality. And both will and resistance are *themselves part of reality* (II 61-62).

Within Bouterwek's "absolute reality principle", the only unconditionally grounded reality that exists is the "unity of forces" that emanate from our will on the one hand and from the resistance of the world around us on the other. This reality is not actual but virtual because we, who feel these "forces", are ourselves a part of this reality. There is no exterior point from which this reality can be measured, but any knowledge of this reality remains grounded in the opposition of force and resistance.

Bouterwek's "Absoluter Virtualismus" draws on reality as a virtual quantity because perception can be defined in terms of neither subjectivism (solipsism) nor objectivism. Within this reality, subject and object are absolutely interdependent, and no idea of reality can be traced to one alone.

Today this reality can look like a posthuman narrative, or one of reality effectuated through virtual immersion in a "fictional world" with all the postmodern parameters we attribute to such experiences (semiotic blindness, passivity, self-enclosure, etc.). Or perhaps Bouterwek anticipates the "reality" of the people in *Brave New World*, which is, as mentioned in the introduction, a dreamworld in which people no longer 'really' struggle, aspire, love, feel pain and in which nothing ever signals that things do really exist. It is, of course impossible to suspect that Bouterwek had any of those things in mind. However, in any case it remains clear that Bouterwek did more than just refine a Humeian subjectivism (at which Kant stopped), which holds that the whole world is simply in our minds. More radically than that, Bouterwek took a clear step towards a posthuman vision of reality for which the traditional division between mind and reality no longer makes sense.

### 3. Bouterwek's Reception

Bouterwek is not an important historical figure. Not even among the minor figures on the ladder leading from Kant to Hegel is his position outstanding; nor did Bouterwek's German contemporaries find much inspiration in Bouterwek's ideas about the virtual. Hegel wrote a long but cynical review of Bouterwek's book *Anfangsgründe der spekulativen Philosophie* in which it becomes clear that Hegel did not appreciate or even grasp those of Bouterwek's arguments that concern Virtualism. Bouterwek's design of a science which recognizes itself "as thinking essence through thinking itself" is searched by Hegel for a "fixed point" from which "consciousness could be constructed". According to Hegel, Bouterwek mixes Kant's pure reason and reason in the idealist sense (Hegel 1986: 144 and 149), which is unforgivable.

Philosophers of the next generation were slightly more willing to develop Bouterwek's thoughts, which leads to a possible characterization of Bouterwek as belonging to the generation of post-Kantian thinkers led by Schopenhauer and Nietzsche, who felt no longer bound, when conceptualizing the human will, by a deeply ethical outlook (this is, for example, Eric Roman's characterization of Bouterwek's place in the history of philosophy; Roman 1975: 59). When Schopenhauer (1788-1860), who had attended Bouterwek's lectures in Göttingen as a student (Espagne 1988: 281), emphasized, under the influence of Fichte's metaphysics, the moment of knowledge (*Erkenntnis*) that would flow out of the conception of a world conveyed through "will", he takes the notion of "will" right from Bouterwek (Windelband 1957: 505-506). In a way, Schopenhauer's voluntarism is the continuation of Bouterwek's Virtualism. However, the decisive modification is that Schopenhauer filled virtuality with a subjective content and called it "will", which changes, of course, the philosophical program. Bouterwek's notions of "force" and "resistance" are abstract while Schopenhauer's "will" and "representation" are concrete because grounded in subjective experience. This leads, in the end, to a decisive transformation of Bouterwek's idea of Absolute Reality. For Schopenhauer, reality is *only will*, while the world of representation (*Vorstellung*) is defined as appearance, that is, as a "mental phenomenon" (*Gehirnphänomen*) that does not contribute to reality (Schopenhauer 1948-61). In Schopenhauer, the *resistance* of the real world – through which, for Bouterwek, the sensation of "will" becomes possible – does not appear. For Schopenhauer the world is one of will on the one hand and of a representing screen on the other, into which the subject is not integrated but which it can watch. Finally and for this reason, Schopenhauer's philosophy can very well be grasped through current criteria of traditional Western metaphysics. Bouterwek's "World of Will and Resistance", on the other hand, avoids these moments of *representation* by declaring that *everything* is virtual.

It is possible that a little more of Bouterwek's Virtualism has survived on the French side. Bouterwek's writings were well known in Paris because they had been spread by the Schlegel brothers during their stay in France (cf. Windelband 1957: 548-549) as well as by Heinrich Heine who had also attended Bouterwek's lectures in Göttingen.[8] Bouterwek's former French students from Göttingen also played an important role, especially the historian of literature, early enthusiast of comparative literature and "inventor" of the word "indoeuropéen" Claude Fauriel (Espagne 1988: 284), and the historian of religion and "inventor" of the word "esoterism" Jacques Matter (Espagne 2004: 81, 94).

Bouterwek's influence can be found in Maine de Biran's (1766-1824) psychological metaphysics of the "primacy of the will" though lack of historical evidence prevents us from establishing a connection between Bouterwek's and Maine's philosophies. However, it remains an interesting idea to read Maine's reflections on the immediate link between "habits" and the act of thinking in the light of VR created by a perfect interplay of both. When "will" and bodily resistance are sublated within habit, reality acquires a virtual character.[9] Maine's examination of the nature of our consciousness establishes the notion of habit as a "center of activity" that can be crystallized within the ever changing states of the world. In *Influence de l'habitude sur la faculté de penser*, Maine de Biran advances habit as the primary aim of education and defines habit in this way not only as a necessary component of seeing, thinking and imagining, but also as an important cultural phenomenon that is present in physical, intellectual and moral life (Preface). He criticizes the metaphysicians who believe in abstract principles existing outside the concrete context of habits.

These thoughts are, of course, also reminiscent of Bergson which is not surprising because the philosophical line of French thought continues through a tradition that Emile Bréhier has named "spiritualist positivism" and which is represented by Ravaisson, Lachelier, and Boutroux. Most clearly Maine's ideas were developed through the metaphysics of Victor Cousin (who gave them a "spiritualist" turn) from where they made their way more or less directly to Cousin's disciple, Bergson. And Bergson is today extensively linked to the subject of VR.

**Conclusion**

The fundamental point for us today is that Bouterwek wanted his theory to be a method leading to the knowledge of reality. He could not have guessed that 200 years later his ideas will be read in the light of an artificial reality that openly claims to be virtual; he could not have guessed that there will exist a reality which is, simply because it is "really" virtual, not real.

However, the subject still provides a supplementary interest. Bouterwek abandoned his own ideas about the virtual character of reality after 1810 because he found them too "rationalist". Already in his *Aesthetics* (1805), he attempted to establish this discipline as an activity linked to play on the one hand, and to the capacity of perceiving that which "cannot be seen" (or of that which exists on the level of "pre-sentiment") on the other. In his *Ästhetik* he writes: "All aesthetic intellectual activity starts with free play; and when play ceases, all aesthetic activity dies" (42). And: "Greek artistic imagination made of religious faith an aesthetic dream that was free but not without rules. No dogma limited this dream and it became the soul of Greek art. It had all attractions of youthful play, though in the end the Greek demanded more from art than only play" (243).

Bouterwek switches here, perhaps without being even aware of it, from *rationalist* virtualism to *aesthetic* virtualism. A Schiller-like notion of play linked to the "vision" of something "aesthetic", even if this "aesthetic" cannot be grasped in a physiological, subjectivist way, inspires a quality that Bouterwek deals with on the last pages of his *Ästhetik*: dream. Bouterwek decides to establish dream as playful aesthetic realm that remains undogmatic (in the Kantian sense) because it expresses things "virtually", that is, without "showing" them within the realm of visible reality. Aesthetic feeling remains, since beauty is a pre-analytic intuition, a "mystical" idea, that is, it is conveyed through the feeling of a virtual element in reality.

In principle, in the following chapters, I intend to reconsider the possibility of an "aesthetic virtualism" opposed to a rationalist, Kantian one. "Dream", as an "aesthetic virtuality", represents, because of its visual and existential quality, a convenient subject of reference in any critique of technological VR. The detail from the history of philosophy, through which these chapters are introduced, juxtaposes the phenomenon of the virtual with the idea of play as well as of dream.

These two phenomena, play and dream, are certainly "as old as the world". In the following chapters these phenomena are reflected against contemporary subjects such as autism, globalization, and biogenetics. The opposition of "one kind" of VR to "the other kind" of VR remains constant. It has been inspired by Bouterwek.

## Notes

1. In intellectual history Bouterwek's name is usually associated with another achievement. Later in his life, somehow tired of rationalism though still continuing to work in that domain, Bouterwek engaged in a multi-volume project on *The History of the Newer Poetry and Rhetoric*. The volume called the *History of Spanish Poetry and Rhetoric* became internationally renowned and is still reedited and read in Spain today. A new French edition of the book appeared in 2002 (see bibliography).
2. Herder, Hamann, and Jacobi can be considered as the first generation of philosophers who accepted Kant's challenge.
3. The Austrian philosopher Karl Leonhard Reinhold (1757-1823) taught at the Universities of Jena and Kiel and attempted to expose Kant's transcendental idealism in a most systematic way. His main book is *Elementarphilosophie* (written 1789-91).
4. Wilhelm Traugott Krug (1770-1842) followed Kant on the chair of philosophy at the University of Königsberg. Jakob Friedrich Fries (1773-1843) taught in Jena and Heidelberg and was critical of most post-Kantians.
5. See the bibliography for Bouterwek's works. The philosopher should not be confounded with the famous German painter Friedrich Bouterwek who worked in Paris and was his nephew.
6. See Fichte's *Intelligenzprinzip. Sämtliche Werke*, Abt. 1, Bd.1, 440, 458-63. It needs to be pointed out that Bouterwek's virtuality system and Fichte's subjective idealism are incompatible at least with regard to one major point. For Fichte, reality is identical with the 'I' whereas for Bouterwek, Absolute Reality (that is, Virtuality) can exist without any 'I'. As will be explained in 2.3., the 'I' is a *force* that exists *only* through resistance. Therefore Bouterwek's Absolute Realism is opposed to Fichte's subjective idealism.
7. I follow here Bouterwek's thoughts as developed in the two volumes of *Idee einer Apodiktik*.
8. Heine mentions Bouterwek in *Harzreise* and *Die Religion der Vernunft* (Espagne 1988: 281).
9. Perhaps we find Bouterwek's ideas even more clearly expressed by Maine's contemporary, Jullien Offray de La Mettrie, who announced that a unity of judgment, reasoning, memory could be contained within a single concept of imagination (La Mettrie 1865: 67). Pierre-François Maine de Biran: *Influence de l'habitude sur la faculté de penser*, in *Œuvres* Vol. II (Paris: Alcan, 1922). Engl.: *The Influence of Habit on the Faculty of Thinking* (Baltimore: Williams and Wilkins, 1930). On the reception of Bouterwek in France see also: Michel Espagne, *En deça du Rhin: L'Allemagne des philosophes français au XIXe siècle* (Paris:

Cerf, 2004). On Maine's concept of habit see Chapter 3 of my *Place and Dream: Japan and the Virtual*.

# 2. Posthumanism: The "Autistic Condition?"

Bouterwek's foundation permits a further development of the virtual as an abstract, philosophical notion. Before showing how this virtual affects the culture of those societies that make use of VR it is necessary to establish the virtual with regard to its precise linguistic and philosophical meanings. In this chapter the virtual will be opposed to the tragic, a distinction that permits to reflect the virtual against a condition that I see – in a metaphorical way – as closely linked to autism. As mentioned in the introduction, autism is not referred to here as the concrete manifestation of a neurodevelopmental disorder, but is used in a metaphorical way in the context of a specific social critique. Roughly it stands for self-enclosure and impaired social interaction. The French newspaper *Le Monde* recently reported that five French youngsters had devastated a Jewish cemetery by smashing two hundred-forty tombs. The young people are not known as hooligans but are above-average students. One of them is even known to have antifascist political tendencies. So why did they do it? The local rabbi (the Grand Rabbi of Strasburg) discards anti-Semitic motives but believes that "the act is due to those young peoples' incapacity to perceive something like a 'before'. They are living in a world that is virtual and autocentric. All there is is them and the present; they don't see their parents, their grandparents. This is emblematic for our time" (Van Renterghem 2015). Though the comments are reminiscent of "technological suicide through virtualization" scenarios produced by a networking culture and artificial intelligence known from Paul Virilio's writings, it is necessary to recuperate the human also in this culture. I suggest retrieving the human in the form of the existential.

## 1. The Virtual, the Existential, and the Imaginary

The virtual is essentially distinct from the simulated. While the latter represents an unreal place aiming at the simulation of an already existing reality, the virtual establishes an autonomous reality supposed to be lived *like a reality*, independent of any resemblance it could have with a preexisting reality. The virtual thus represents a *total* reality annulling all interferences between interior and exterior, and, in this way, any activity of simulation as well as of dissimulation. Its particular effect of *reality* and *authenticity* is acquired by an integration of the spectator into a virtual place by trying neither to simulate nor to dissimulate outside reality. This means that the virtual does not try to produce an *actuality*, but exists *beyond* the distinction between the actual and the non-actual. Thereby it is also distinct from the *imaginary*.

How can one characterize the imaginary in opposition to the virtual? In Western culture, the imaginary is often seen in connection with artistic expressions. The imaginary is an actuality that appeals to a stylistic rhetoric. The virtual, on the other hand, does not appeal to an artistic rhetoric of persuasion trying to act *from the outside* on the *interiority* of the spectator. More efficiently, it seems to *absorb* the spectator through its character of pure interiority. Marie-Laure Ryan mentions that this immersion has often been compared with an "entrapment of tourists in self-enclosed realities of theme parks" (Ryan 2001: 11) and does not agree with this comparison because immersion can also involve a considerable amount of interaction.

The question is whether this interaction can also provide an "existential" sense of experience including various intellectual and emotional stances such as imagination and self-reflexivity.

Among the main sources providing an abstract analysis of the meaning of "the virtual" that have so far been offered by critics of VR, is French linguist Gilles-Gaston Granger's book *The Probable, the Possible, and the Virtual*. Granger notes that despite its effect of total absorption, the virtual never reaches the degree of "existentiality" that imagined reality seems to reach with relative ease (Granger 1995: 14). "Existentiality" signifies here a state in which the self is aware of its own position within the everyday world. This everyday world is composed of concrete being and not of abstractions. In this sense, French philosophers like Sartre and Camus representing French Existentialism were interested in the kind of awareness of existence provoked by profound emotional experiences leading towards the discovery of the self's own position within a concrete world. If we understand "existence" in such an "existentialist" way, we will always be inclined to describe it as linked to either an actuality or a possibility.

The problem that arises is that while the imaginary seems to know how to "catch" this actuality through artistic expressions, the virtual, by definition, does not. The reason for this is that the virtual's declared aim – with regard to its linguistic definition – is to cancel all distinctions between the actual and the non-actual (potential). Any opposition of the virtual and the imaginary turns out to be paradoxical as soon as we try to define the relationship that the two opposing elements maintain with "real" reality. On the one hand, there is the virtual to which one is ready to confer the status of "reality" simply because it is "not imagined". At the same time, this VR, whenever it is experienced, has no effect of actuality (or of existentiality). On the other hand, we are inclined to place the world of art on the side of the "non-real" because this world is "only imagined". However, this world can, as a non-real world, have existential effects on the real life of humans. Many of the problems of cognitive, aesthetic or stylistic order that have been detected in the realm of VR created by a computerized cyberspace can be traced to the above paradoxical constellation.

Before continuing, let us take a brief look at East Asian art because this makes the above points clearer. It is interesting to note that the virtual vs. imaginary constellation remains typically "Western" and is far from rooted in the perceptive nature of the human being. Granger insists on the necessity of "the most radical disappearance" of the virtual in the work of art. This exigency is perhaps excessive, the more so since the French epistemologist Gaston Bachelard claims that he needs "the image of the poet like a grain of virtual haschisch" in order to "enter the rule of imagination" (Bachelard 1961: 197). Still, Granger's observation remains correct with regard to Western art. We are thus surprised when we hear that specialists of Far Eastern art explain that in the East, art is always *necessarily* virtual. As mentioned in the introduction and as I have also shown in my study on Russian orthodox aesthetics and Japanese aesthetics (Botz-Bornstein 2008), Japanese culture attempts to attain a vision of the *real world* as something virtual. Sinologist François Jullien locates a similar aesthetic quality in traditional Chinese painting that he names "insipidity" (*fadeur*). This insipidity represents a "beyond"; however, it does not lead the spectator into another, metaphysically determined world, but it appears as a "virtual" quality, providing a "special type of intuition of existence".[1]

It thus appears that VR in the modern "Western" sense, especially as a product of a globalized capitalist society, is directly opposed to the traditional Eastern use of the model of a "virtual world". In traditional Eastern thought one is ready to admit that the "real" reality is only an irreality that must be called reality but which, once it is approached with the help of more "existential" considerations, turns out to be virtual. The Western approach goes in the opposite direction because here one attributes to a reality, which obviously *is* unreal (the computerized VR), the status of a stable and present reality.

## 2. The Tragic

Let us advance more slowly and first discuss the distinction of VR from "real reality" as well as from simulated reality. As an existential phenomenon, reality is not a stable quantity but constantly changing. The changes lived through in real life can have a tragic character. I understand "the tragic" here in the way in which it has been established by Aristotle in his *Poetics* [G. 1449b24], that is as a mental participation, or a suffering, sparked off through enactment. Aristotle opposes this experience of the tragic to that kind of suffering caused by a confrontation with a narrative when writing: "Tragedy is the mimesis of an action which is elevated, complete, and of magnitude; in language embellished by distinct forms in its sections employing not narrative..."[2]

If we draw a link from the existential to the tragic, we can state that VR is different from real reality because of the absence of that "sense of the tragic" that is essential for life and which humans so often strive to transfer, by means of their imagination, to art. This would be one of the constitutive differences between a human, existential-tragic reality and a VR. Michael Heim has brought this lack of the tragic in VR to the point by writing:

> Our full presence in the world comes not only from manipulating things but also from recognizing and being recognized by other people in the world. Our involvement increases dramatically when we feel that we are, in fact, in a drama (the word drama in ancient Greek originally meant action or deed). (Heim 1998: 23)

Heim specifies that a drama must include "dramatic situations where someone—an agent in our world who recognizes us as an agent in the world—watches what we do and responds to our actions" (ibid).

What other differences between the two realities can be stated? One main difference has to do with time. In principle, virtual time is a rational construction produced by the computer. Philippe Breton has said that, as such, virtual time remains "closed to every mode other than that of logic" (1992: 101) because it does not strive towards an existential structure of tragic changes but towards continuity. The "virtual" tendency to eternalize or accumulate within the same "absolute present", a maximum of elements coming from the past, present, and future, opposes the structure of "existential" time as it is lived in real life. It goes without saying that this idea of the virtual is also opposed to the Eastern idea of virtuality, whose aim is to retrieve the ephemeral character of reality itself.

To clarify the point, let us say that virtual time is constructed according to the mode of Zeno's theory of time. In Zeno's aphorisms commentated by Aristotle, Zeno explains that temporal movements do not exist, because as soon as one cuts time into "pieces" (instants), one notices that inside these instants there are no movements at all. As a consequence, time itself must also be a phenomenon that contains no movement. The idea of the immobility of time implies that the instant remains, because of a lack of movement, the same all over.

The French philosopher and specialist of Aristotle, Victor Goldschmidt, has analyzed this aporia of the existence of time as it appears in Aristotle's *Physics* (VI 218a 14) and concludes: "If 'to be simultaneous' signifies to be in one and the same instant, and if the anterior and posterior events were in that same instant, there would be simultaneity between the events of 10.000 years ago and those of today, and nothing would be anterior or posterior" (Goldschmidt 1982: 14). An absurdity for common sense, this description seems not far removed from a vision of computerized "virtual time". Interestingly, Goldschmidt distinguishes in Aristotle's philosophy between "physical time" and "tragic time" (his book is called *Physical and Tragic Time in Aristotle*) and points out that in Zeno, physical time (made even more abstract and mathematical through an intellectualist aporia) excludes the perception of a "place" in which time can unfold itself "tragically" as a permanent loss of every instant. This means that when "physical time" wins, we observe, through its transformation into simultaneous instants, the destruction of time as "tragic duration".

I would claim that this destruction of a "temporal place" also happens inside the computer which contains, as a being without body and extension, a time "as such" which manages to exist "posthumanly", that is, independently of all human, real and tragic development of concrete time. This is not human time but posthuman time.

In this sense, the computer, as a producer of posthuman synthetic time, achieves the project that photography and even cinema could not even begin. Rodin could still be puzzled in front of photographs because in these "scientific images" he felt time as being "suddenly suspended" (Rodin 1911: 74). The virtual image suspends nothing, simply because it lacks any real time to "suspend". To say that the virtual image is "outside of time" does not really hit the point. The virtual image rather *possesses* time itself as it stops it inside a virtual world where past, present and future overlap.

We know that the "suspension" of time as a stylistic gesture can appear tragic and that photography (like all arts) makes use of this tragic element. The virtual, on the other hand, cancels those suspensions of time that could, through its tragic or stylistic character, confer to time an existential value.

## 3. The Virtual World: A World of Dreams?

As strange as the idea of virtual time may appear due to its ludic moment of absolute simultaneity, usually we do not see virtual time as opposed to "reasonable" time, measured by the clock. Rather, virtual time seems to oppose those conceptions that evoke time as a movement of tragic vertigo ("*Rausch*"), as it is preached, for example, by Baudelaire and Benjamin (Benjamin 1982: 57). However, it is wrong to believe that virtual time is opposed to real time only because the real is lived and the virtual is not. On the contrary, I would like to show here in what sense the virtual is a phenomenon of a "hyperrealist" order. I also aim to elucidate the reasons for putting real life, as opposed to "hyper-reality", willingly on the side of dreams. It becomes clear that, when speaking of the difference between VR and "real" reality, what matters is not the "realistic character of things". VR is distinct from "reality" for the same reasons for which it differs from dreams, though there are also essential resemblances between dreams and the virtual. Dreams resemble VR due to the absorbing force with which they cheat the dreamer. At the same time VR is different from dreams because it strives towards continuity and eternity. For the same reasons it is also different from "real reality". Dreams and real life do not strive towards continuity, but are part of the "tragic", human everyday world constituted by the alternation of sleep and the state of being awake.

In this way, dreams also parallel imagination. The romantic slogan that "life is a dream" expresses the intimate appreciation of life's tragic character that has often been linked to the irony with which we sometimes recognize the definitely ephemeral character of worldly things. The sentence "life is virtual", on the other hand, should it ever be chosen as a slogan by certain techno-romantics, evokes a feeling of indefinable *Angst* as if here the world can definitely get lost.

What is it that makes us afraid of the idea that reality will be lost and replaced with VR? Why do we feel anger instead of associating it with a kind of life eternally lulled in dreams? It is not the possible and unforeseeable surprises that make us afraid. There are nightmares that regularly haunt our sleep, but this does not make us fear dreams in general. It seems rather that the eternal life within VR (as it is proposed, for example, in the Diesel advertisement presented at the beginning of this book), suggest a Matrix-like life *without existence*, that is, without those tragic changes that make "real" life feelable.

Since ancient times, dreams were believed to establish an essential link with the gods. Dreaming as well as carrying out rituals were "transcendental" approaches for humans that enabled them to feel closer to their gods. Is it wrong to say that, after a first phase of technological development during which humans were looking for God in the skies, they seem now to have created their own "synthetic" dream, that is, a VR which *seems* to have the transcendental characteristics of dreams?

There are several differences between the virtual dream and the real dream dreamt at night. First, VR is a reality desired by humans, it is what Freud used to call a wish-dream (*Wunschtraum*), which is the realization of human desires through an intellectualist act. Dreams, on the other hand, come "from elsewhere", they are neither predictable nor measurable. This is why humans do not trust dreams. The further problem is thus that dreams, like madness, cannot be controlled. As Foucault has shown (1961), madness has almost definitely been eliminated from the daily life of "normal" people in modernity while the dream still subsists. Is it not right to say that the dream is one of the last *pharmaka* that we encounter in the modern époque and that man, exasperated, attempted to control also this last *pharmakon* by inventing VR? It would at least be an interesting hypothesis: humans found the most efficient remedy against this last remaining *pharmakon* by synthetically creating a substitute dream destined to replace real dreams.

The above scenario is polemical but it contains some truth. Dream remains, like games and madness, one of the last "tragic homes" (Foucault) of our civilization. To call the virtual world a virtual "*reality*" and not a virtual "*dream*" can almost be understood as rhetorical scheme. The producers of psycho-pharmaka do not say either that they want to engender a second madness but simply "normality".

The above points about the treatment of madness by Western society come from Foucault. On the first pages of his doctoral thesis *Folie et déraison* (published in 1961)[3] Foucault explains how "the freedom, even terrifying, of his dreams [and] the phantasms of his madness,

[were] for the man of the fifteenth century more attractive than the desirable reality of the flesh" (24). According to Foucault, it is

> in the way of doubt [that] Descartes finally encounters madness next to dreams and all forms of errors. This possibility to be mad, does it not run the risk to disown him of his own body, like the outside world can slip into error, or consciousness, by falling asleep, slip into a dream? (54)

Descartes will ban "madness in the name of the one who doubts", but he will also ban, as is well known, the dream (for more on Descartes' "malicious demon" theory see Chapter 5 of the present book).

What subsists in the history of modernity (and what also fascinated Foucault) is a sort of "deaf tragic consciousness" (35) whose voice we still hear in Nietzsche, van Gogh, and Artaud – those "mad" thinkers and artists who never cease to remind us that "our culture [has] lost its tragic home (*foyer tragique*)". For Nietzsche the tragic was the objectification of a Dionysian state that he opposed to the Apollonian redemption. Learning signified for him tragic insight into life, because in tragic experiences man's relationship with Being turns out to be more primordial. However, the tragic consciousness becomes manifest also in the writings of the great specialist of dreams, Freud, who attempts to symbolize this consciousness through the "mythological combat of libido and death instinct" (Foucault, ibid.).

In conclusion we can say that madness, dreams and games have often been banned from man's vocabulary, only to reappear in a denatured form, widely emptied of their original meanings. It suffices to think of the malediction of games in the Middle Ages and still much later by the Christian church and of the mechanic ludism that is now practiced in pachinko parlors of industrialized countries. It is not difficult to see here a parallel with the treatment of dreams in a virtualist society.

The chanters of the tragic no longer seem to be demanded. Dreams and madness have been cleansed of everything that could still be reminiscent of the "death instinct" or other subversive powers. Amazingly, this project has not been advertised as a political ideology, as art or as a scientific vision of the world, but, more radically, as the establishment of a "reality". That this reality is not "real" is not its main problem. Rather the problem resides in the fact that it is a "dream without a dream", a "madness without madness", or a "game without game", and, thereby also a "reality without reality".

But let us proceed more slowly in our analysis of what is lacking in VR as compared to dreams. The British Kleinian psychologist and specialist of dreams, Donald Meltzer (1922–2004), said that "machines do not speak" and that "airplanes cannot fly". One can also say that computers cannot dream. First, VR has difficulties reproducing certain dreamlike, ludic, ritual, and transcendental components that dreams, as well as the "lived" perception of reality, use constantly. The problem is that the "power of the technological dream"[4] has no "beyond": it is a presence that is dense but "pure". Therefore it may relatively quickly appear as banal.

The builders of VR seem to be aware of this. They strive not only to reinforce the "realist" components of this reality, but also its oneiric components (without noticing that both are coordinated by one and the same aesthetics). Realism will thus be created through an assimilation of virtual images to reality while dreamlike re-enchantment will be obtained through the multiplication of ludic devices allowing this reality to appear as a permanent game. I am not only thinking of computer games but also of a large part of the "reality" that we experience on the internet on a daily basis. Finally, the "subjective" and "too human" character of this reality seems to have been neutralized; it seems that one has wiped out all traces that could testify to the fact that this reality is, in the end, only a reality constructed by humans. In some cases, we look at this reality and are imbued with awe: "Man has no clear consciousness [...], he does not know what it is [...], he is unable to understand the change that is taking place but he knows that he is at the threshold of a great mystery". Jacques Ellul said this with regard to the perception of VR.[5] However, the fact that all this is still not more than a *calculated* effect distinguishes this VR from the reality of dreams.

What are the principles of the "aesthetics of the virtual"? As an example let us take a "virtual landscape". Bergson once said that there is "no comical beyond the properly human realm" (Bergson 1940: 2). What he meant is not only that only humans can be ridiculous but also that ridiculous objects must always be linked to the human realm. Clothes and houses can be ridiculous while nature cannot be ridiculous. As an object that can *never* be ridiculous because it is mainly linked to nature, Bergson introduces the "landscape" which "can be beautiful, gracious, sublime, insignificant or ugly" but never ridiculous (ibid.).

Obviously, Bergson could not imagine at his time the reality of landscapes that has been synthetically produced. Today we see that a virtual landscape *can* be ridiculous – not because it is no *real* landscape but because it is the product of a human spirit. The virtual landscape is not a painted landscape, recognizable as an imagined non-reality, but it is a mind-landscape (and, admittedly, what trouble would a painter have were he to paint a "ridiculous landscape"!). The explanation why a landscape produced through virtual effects *can* be ridiculous is as follows: while the virtual landscape is "real", it still lacks the inner necessity displayed by real or painted landscapes. By "necessity" I mean *the indisputable necessity of being a landscape*. Or perhaps we should call it the existential *feeling* of necessity that usually accompanies the perception of such a landscape. Virtual landscapes are lacking this necessity and therefore they *can* adopt the quality of being failed and ridiculous.

Of course, retrospectively, those virtual landscapes can be equipped with an artificial "stability". This will usually be obtained with the help of stylization or *Verfremdung*. A virtual landscape can, for example, appear as dreamlike. The problem is that, in spite of the various stylizations, a realist *or dreamlike* effect of the landscape that excludes by its nature every possibility of the "ridiculous" will never be obtained because the stylizing procedures remain arbitrary. In other words, the stylized landscape will have no inner necessity. The "virtualist" is trapped by the fact that – by the nature of things – the criteria of the arbitrary and of the possible have no importance for the virtual. Granger said that every calculation with the "possible" is by definition detached from the phenomenon of the virtual (Granger 1995: 33). So what would be the use of installing a dimension of "necessity" into VR by introducing a stylistic structure?

The above problem becomes clear through the account of graphic designer Milton Glaser who describes the difficulties coming with the use of computer technologies in the realm of design, architecture, and other plastic arts. In Glaser's opinion, the quality of a given piece of artwork stands initially in inverse proportion to the ease with which its material can be molded to the artists' desires. In other words, there must be the resistance of the "real" able to spark in the artist the existential experience of "being creative". The existence of such a necessity is essential for art in general:

> Increasingly, my students and other young people are beginning to realize they can't use the computer for everything, and they can't start with the computer. They have to start by making things, by drawing things, by conceptualizing things. I have the long rap on the computer, but the problem with the computer finally is there's no chance to develop ideas. Things become clear too soon. The interaction between a sketch and the brain is such that you try something, the brain corrects it, you revise it, the brain corrects it. That dialectic is totally missing from the computer, because as soon as you have an idea, it becomes

> clear. There's not enough fuzziness in a computer solution, so you figure it out too early, and what you get is a very well-executed ordinary idea. Because there's no development in this system. That's not entirely true, but it is characteristic. It's hard to do things that are, it seems to me, fully developed in a thoughtful way on the computer. (Interview with *The Believer*, quoted in Esposito 2013)

Strictly speaking, in VR any reworking of "possibilities" or "necessities" remains a senseless undertaking simply because in a totally arbitrary world even the attempt to go beyond the arbitrary remains arbitrary. The alienation effect created by this deficiency might be taken for a dreamlike effect. It might be taken for the search of a certain "style" of VR as virtual images are indeed sometimes said to look dreamlike. However, in reality, no "subjectivity of expression" has been transcended here and, as a consequence, VR cannot claim to be reality or a dream or art. This means that VR does not attain the degree of "real" playfulness or oneirism that art (especially cinematographic art) can attain. Paradoxically, this follows just from the fact that the project of VR is to create a "real" reality and not only a film or a work of art.

Other, even more essential elements are also lacking. Jean-Clet Martin, in his book on VR, evokes the idea of the philosopher Eugen Fink who talks about a "game without player" or a game deprived of all finality (Martin 1996: 100-101). Significantly, Fink likens play to dreams, because the "doing as if" that is proper to play is more than just an imitation of reality. For Fink, play is a dream and we move within the space of the play with the assurance that is proper to dreamers (Fink 1960: 191). In play, says Fink, the player and play are one, just like in the real dream dreamer and dream are one (192). This means that play is not the product of a subjective consciousness: "Whilst playing, the human being does not remain enclosed in himself, in the limited domain of his own psychic interiority but, through a cosmic gesture, he leaves his own self and interprets the whole of the world".[6]

It is in this context that Jean-Clet Martin suggests that, if VR grounds itself on the model of the game, it could attain the status of a "marvelous cosmic harmony". This idea suggests the following anthropological considerations about play: from the moment humans first experienced play as an activity able to help overcome suffering, they must have desired means of eternalizing this play, or at least of incorporating it in a more fundamental way into their lives (the phenomenon of "lifestyle" is probably still one of the remnants of this ambition.) However, the people of ancient times, as they were living a fundamentally tragic life, must also have known that the charm of every game flows out of game's ephemeral character, that is: out of their opposition to non-games. Only the tragic proposition that every game must end and that suffering will start again, creates – within games – an attractive tension. This tension determines game's style or, in the realm of art, the work's artistic value. For example, it has been shown above that the "suspension" of time (which is a stylistic gesture) can appear as tragic and that photography makes use of this tragic element through which it becomes artistic.

It has also been shown that the virtual cancels all those suspension of time that could be able to confer to time an existential value. Today humans have the possibility of creating for themselves a played world in the form of a "virtual world". But have they really understood the ontology and the existential value of games and of dreams? The aesthetization of life, the idea that "life should become art" is a dream dreamt not only by aestheticians and proponents of lifestyle philosophy but also by highly "existentialist" thinkers like Nietzsche.

What can be said about the creation of style in the realm of the virtual? Necessarily, in a perfect "virtual" reality that is disconnected from anything tragic, stylization will turn *everything* into style; this world will reproduce itself with the quasi-absolute lightness that one can normally find only in games and in dreams. In this sense, VR can be seen as the "dream of the world". Critics will find this approach is too direct or simply too pragmatic because of the exclusion of the element of the tragic. Every phenomenon, before becoming a dream, a ritual or a style, must first exist in the form of a (tragic, existential) culture. Granger said that stylistics always passes through the "concrete realization" of a code (1988: 190). This means that before any creation of style is possible, a cultural reality must *preexist*. The dream of VR, on the other hand, is too absolute to constitute a corresponding "style". Nothing preexists here and a style is somehow created out of nothing in the same way in which Milton Glaser's students try to produce art "virtually" without experiencing the tragic conflict inherent in creative process that proceeds from the attempt to correction. This process involves doubt, crisis as well as other existential stances.

The above reflections also join Edmund Husserl's thoughts on the phenomenological task of getting a "grasp [of] this style, this purely subjective and apparently ungraspable Heraclitean river" (Husserl 1954: 159) of the experienced world. Husserl believed that the eternal flux of what cannot be grasped in life (because one cannot enter the same river twice) should be made accessible through phenomenological reduction. Husserl did not suspect that one day humanity would be able to engender a world where *phenomena have become* reality, a world where no deeper reality behind phenomena exists, and where the "phenomenological style" completely overlaps with the "things" and the "reality of the world". In a sense, VR is indeed a world of phenomenological reduction. Also Michael Heim describes VR as "the Heraclitean stream [where] nothing stays the same" (Heim 1998: 59). In VR, this world-river is supposed to be absolutely ludic and Heraclitean, so much that it has become useless to look in this river for the "phenomenological style" of things.

At the same time, society of communication makes considerable efforts to raise VR on a cultural pedestal in order to make it more "real". As mentioned above with regard to Bergson's "landscape", VR is unthinkable without the multiplication of ludic procedures, be it on regular websites or in games. In principle, one forces alienation upon a reality in order to make it look less synthetic. However, in spite of all efforts, the great wish-dream that is VR does not seem to have become a *dream*. Being unable to conceal the simple desires hidden at its origin, the game often appears as rather childish. It does not become cultural or spiritual. It seems that the game of VR cannot develop the kind of existential force that rituals or children's games manage to deploy rather easily. Even an "ontological" stylization that tries to perceive VR like "a dream in a dream" (cf. Martin: 11), cannot constitute a true ontology of non-foundation that is underlying regular games. The same is true for the introduction of elements of contingency. Contingency, this essential ludic element and great *pharmakon*, represents, according to the mathematician and author of *Cybernetics*, Norbert Wiener, the enemy of modern society. VR uses plenty of it but still it does not provide the existential experience granted by dreams or by real life. The only movement able to reveal the tragic, human, state of reality's non-foundation is a "really" ludic movement as it is produced, for example, by madness. Only an oneiric, non-reasonable element can create the kind of "strangeness" that permits an alienation from what otherwise is condemned to appear as a pure, posthuman presence.

## 4. Virtual Time

Let us define this presence more closely by focusing again on the phenomenon of time. The world of virtual time might present itself a little like the world of schizophrenics for whom everything is present and who are, thereby, unable to leave the realm of their own receptivity. The psychologist Ludwig Binswanger has described such a schizophrenic relation between humans and the world. For the schizophrenic, he says, "*presence* is imprisoned in simple receptivity because he falls victim to all influences of the world of the other; he cannot 'step out' of this imprisonment or step back from it because this 'distance' implies the fact of being able to take aim, to state, to compare, to establish the limits" (Binswanger 1957: 69).

VR as a pure, immersive presence absorbs its players which makes it similar to games and dreams but which, paradoxically, also makes it unreal. As a matter of fact, builders of VR constantly think of developing procedures that permit to "leave" the pure presence. "Interaction" is a common device and it has been very much analyzed by Ryan (2001). As mentioned, certain stylizations of this pure presence or the ludic use of the presentation of different parts of this present (which is also a kind of stylization) are means to make the posthuman reality more "human", that is, to install an "existential" dimension of experience able to include imagination and self-reflexivity. The overcoming of the "simple receptivity" that Binswanger speaks of, however, or the "stepping back" from the prison of an absolute presence and the establishment of a distance between the 'I' and the world it is immersed in, is a matter of "spirit". The problem is that this spirit, which is the typical product of a cultural, human world, cannot be obtained simply through "interactive" procedures, stylization, and the artificial introduction of contingency. An existential, spiritual reality containing a transcendental distanciation between the 'I' and the world exists in the real world and also in games as well as in dreams but it does not exist in immersive Virtual Realities.

It is indeed possible to characterize this as the particularity of the posthuman condition: as a permanent accumulation of facts that are stable because not varied through an existential process of distanciation (though stylized and disguised by a calculated ludism), VR refrains, or is rather bound to refrain, from recognizing any tragic element underlying cultural reality. Because of this structural lack, VR does not assume the status of a game or a real dream but remains a childlike wish-dream, or simply a formalist game "badly played" by adults. Children do not know that life is tragic, and adults make huge efforts to forget this fact by hiding it behind constructs of technological civilization. For children as for technocrats, every action is supposed to lead towards permanent stability. If children still manage to play, it is because, being "cherished by the gods" (Fink), they are able to abandon their own subjectivity. Children's *daydreams*, on the other hand, fully reveal their immaturity through their character of a wish-dream that has not yet been purified of its childlike subjectivity. Adults' daydreams are not very different from the daydreams of children.

Through the systematic production of a VR, humans believe to be able to create a playful reality or a dream. However, they do not recognize that the virtual as an intellectual phenomenon is unable to reproduce the paradoxical ontological constellation contained in dreams or in play: in play every action is also a non-action, every aim is also a non-aim, and being is also non-being. For most philosophers and psychologists who were working on the ontological nature of play, those points constituted the main characteristics of play.

### 5. Bergson's Virtual: "*Onirique*" or "*Ordinatique*?"

The above philosophical considerations of "the virtual" touched upon the idea of time as an "absolute present", upon Zeno's concept of time as well as upon the experience of time in dreams and reality. It is obvious that those themes are also central to the philosophy of Bergson. What might look like a digression into the subtleties of Bergson's philosophy is actually essential for the understanding of the links that exist between the virtual and dreams. Gilles Deleuze (1966), Jean-Clet Martin (1996) and others have noted the resemblance between the virtual and central concepts of Bergson's philosophy. Most of those concepts can be found in *Matière et mémoire*. Strangely, this philosopher who was so clearly opposed to the "scientification" of reality can now also be considered as the precursor of an abstract reality produced by computers.

The world of communication is clearly marked by the element of the virtual, and the virtual image as well as virtual society, are constituted by a dynamic accumulation of elements reminiscent of Bergson's concept of *mémoire*. Martin speaks of an "ensemble of elements, the infinite sum of their relations, an arrangement of parts or a composition of relations that Bergson ranges on the side of the memory (*mémoire*)" (22). The "communicative continuity" (Philippe Breton 1992) in which humans find themselves nowadays more and more implicated, engenders a VR reminiscent of the immanence of *succession* as well as the immanence of *coexistence*. This means that the absolute immanence represented by cyberspace reconstitutes a "living and flowing bath [uniting] signs and bodies" (Pierre Levy 1994: 2).

It is indeed interesting to compare the electronic, pluri-dimensional, and gigantic image of VR with Bergson's *durée pure* in order to detect the specific characteristics of VR, and to subsequently link those findings to the aforementioned themes of the "posthuman loss of the tragic" as well as to that of "virtual reality and dreams". In his early *Essai sur les données immédiates de la conscience* (1888), Bergson criticizes our "ordinary" conception of time, which is always spatial and homogenous and postulates that *durée pure* (pure duration, "real time" or "living time") is not spatial. His distinction between mathematical time and *durée pure* has become famous. In the *durée pure*, time is not a spatio-temporal product but it is mere consciousness as we are constantly aware of time in relation to ourselves. Most interesting are Bergson's ideas about the formal character of this conception of time. In the *dureé pure*, perception does not cut time into pieces but past and present form an organic, dynamic whole. In music, for example, succession is not linear but we perceive a melody as an indivisible whole in which all units interpenetrate each other. The same goes for other temporal series: "When we hear a series of blows of a hammer, the sounds form an indivisible melody in so far as they are pure sensations, and here again give rise to a dynamic progress" (1888: 57). Duration preserves the "wholly qualitative multiplicity, an absolute heterogeneity of elements which pass over into one another" (50).

In *durée pure* matter presents itself through an "entirety of images" (*ensemble d'images*, 1939: 17), which is stable in itself but characterized by an interactive mobility at the inside. This constitutes a "true" reality but it can be commented upon on two levels. The question is: is the "Real Time" (one of the possible English translations of *durée pure*) "real" as *opposed* to "virtual" or is Bergson's *durée pure* a sort of precursor of VR? The problem is that Bergson's conception of Real Time remains ambiguous. Though an important part of his system works in favor of the real as opposed to the scientifically constructed, at the same time, the layout of Bergson's "real" often looks like a self-enclosed entity. Also in VR matter presents itself through an "entirety of images", but the tragic as the predominantly "real" quality of life does not appear in this "*ensemble d'images*".

Certainly, Bergson wanted to oppose to the particularistic immobilism of scientific thinking an idea of a mobilism that is dynamic because it is "universal". However, it is not self-evident that a "universal mobility" will become dynamic in such an automatic way as Bergson supposes, simply because it is "universal". In this sense one can be tempted to say that *durée pure* presents itself too clearly as a simple inversion of the scientific conception of time. For the scientific conception of time that Bergson combats, everything that is "past" is lost. As a matter of fact, it is so systematically lost that nobody would ever consider this a tragedy. For Bergson's *durée pure*, on the other hand, *nothing* is lost – and this does not permit the appreciation of tragedy called life either. Bergson wants to grasp "real life" but what he calls "life" remains a simple accumulation. No matter if it is *durée pure* or another kind of duration, real life is by definition *opposed* to duration, and this is also why the Bergsonian intuition cannot grasp more than an abstraction.

The Japanese philosopher Nishida Kitarô has brought this to a point. He criticizes Bergson, arguing that his concept of *durée pure* "cannot be considered as true life. Life includes death and death includes life" (Nishida 1970: 67). Another Japanese critic of Bergson, Kimura Bin, looks in vain for an "interfacial" quality in *durée pure* because here everything is seen from a subjective point of view that excludes the playful interchange between one and the other, the play by which (spatial and temporal) duration is normally constituted. Kimura writes: "Duration, from the moment it constitutes itself as duration, provides also the constitutive space of its own alterity. *Durée pure* is only realized as the death of duration which is the death of time".[7]

Everything seems to announce a lack of the "tragic" because Bergson consciously avoids, at the inside of *durée pure*, any confrontation with tragic elements that could perturb the pure character of the *duration*, but which continues to constitute duration in human life.

A comparison of Bergson with Freud shows what this conception of time as an accumulative *durée pure* means for civilization in general. As a matter of fact, nobody has ever insinuated that Freud contributed in any way to the idea of VR, though Jean Piaget remarks – rightly – that "the Freudian memory is not very far from the Bergsonian one" (Piaget 1978: 198). It is true that Freud and Bergson believe in a sort of accumulative memory, but what distinguishes these two memories from each other is that in Freud's there is forgetting whereas the unity of the Bergsonian spirit, which presents a "mixed becoming" (*devenir mixte*, 1939) of being and non-being or of the one and the many, intends to be a *permanent* entity.

In Freud's memory there is the deep regret that everything humans create, in the world as well as in memory, has the potential for either bad or beneficial effects. Memorization itself is linked to a certain discontent, and all cultural dreams that humanity has created for itself in the form of "civilizations", are – for the good or for the bad – not permanent. In Bergson, on the other hand, the permanent presence of *durée pure* seems in a strange way to avoid any cultural criticism but considers itself superior to all possible discontents of civilization. There are no regrets in this philosophy of time and an appreciation of time as *durée pure* becomes a fulfillment of time itself.

This is what can make us feel uneasy with Bergson's philosophy since in contemporary society an absolute memory *is* often linked to discontents of civilization. We have this feeling, for example every time we are confronted with the large stock of electronic information that governments today accumulate almost automatically; we perceive the same kind of vertigo when we think of the gigantic electronic memory constituted by VR itself with bits of information that some would perhaps rather prefer to be forgotten. Or we might associate the *ensemble d'images* with the "industry of telepresence" which, constantly facing the most sophisticated forms of voyeurism, has developed a real "art of presence" (Paul Virilio 1997) in which too many things are *constantly* exposed.

It is probably for this reason that we feel closer to the human Freud than to the posthuman Bergson: Freud knows the blessing of forgetting. Freud was interested in dreams because he intended to reveal those secrets that one always appreciates *as secrets*. In VR, like in media reality, there are no secrets and everybody has become a "naked king".

When Bergson enters our intellectual imaginary in the context of VR studies it is not, in the first place, in the form of an anti-technological humanism or (Freudian) criticism of civilization. Still there is an element that Freud and Bergson share, and this allows a delimitation of *durée pure* from VR. It actually represents the second level of the critique of Bergson. Bergson and Freud see *dreams* as phenomena in which memory can be retained. "One must be willing to dream to see the past" ("Il faut vouloir rêver pour voir le passé", 1939: 87)", says Bergson. Considered from a contemporary point of view, one can say that the "humanism" of Bergson's philosophy is constituted by the idea that the mobility of *durée pure*, which inspires intuitive approaches can also be grasped through the metaphor of the dream. The "virtual multiplicities" that according to Deleuze have animated Bergson's thought since the beginning are perhaps not purely dialectical, purely abstract and posthuman, but also *cultural* and stylistic or even ludic. Perhaps they even have, as Vladimir Jankélévitch once enthusiastically noted, "the sinuous flexibility of the curbs and the living grace of free actions" (Jankélévitch 1959: 70).

Regardless, it is certain that only when *durée pure* reveals itself as something other than an actuality enlarged to a point beyond its character of actuality, that only when it manages to become a "real reality" will Bergsonian idealism avoid abstraction. And this will depend on whether the "simplicity" of "Unity" or the simplicity of the "Unique Time" mentioned by Deleuze, is represented by a simplicity that is purely *scientific* or by the mode of being – that can also be simple – represented by dreams. The unstable and fleeting quality of dreams that can never be transformed into a narrative because their state of reality is constituted by intersubjective cultural experiences will always remain different from the calculated flow of VR.

I have given two general interpretations of Bergson's philosophy in connection with VR. As a matter of fact, it is difficult to decide which one is more important for an understanding of Bergson's philosophy. The first interpretation seems most appropriate for VR. It concerns the Bergson of duration as a stable accumulation, which is an abstract mobility, or simply, the "computational Bergson" (in French, "Bergson *ordinatique*"). The second one is the "oneiric Bergson" ("Bergson *onirique*"),[8] who traces the tragic simplicity of the world through a concept of *durée pure* just as if the world were a game. This interpretation highlights a Bergson willing to go beyond Platonist idealism and science in order to reflect upon the intermediaries of the absolute and the possible. To an absolutely pure VR in which everything is *absolutely possible* Bergson prefers "mixed" virtualities as they are represented by Plato's *chôra*[9] and by the dream. Instead of making a decision about who is the "right" Bergson, I prefer to adopt the distinction between these two conceptions of virtual space and virtual time as a basis for further analyses of two subjects that are linked to the virtual in contemporary society.

## 6. The "*Condition Autiste*"

Let us start with some reflections on urbanity and community. The metaphor of the "global village", very much used in the 1970s, still fails to evoke the idea of a "global *city*", and it is perhaps not by coincidence that urban metaphors have been avoided here.[10] The global *village*, if it has ever been realized by VR, appears more as an idyllic space, a wish-dream ignoring urban responsibilities.

Philippe Breton is convinced that the phenomenon of the "modern *homo communicans* would not have been possible without the preceding fixation of the nomadic impulse through which a part of human creativity was going to express itself" (Breton 1992: 86). However, before arriving at the state of a society of communication, the modern human built cities. That is, she left the state of nomadism and founded cities in which she could act in permanent contact with the others. The ever-changing space of the nomad was replaced by a place not subjective and stagnant, but by the dynamic and tragic space of a social, urban life.

While evolving within this process of civilization, humans attempted to reintegrate nomadic elements in their sedentary lives by inventing imaginary worlds, adding an interesting existential dimension to their sedentary lives by dreaming about other places. Still, humans do not seem to have been satisfied with the nomadism offered by imagination, but invented a sort of disproportionate romanticism, which inspired the adventure of *virtual nomadism*. The new destinations were idyllic places free of tragedies.

The virtual community of cyberspace represents one of the most idyllic versions of human "cohabitation" that can be imagined because it avoids, through the total sublation (*Aufhebung*) of the tension between general and individual, all tragedy.[11] Within these spaces psychological conditions of individuals can develop into certain, at times, peculiar directions. Philippe Breton speaks, in his book *L'utopie de la communication,* of the "eminently contemporary character of certain forms of [metaphorical] autism" (128) which is connected to the rise of the new media. Lucien Sfez has even created the term "tautism" referring, through its double reference to tautology and autism, to man's posthuman enclosure in representations referring to nothing other than themselves (Sfez 1990: 132; see also Breton 1992: 132). The French psychiatrist Pierre Fédida rejects Sfez's claim by insisting on the idea that autism itself has nothing tautological because the autist is not shut into a cognitive fiction like the "double-self of the computer" (Fédida 1990: 408). In spite of the – certainly justified – reservations of specialists of psychopathology, one cannot refrain from thinking that a real link between mediatized or even virtual society and a general idea held about autism does exist.

On the one hand, the contemporary fascination with autism allows the supposition that this phenomenon has been exported from its clinical context (just like what happened to "hysteria" at the time of Freud) in order to become a "concept" or even a popular metaphorical expression. On the other hand, in spite of the phenomenological distortions that this implies for autism itself, the reason for the "popularity" of this psychic anomaly must be that autism as a kind of "discontent of civilization" is felt independently of the clinical discourse. Without denying any possibility of distortion of the concept of autism itself, I would like to present here, in the context of the discussion of posthumanism that has been established, reflections on autism and VR.

Everything that has been stated in the present chapter about dreams and play directly leads to the subject of autism. Autists do not play, at least they do not engage in games in which one needs to imagine or pretend (according to the British psychologist Michael Rutter, 1978: 1). They are thus unable to simulate. Their lack of imagination makes them "hyperrealistic" in a sense coming close to the phenomenon of "pure presence" discussed above. Moreover, according to the French psychologist Jacques Hochmann, autism can appear as a caricature of schizophrenic functionality (1994: 33).

If one considers the "scientific character" (Donald Meltzer) of the "autistic method" of exploring the world, and at the same time the obvious lack of abstraction with regard to space and time that is characteristic for autists, one can define autism, through this very paradox, as a "Hyper-Bergsonism". Of course, what is in question here is what has been called above "bergsonisme *ordinatique*" and not the "bergsonisme *onirique*". For autists, everything, including space and time, is concrete. But this absolute concrete becomes, just because it is absolute, a kind of non-world very similar to the scientifically established, posthuman world of VR. As shown above, Bergson wanted to avoid this abstraction and he did so by creating the image of the "mobilité universelle". I have likened this image to the image of the dream. Autists, on the other hand, lack precisely this kind of imagination that would be necessary for the perception of temporal, "globalized" images within which a true timely dynamism can develop. Bruno Bettelheim, one of the early initiators of research into autism, has analyzed up to which point "the [autistic] child does not create for itself a global, simultaneous plan of these different successive images. To do that, one must first mentally represent an object that has been taken away and is no longer visible" (Bettelheim 1967: 554).

Hochmann claims that the time of autists is "without duration". A time which has absolutely no duration, becomes, as Hochmann also says, a circular time representing a ludic form of time. There is no "succession" in the time of the autistic child, says Bettelheim (119), which means that the lack of an *imagined* "global image" of time makes the past *present*. The past is there, but it is not recognized *as a past*. The autistic child lives in a "total immanence" or in an absolute present, as describes Bettelheim:

> When I say that Marcia started to recognize some isolated events of her past, this does not mean that for her they belonged to the past. The past experiences still dominated her present life too much as that she could have thought that something would be finished once for always. For an experience to be really past, we need to have the feeling that the past and important events can no longer act on our present. […] for her, nothing belonged to the past. (253)

The "advantage" of this absolute present, which knows no succession, is that any possible "tragedy" is naturally excluded. It is possible to interpret autism as caused by a general "hyperselectivity", allowing the autistic child to appear as a hypersensitive being, obliged to reject certain immanent stimuli in order to avoid too "tragic" feelings when facing reality. Some studies[12] support this characterization of the autistic child.

The "tragic" can be avoided, but efforts to live in an eternal present will not succeed, and this happens for interesting reasons. The loss of time is tragic and the child tries to make up this time by what appears as a game, but which in reality, as is typical for autistic "rituals", has no ludic quality. Hochmann describes these children's "desperate attempts" to

> painstakingly reproduce a happy experience, [as well as] the painful anger which overcomes them because they don't manage to do so. The second time, simply because it is the second time, is, according to Heraclitus' principle, never identical with the first one. (Hochmann 1994: 35)

It is the reproduction of what Husserl has called the subjective "style" of things, and which he, too likens to the Heraclitean River, which remains ungraspable for the autistic horizon. The child makes the painful experience of an existing gap between the present and the past that she cannot bridge because of her incapacity to join and reproduce the real, "actual style" of the world. Finally, the autistic child decides to live in an absolute and circular time in which even the flow of the Heraclitean River has no duration. The child remains "insensitive to the poetry of the world" and "closes its ears and its eyes to the call of the original" (Hochmann 1994: 40). In the circular time in which the autistic child has decided to live, all "stylistic suspensions" of time, even small "delays" or "projections", appear "like a disaster" (Bettelheim 1967: 253). The autistic child decides to spend its time "playing" according to empty rituals taking place within a duration so pure that for the one who enters, even the physical body ceases to exist and physical pain is no longer felt.

The above considerations of play in the context of autism lead to further considerations of dreams. The research on the "dream capacity of the mother" (*capacité à la rêverie de la mère*) pursued by Hochmann, Serge Lebovici and others shows that "the baby's actions develop along the lines of a temporality, a *before*, a *while*, and an *after*" within the "maternal reverie" that the mother exposes to her child: "They succeed on a line of causality" (Hochmann 1994: 42). Hochmann points to the importance of the (maternal) dream for the cognitive development of the child:

> The language of maternal reverie, to which the child is, originally, exposed, seems to have a double polarity. It is an interior language, a *récit* the mother makes to herself and which, as said Novalis, 'dealt only with itself'. But it is also a text addressed to a third person whose absence is essential to the production of the *récit*. (43)

According to Hochmann, at the beginning there was not the myth but the "reverie of a mother".[13] In places where this dreamlike experience has not installed a temporally and spatially correct vision of reality, distortions will occur later. It becomes here particularly clear how important the activity of dreaming is for the human capacity to "feel" time as *durée pure*. The loss of sense suffered by the autist overlaps with the loss of a generality. The feeling for style or for the "poetry of the world", for example, is linked to this. The loss of a general vision creates a sort of "surrealist reality" characterized by an insensitivity for the "general style" of things; very often it will end up with an obsession for details.[14]

**Conclusion**

The present chapter has attempted to point out resemblances between the (metaphorically) "autistic" symptoms described in the last section and the virtual world. First, I hope to have shown how dreams and play produce a sense of a world that claims to be human and that posthuman realities, as they are rooted in virtuality, need to face this challenge. Meltzer describes dreams as a "theatre aiming at the production of sense" and insists that they are able to provide a sense to the non-dreamt world. We can conclude that one of the characteristics of autism is the incapacity to develop a dreamlike, imaginary scene of time and of space, a scene representing the necessary foundation for every production of the "stylistic sense" of phenomena. Meltzer adds to his passage on "the dream as a producer of sense" a further commentary on autism[15] saying that the study of the behavior of these children has shown that the "loss of dreams" signifies also the "loss of sense" (Meltzer 1984: 112).

The French poet Roger Lewinter, commenting on the relationship between surrealism and dreams, speaks of "the autism" of that part of surrealist painting that strives in vain to reproduce dreams because it stops short at an "interpretation of dreams instead of recognizing the dream in its generality: "The painting joins here the autism of the dream. Here one must situate this important part of all surrealist painting or deviated dreamlike forms [...]. At that moment, dream painting, dream literature, and dream music contain only the [dream's] autism but ignore its generality" (Lewinter 1972: 55). This certainly has to do with the fundamental difference between the dream and the "dream content" or between what Jung calls the "authentic" dream and the "inauthentic" (symbolic) dream (Jung 1946: 200). I hope to have shown that, while dreams, art, or especially certain forms of "dream art" manage to leave this labyrinth that locks human beings into an intellectualized and autistic "inauthenticity", VR is condemned by definition to stay inside this labyrinth.

## Notes

1. Jullien 1991: "La richesse (virtuelle) de la fadeur est indissociable d'une intuition particulière de l'existence" (115).
2. Trans. Stephen Halliwell "The Loeb Classical Library" Aristotle XXIII (Cambridge MA: Harvard University Press, 1995).
3. For the 1972 edition, Foucault abandons the title and turns the subtitle *Histoire de la folie à l'âge classique* into the book's title. A complete English translation has been published in 2006 with the title *History of Madness*, transl. J. Murphy (New York: Routledge). The editing history of the book is more complicated. For example, in the numerous English editions, Chapter 2 is not equivalent to Chapter 2 in the 1961 version. The below extract dealing with Descartes has been taken from the 1961 French version and corresponding English passages could not be found in any of the translations of this chapter. Therefore the translation is mine.
4. I use this phrase in the sense in which it has been developed in the numerous works of the French futurologist Thierry Gaudin, especially in *Les Pouvoirs du rêve* (Paris: CRCT, 1984), which analyses the importance of dreams on technology. Gaudin's idea is that "modern technology realizes age-old dreams: flight, mentioned by witches and wise men throughout the ages; ubiquity, through the proliferation of sound and images; even the Apocalypse, to which humanity has never been as close as it is now. All of man's great dreams, whether exhilarating or dreadful, are materialized in modern technology" (13).

5. Ellul 1991 quoted by Philippe Breton & Serge Proulx (240). See also Breton's description of the marketing of virtual reality at the end of *Utopie de la communication* [The Utopia of Communication] which is, in my opinion, part of its "ludisation":
6. "They keep harping about [...] how this time really revolutionary changes like high definition television, cellphones, new multimedia, virtual universes, machines featuring an 'artificial consciousness' will be provoking. Those themes absorb more or less all representations of the future suggested by 'specialists' and taken over by the press. [...] However, one does not find anything very original or anything new" (144, my trans.).
7. "Whilst playing, man does not remain in himself, does not stay within the closed area of his mental interiority, but, through a cosmic gesture, he leaves his own self and meaningfully interprets the totality of the world". German: "Spielend verbleibt der Mensch nicht in sich, nicht im geschlossenen Bezirk seiner seelischen Innerlichkeit – er tritt vielmehr ekstatisch aus sich heraus in einer kosmischen Gebärde und deutet sinnhaft das Ganze der Welt" (22). For further explanations of Fink in this context see Botz-Bornstein 2007b.
8. Kimura Bin: *Jikan to Jiko* (*Time and Self*, 1982), 32. Kimura develops the concept of "*aida-ity*" (from the Japanese *aida* = between) as fundamental experience of "things" always made in the "between" of subject and objet.
9. In an earlier French version of this Chapter ("Réalité virtuelle et rêve. Vers la condition autiste?" in *L'Aleph* 12, déc. 2003) the opposition of *ordinatique* and *onirique* has been important.
10. For an interpretation of the *chôra* in this context see my "Khora or Idyll: The Space of the Dream" in *The Philosophical Forum* 33:2 Summer 2002.
11. Marshall McLuhan coined this term in his books *The Gutenberg Galaxy* (1962) and *Understanding Media* (1964).
12. One can understand the particularly infantile character of this community through a reflection on infantile society as a whole as it is produced by the Japanese sociologist Takeo Doi. In his famous study on the phenomenon of the *amae* in Japanese society, Doi shows that to be voluntarily dependent of others is often idealized by society and can become a cultural specificity. *Amae* is the "coaxing" done by children who refuse to recognize, in an adult way, their responsibility towards the world. These children aspire to be wrapped in the dreamy tenderness of their mothers who will not refuse their *amae* and provide an environment adapted to the needs of the children's *amae*. Society of communication engages in the creation of a virtual society as an accumulation of individuals within which everybody, through an act of ludic communication, depends on the other. The soft and idyllic *rêverie* produced by an absolute interdependence of individuals is indeed reminiscent of Takeo Doi's cultural criticism of *amae.* By using a "pure intuition" within the universe of electronic communication, humans look for the confirmation of their *amae* vis-à-vis a mass of individuals forming an opaque and oneiric bloc named VR. As a counterweight to *amae*, and as a procedure able to assist the individual to leave the prison of its ego-centric rêverie that transforms the world into a superlarge, dreamed 'I', Doi introduces the notion of *iki*, generally translated as "style". It is thus a work of stylistics that, according to Doi, shows individuals the way out of the prison of their ego-centric rêverie. However, in a society populated by children who freely engage in the coaxing of *amae*, this "style" can never be engendered as a cultural force (cf. Doi 1973). Doi's analysis of *iki* appears in the work quoted on p. 80. It should be mentioned that in Doi's analysis

the opposition of *iki* and *amae* is backed by the linguistic parallels of both words: *amae* signifies, apart from the meaning given, also "sweet", and *iki* also signifies "harsh".

13. Cf. Marion Leboyer: *Autisme infantile: Faits et modèles*: "[the authistic child] responds to a limited number of stimuli. One says that the child 'hyperselects' a certain type of information among those available in her environment" (56, my trans.). Cf. also Lorna Wing: "Approche épidémologique des caractéristiques sociales comportementales et cognitives" [Epidemological Approach of Comportmental and Cognitive Social Characteristics] in Rutter & Schopler (*op. cit*) who relates the works of C. Hutt, S. Forest, and J. M. Richer: "According to this research, the autistic child is hyperstimulated by social approaches. In particular, a direct eye contact sparks this hyperstimulation. As a consequence, autistic children tend to avoid social proximity and the glance of the other" (35, my trans.). See also the works of Kimura Bin on this subject. Kimura defines autism primarily as a "protection" towards others.

14. As an introduction into this subject the special issue of the *Revue Française de la Psychanalyse* Nr. 5, 1987 ("La psychanalyse et la capacité de rêverie de la mère" Colloque de Deauville 1986") is very useful.

15. There is still one more important parallel, which is the problem of the body and of "bodilessness". In the virtual world the communicating being is a computer and has no body. However, to have a body in real space and real time is important for the perception of a reality that is equipped with an aesthetic or stylistic meaning. In the same way, the frequent absence of the 'I' in the vocabulary of autists is linked to this non-corporeity. Where everything is 'I' (as it is the case for autists), there is no 'Thou' either. As a consequence, a social and urban 'We' corresponding to a political reality cannot develop. All that remains is an idyllic 'We' that is nothing other than the prolongation of the own self.

16. Pierre Fédida, on the other hand, makes an effort to see the "silence where bodies receive a strange visual evidence" and where there is no "mimetic of the same" as an expression that remains *oneiric* in the Freudian sense. But the fact that he encounters large difficulties to do so make us suspect that there is a real distance, between the autistic world and that of dreams. Cf. Fédida 402-403: "The other is a projection of the self. In the case of autism, everything is called into question. Is it possible to operate such a mimetic facing this silence where bodies receive such a strange visual evidence? [...] The aesthetic topology of observation requires of words that they be sensorial acts of signification. But are we so far removed from the Freudian requirement to listen to the psychotic like one should listen to dreams? And is it not here once again the paradigm of the dream that assures the figurability of forms?" (my trans.)

# Feature Scene II

## "Your Face is a Scape": An Exercise in Facial Geomorphology

International realities, some of which are imagined and some are not, interfere with each other up to a point that "virtual ethnicities" become real. This means that even the *ethnos* is no longer necessarily linked to the human realm but can be posthuman.

First there is geographical dislocation. The sociologist of Indian origin, Arjun Appadurai, invented the term "ethnoscape", a notion which successfully grasps the *ethnos* as represented in the new global cultural economy which, as Appadurai writes, "has to be understood as a complex, overlapping, disjunctive order" (Appadurai 1990: 33ff). According to Appadurai, it is no longer possible to speak of *ethnos* as a quality settled in a locality. The more suitable word "ethnoscape" describes "landscapes of persons who constitute the shifting world in which we live". They are represented by all those people who are constantly on the move, that is, "tourists, immigrants, refugees, etc". (297).

The notion of "ethnoscape" is indeed impressive. However, how should we imagine these "landscapes of floating persons?" Should we imagine them as hovering through the air like herds of balloon-like faces, appearing like more or less regularly shaped clouds, each shaded in a different color?

The problem is that when Appadurai launched his notion of the ethnoscape as a metaphorical derivation of the landscape, he seemed to have forgotten one essential point: that landscapes no longer exist. Submitted to the impact of civilization, natural scenery no longer offers the coherent setup permitting a wide view that inspired traditional landscape painters. This unavoidably leads to a disconcerting question: will the ethnoscape suffer from the same symptoms from which the landscape suffered and will it, finally, disappear?

Let us first check Appadurai's metaphor itself and see if what the landscape did to "the country" is comparable to what the ethnoscape does to the human face. "Landscapes are without destiny" said Jean-

François Lyotard (1991: 183). Still, no landscape is thinkable without a minimal dialectics aiming at a reconciliation of antagonisms. What characterizes landscapes is that they are peaceful and temperate. Though they have been shaped by the forces of nature their appearance is peaceful. When looking at a landscape, we simply *cannot imagine* all those basic elements like the water eroding, the wind displacing, the frost crunching, or the heat drying. The powers that formed the valleys, the canyons and the cracks in our regions are automatically eliminated from our imagination as soon as we see the region no longer as a geological-cultural given but as a – landscape. In other words, the landscape is a cemetery of signs. Signs of earthquakes and tragedies might exist or not exist (did you know that in the suburbs of Paris there was once a huge sea?), but, if they existed, they are covered under a heavy "make-up". And usually they remain unconsidered by the meandering view of the contemplator of the landscape: when looking at landscapes, the eye never clings to the detail.

The *view* remains a unifying system and details are usually "viewed" according to a common norm. This norm can even become linguistic. All villages are "perched on a crest" has mocked Alain Robbe-Grillet, and landscape language is often haunted by absurd anthropomorphisms.

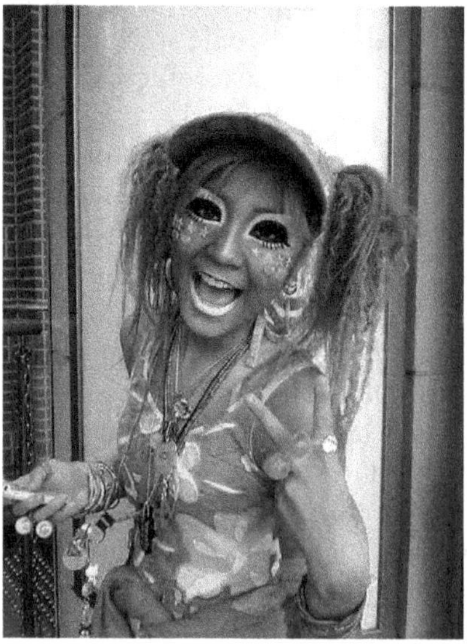

Fig. 5: Ganguro

My point is that, *in reality*, the landscape as a unifying system is no longer functional because the landscape as such has disappeared. Today landscapes are interspersed with electric cables, warehouses, factories and motorways. This means that, while, already in the nineteenth century, landscapes were to a large extent a matter of imagination, today they tend to become, since they no longer exist, a matter of the virtual.

Would it be cynical to say that, in parallel, all those local, human, and ethnic faces, with their natural cracks, valleys and canyons, are bound to turn into posthuman virtual ethnoscapes?

In Asia, a certain "neo-Asian" cultural style dominant in youth culture is concerned not at all with national or political identity but rather with a *personal* – "facial" – identity. The *ganguro* movement of young women in Tokyo attracted international attention in the late 1980s not only because of the eccentric style of clothing, but especially because these women colored their faces in a very dark taint (*ganguro* means "blackface"). Combined with hair dyed in blond or other clear colors, the *ganguros*' look was indeed "exotic" up to a point that it was explained as derived from a Caribbean ethnic outfit.

Though revolutionary in its appearance, the *ganguro* movement was most probably only the – so far – last step of an evolution that the sociologist Takeo Doi had defined in the 1970s as the Japanese ambition "to shelve all distinctions, male-female, east-west, adult-child". The "binarism" that Félix Guattari still put forward in 1979 in his *L'Inconscient machinique*, and through which capitalist society was supposed to maintain the facial hegemony of the "either/or", has definitively been deconstructed. Guattari affirms that capitalist society does not tolerate faces which do not clearly announce their racial or sexual option: "Not only is it necessary to immediately recognize if this is a man, a woman, or a homosexual, but also which kind of man, woman or homosexual" (Guattari 1979: 97).

Posthuman faces relativize these cultural barriers and this not only in Asia. In the Northern hemisphere the white population prefers a tanned skin; in Africa, black people bleach their skins and the clearest taint they can achieve somewhat resembles that of the *ganguros*. If we look at the Jacksons (no matter if Michael or Janet) the resemblance with *ganguros* is really amazing.

A new international, non-authentic, ethnically-universal, posthuman face populates the landscapes of the streets and of the media by becoming what Bruce Clarke has called "narratives of bodily metamorphosis" (Clarke 2008: 1). Critics might find that in these faces, in these "cemeteries of signs", we have difficulties to imagine what conservatives would perhaps call "ethnic reality": the water eroding, the wind displacing, the frost crunching, and the heat drying. However, since the main occupation of ethnoscapes is to "float" within the classical region of landscapes, (that is "where earth and sky touch"), the shift from the real ethnoface to the virtual ethnoscape is probably one of those things that we have to accept as unavoidable.

# 3. From Civilization to Culture: About the Dreamlike Character of Global Civilization

## 1. The Clash of Civilizations

In his best-selling book *The Clash of Civilizations and the Remaking of a New World Order* (1996), Samuel Huntington attempts to explain troubles arising in globalized society by "clashes" occurring violently or non-violently between different civilizational blocks. Huntington suggests that in a society in which no cold war opposition of superpowers is able to establish structural order, international order will be furthermore based on the particularity of the civilizations and not on political ideologies. This would finally serve as a "safeguard against world wars" (Preface and last sentence of the book).

Seen from a philosophical point of view, Huntington's book comes along as a strange paradox. In philosophy classes one sometimes divides the entire body of human thought into two halves: first the "egocentrist" group of thinkers looking for "given", indubitable, self-evident facts that can be systemized (as do for example materialism, skeptical nihilism, positivism, or certain forms of idealism); and second, the "non-egocentrist" group that remains critical towards all givens and, finally, prefers to remain *relativistic*. It is difficult to decide into which school Huntington's theory belongs. Taking "culture" as a primordial subject and highlighting it as by its nature opposed to abstract, structural analysis, he obviously takes a "non-egocentrist" relativistic stance. At the same time, however, his approach appears as materialist with regard to the "culture" he examines since the cultures appear more or less as "given" facts that cannot be doubted.

Huntington could be classified as an "Egocentrist Relativist", a paradoxical combination that might also account for the book's great public appeal. In a way, Huntington manages to have his cake and eat it too. Yet this also has its drawbacks because this book provides neither the "essentialist" assurance usually provided by egocentrist absolutists, nor the therapeutic function usually provided by non-egocentrist relativists.

The main shortcomings of Huntington's view flow indeed out of this "have your cake and eat it too" attitude. They become obvious when looking at his arguments not from a technical, but from a wider historical-philosophical point of view. As mentioned, in spite of the "relativistic" attitude, Huntington's concept of civilization is basically "materialistic" and appears, for that reason, as flat and un-reflected when applied to actual problems of culture in their complexity. Since the book has attained such a high amount of attention one can conclude that a great number of people share Huntington's concept of civilization. Apart from that, those standing on an "other" political shore and who would rather speak out for Western "inventionism", submitting all civilizations under a single "liberal-democratic" roof, do not seem to exhibit a concept of civilization different from Huntington's.

The root of Huntington's misinterpretations is his failure to define the phenomenon of civilization that for him continues to be a fixed entity of materialized consciousness, widely ignoring the complexities of human self-consciousness. Therefore, Huntington's approach to civilizations appears on several levels as too hastily adopted, giving the impression of wanting to explain too many things with the help of one limited theory.

In general, Huntington's attitude appears as characteristic of an objectifying attitude seeing civilizations as something "made", consisting of, as Huntington writes, "objective elements, such as language, history, religion, custom, institutions" (43) on the one hand, and of "subjective" elements like "self-identification" (ibid.) on the other. The problem with this account is that the "subjective" side looks equally as "objective" as the preceding objective elements. The idea of cultural *experience* as something immediate and *inter-subjective*, that is particularly *human*, is from the beginning excluded from these systematical considerations.

Paradoxically, it is too much and simultaneously not enough to say that Huntington's attitude is due to his unfamiliarity with the subject of culture, often apparent in social studies and international relations studies.[1] It is too much because cultural ambitions in sociology have existed (Parsons and Bourdieu, for example); and not enough because Huntington's way of treating global culture is particularly out of place in a sphere today, which is essentially composed of *virtual* elements. More than ever the cultural sphere is to a large extent *immaterial*. Huntington should know that the phenomenon of "culture" which, even traditionally, is difficult to grasp objectively, is even more difficult to establish once we are confronted with virtual, "global culture".

While Huntington's cultural materialism is unacceptable, his treatment of the virtual sphere of the global as if it were a given "something" is perhaps pardonable. Presently, there simply are not many theoretical tools that permit a firm grasp of this "culture". In this sense Huntington's attitude testifies no more than to a typical kind of helplessness present in many disciplines. Kenichi Ohmae has called the new global sphere which represents for him the theatre for international (internet-) business, the "Invisible Continent". In his opinion, on this "continent" a new cold war could transpire (Ohmae 2000). In principle, one cannot deny that ideas like these are temporarily interesting and effective for studies of economics and politics. However, *philosophically,* these attempts to theorize the new geopolitical situation are extremely clumsy since they abandon, once they have given the "ungraspable" a new and concrete name, any further ontological research into the character of the "virtual world of globalization" and the "culture" which is about to arise. The "things that are fleeting" (and which are effective only *because* they are fleeting) are materialized and turn into concrete phenomena. The point is that a new cold war played on the "Invisible Continent" will follow completely different rules not because it is *another* continent, but because it is no continent at all.

Huntington does not write about the virtual input of the new international order. Actually, judging by the tone of *The Clash*, it would be difficult to imagine what he would even have to say about it. In his approach, even "conventional", "non-virtual" culture is materialized. He tries to establish a "map" of civilizational continents, as if civilizations were *visible*, material goods that can be drawn on paper like expressways or mountains. In this way, he establishes parallels between what appears to him as an international reality on the one hand, and conventional "real" civilizations on the other, believing that the first follow the same rules as the second. From there one of his fundamentally false assumptions that civilizations would form groups and oppose themselves to other civilizations also arises. In philosophical terms this represents an immense simplification of the phenomenon of the *perception of the other* which can, on the consciousness-level, already when played with only three individuals, develop constellations close to paradoxical conundrums. How much more complex will it be with civilizations?

Let me sum up my argument. The first part of my point is that even without taking into consideration the existence of the Internet, e-commerce, VR, and so forth, the global situation as it presently appears has something virtual in itself. After all the "cold war" was a widely virtual phenomenon, since it never "really" took place. Second I hold that any "reworking" of this situation with the help of computer technology will only *reinforce*, but not found, this virtual character of the world. In this situation, neo-realist approaches like Huntington's, but also system theories like Wallerstein's,[2] easily appear as passing beside the essential characteristic of "global culture". First because this culture is "global" (meaning to a large extent virtual) and then because, in the new context produced, the concept of "culture" or "civilization" must be elaborated in a more sophisticated way, reflected against the ontological status of "global reality".

Let me start with the latter point – the definition of "culture" – before gradually introducing the "virtual elements" into the discussion. The problematic character of Huntington's theoretical framework may be hidden under heavy empirical studies that speak for themselves. As mentioned, an immensely problematic, as well as characteristic, moment with regard to his theory lies in his idea of "civilization". This is obvious almost anywhere in the book, but I, naturally, am particularly "attracted" to the pages where Huntington tries, obvious to anybody who is acquainted with the problem, to talk away any difference between culture and civilization. It is rewarding to examine this problem from a philosophical point of view since, finally, essential things can be re-learned from classical reflections on culture and civilization especially today when the "global" and the "virtual" invade even our most basic thoughts on civilization.

Huntington writes at the beginning of *The Clash*: "The efforts to distinguish culture and civilization, however, have not caught on, and, outside Germany, there is overwhelming agreement with Braudel that it is 'delusory to wish in the German way to separate *culture* from its foundation *civilization*'" (41). First, there is a difference between separating two things by saying that they bear no relationship with each other, and the *identifying* two different things as being different by clearly maintaining that they remain closely linked. The "German way" has never said that culture and civilization should be "separated" (nor did Braudel believe that they had). The way Huntington puts these matters reveals once more his materialistic attitude towards culture. By quoting Braudel out of context, his statement appears even as bluntly deterministic – normally incompatible with Braudel – suggesting that, because culture is *determined* by civilization, it finally *is* civilization. This does not at all touch upon Braudel's point, let alone upon that of the "German way". As a matter of fact, the purpose of

Braudel's article "On the History of Civilizations" (1969), is to demonstrate the contrary: that culture and civilization are not the same, that the "German persistence is defensible", but that the study of cultures should be integrated into that of civilizations (without saying that the one would be the same as the other). What follows in Braudel's essay is a critique of Arnold Toynbee's division of World culture into civilization-groups, a critique that could easily be adopted as a critique of Huntington's theory itself. Braudel writes:

> That the complex history of mankind could thus be reduced to a score of dominant experiences, what a delightful simplification, if it could be justified! In any case, from this very first contact with Toynbee's way of thinking, from this initial problem of enumeration, it is possible to discern his method of procedure, which is very like that of a scientist looking for a world system, a system whose clear order and exclusive relationships must be imposed authoritatively, for better or worse, onto the teeming mass of reality. (ibid.)

Certainly linked to these fundamental misunderstandings, Huntington adopts Braudel's general outline of the distinction between culture and civilization but omits – though very well developed by Braudel – its decisive subtleties. Huntington describes the German distinction between culture and civilization as the subdivision of civilization into the "civilization part" including "mechanics, technology, and material factors", and the "culture part" including "higher intellectual artistic, moral qualities of a society" (41). The problem with this account of almost a century of German philosophical discourse on civilization is that it is itself materialistic: the "culture part" qualities are described in the same material way in which the "civilization part" qualities are described. This is opposed to the historian's initial intentions. It is thus no wonder that Huntington can conclude with ease, at the end of his elaboration, that any distinction between culture and civilization is unnecessary. The philosophical question behind the distinction has been eluded, by reducing it to one of *classification* and scientific *description*. In reality the distinction between culture and civilization, at the time it was defined, was not meant as an anthropological statement but one concerning the *experience* and *perception* of culture which, with regard to mechanics, differs from that of, say, literature. In other words, while from the perspective of empirical anthropology the distinction between culture and civilization might be inessential, from the point of view of social psychology, consciousness studies, cognitive science, and philosophy, it is not.

This is certainly neither the place nor the time to reanimate the old German discussion about culture and civilization. Certain ideas from Alfred Weber, Spengler or even Nietzsche are no longer valid simply because the context has changed. Still I believe that a certain part of their reflections can provide an original starting point from which to untangle problems concerning contemporary globalization and "virtual culture". Apart from that, it is obvious that the problem of "civilization" in the humanities has not been solved by replacing culture with civilization, but that the difficulties of defining culture as well as civilization persist in all disciplines, including Huntington's.[3] I would suggest that an essential part of human culture and what people in the presently heated discussions on cultural clashes call "civilization", is definitely lost through such a substitution. Also, one should not underestimate the fact that the concept of culture as distinct from civilization, as it was once present in the humanities, has *indirectly* determined other Western disciplines such as linguistics or psychoanalysis, all of which are now used for the analysis of culture.

Let me draw a brief outline of what the "German distinction" between culture and civilization, which Huntington rejects, actually suggests, and how parts of it could be reevaluated. The German word *Kultur* is the older term and corresponds to the Latin form also in its content, whereas the term *civilization* was coined later and developed rapidly especially in eighteenth-century France. During the Enlightenment it ended up signifying perfection, progress and refinement. The optimistic, conquering connotations linked to *civilization*, led in German philosophy since about 1880, to the opposition of *civilization* and *culture*, the latter of which signified human cultural activities which the philosophical tradition liked to link to "soul" and "spirit". An idealist notion of *Kultur* as something "foggy", ungraspable, or, as Mme de Staël would say, "dreamy", was developed during German Romanticism. (I dare to suggest that this fact is certainly interesting with regard to VR as the contemporary cultural mediator.)

Though, in general, France has been heavily influenced by this German notion of *Kultur* as something intimate, local and personal (the French word *culture* is marked off by these connotations ever since), it developed, in parallel, a notion of *civilisation*, excelling through a particularly general and supra-national outfit. In Germany, the traditional distinction between culture and civilization continued to exist and was revived through Spengler, whom Huntington quotes on occasion. Spengler reflected very much upon the difference between "inward-turned cultural energy" and "outward-turned civilizational exposure".[4] In certain passages of *The Decline of the Occident*, Spengler comes very close to the distinction between what I have sketched above as the opposition of cultural *experience* and civilizational *description*. Certainly, as Braudel rightly reproaches Spengler, Spengler systematically neglects politics when defining "culture" – an easy thing to do in Germany where the separation of culture and politics has always been commonplace. Still, this does not represent a reason to say that culture simply *is* politics. Thomas Mann, after having experienced World War II, returned to the formerly rejected designation of culture as something spiritual as opposed to the mechanical "civilization".

The British anthropological approach towards civilization, mainly developed by E. B. Tylor, could not find useful applications for the German distinction, not so much because it would have been proven wrong, but because the angle with which these anthropologists were looking at culture was entirely different. British anthropology focused on social expressions that are measurable, such as customs (Frazer), and designed their notion of civilization accordingly. This British and, afterwards, worldwide accepted notion of civilization was solid enough for the study of "real" *societies*.

As superseded as the German discourse might be in general, the most essential point worth reconsidering today is the distinction between culture as a lived experience seen from the point of view of the people "inside" that culture, and culture as a materialized, "labeled" phenomenon seen as a stable quantity by those who look at it from the outside. Alfred Weber's distinction between "external history" and "internal history" (1946) comes to mind, but even this is still misleading. History or civilization are not *objects* with an inner and outer side, but civilization and culture are *experiences* which, like all experiences, can be either *made* or *observed*. They cannot be visited once from the inside and then from the outside.

There are reasons to suppose that the traditional German distinction between culture and civilization has, among other things, been developed in order to establish the difference *not* between two different and separately existing phenomena, but between two different modes of existence of the same thing, that is of civilization. In this way, Braudel's idea of civilization as the foundation of culture continues to make sense. Others stop making sense, like the "inverting" one which sees "cultures" as primitive phenomena and "civilizations" as more advanced (which Huntington mentions); or the idea of "cultures" as the smaller units embedded in a "larger" civilizational spheres. All these theories are, so to speak, sublated, *aufgehoben* (to use Hegel's term), in the present model of civilization that claims that any civilization can have different modes of existence.

Today, with regard to contemporary global culture that remains difficult to structure on the one hand, and equally difficult to reduce to empirical facts on the other, and which is, furthermore to a large extent "virtualized", any common concept of "real civilizations" can seem overly pragmatic. The "new world order" consists not simply in the abandonment of an old cold war world partitioned into two strongholds and the subsequent recognition of new strongholds according to "civilizational" laws. Instead of describing the globalized sphere as a juxtaposition of more or less blown up indigenous "core elements", today's challenge consists in philosophically defining the "foggy", dreamlike and playful state of "reality" that is suggested through the latest version of globalization made possible through the internet and VR. Of course, I am talking here about the world as an *experience* of global *culture* and not about bits of civilizations distributed over the globe as they seem to be perceived "from the outside" by some analysts of international relations. When, for example, through the effects of globalization, common-sensical notions like the small *Gemeinschaft* and the larger *Gesellschaft* are partly inverted, the intimate process of cultural perception is under more scrutiny than the process of scientific classification. Globalization asks people to form a "global community" with those who are geographically far, whereas *society* represents the more intimate unity by which experience is still mediated through physical access. Even without the use of the internet or a computer, the effect this causes is certainly one of *vertigo*, and comes closer to the experience of a game or a dream than to that of scientific classification.

Goethe wrote already in 1795 that the center of culture could be found nowhere and he meant this in an anthropological sense as well as in a geographical one (Goethe 1999: 287). Is this not reminiscent of the present virtual-global world? For this reason the theoretical focus on these phenomena cannot be one of describing objective "civilizations" but must be one of trying to grasp inter-subjective cultures as cultural experiences which are "intimate" but which at the same time include within their intimacy the constant perception of the other.

But let me return for one last time to "German philosophy". In German philosophy the distinction between civilization and culture was also one between form and content. The ideal culture, as it was first expressed by Nietzsche, was one in which form would absolutely correspond to content. Culture would obtain a degree of "reality" in which it finally *was* what it *appeared* to be. Nietzsche's ambition seems rather far-fetched in the present context as it was meant to criticize contemporary German culture which Nietzsche perceived as too much of an empty form with nothing "real" inside. The distinction between form and content, however, remains interesting, especially when looking at a global map of civilizations today. How much imitation, pretension, and simulation is actually contained in *every* culture or, how much of every "real" culture is actually "unreal"? When talking about culture not as a "label" pitched on different parts of the globe but as the immediate experience of those living in that culture, we see that no style of any culture is actually more than an accepted balance between elements that are real and those that are unreal. In some way, style or even culture itself becomes here virtual phenomena *par excellence*; this once again reinforces my claim that the appearance of VR does not create an entirely new situation but makes the existing situation only more complex.

I have pointed out above that the creation of style in the realm of the virtual creates a reality that is alien to anything tragic and turns *everything* into style. Style is reproduced with the lightness that one can normally find only in games and in dreams. This is the "culture" that Nietzsche criticizes. Also Nietzsche would say that before any creation of style is possible, a cultural reality must *preexist*. The dream of VR, which exists irrespective of any *cultural reality,* however, is absolute; it is a "phenomenological style" described in Chapter 2, which pretends to overlap with the "things" and the "reality of the world".

Had Nietzsche read Huntington, he would certainly have said that Huntington's world appears as an "idyllic place" in which the present corresponds exactly to history (has become history) and in which people behave exactly as they are supposed to do. It is difficult to resist adding that Fukuyama's world, as it is exposed in *The End of History* (1992), appears here as the exact contrary of Huntington's which makes it, however, no more convincing. In Fukuyama's world, three quarters of the world's people behave as they are *not* supposed to behave, though this no longer raises concern since the historical model for the "right behavior" has been definitively lost (history has been abolished). What is lacking in both Huntington and Fukuyama is an essential ironical distance towards any such phenomena as civilization, an irony that was inherent not only in Nietzsche but also in Norbert Elias. Elias, when establishing the "rules" for civilization (self-control, table manners, conditioning, etc.), was aware that no ideal state of such a civilization exists, which means that whenever we discuss "civilizations" we are talking about something inexistent. All that exists is the *cultural experience* of people who live in their culture, who shape their culture by being exposed to influences produced at the inside of their culture, as well as to outside influences (Elias 1969: 229).

It is for these reasons, as well as for their proximity with a kind of contemporary, global, "virtual civilization", that I find the parallel between culture and dream instructive, and I would like to consolidate them here. Given the strategic value that the word "dream" has in the present book, it is worthwhile to establish it in the context of a Freudian theory of civilization. For Freud, civilization came about through the determination and conditioning of the *id* by the *superego*. Would the uncivilized *id* be able to exist without the forming influence of the cultural *superego*, civilization would never have come into being. It is obvious that this model of culture is coined along the model of the dream. Also dreams come about through the intervention of the *superego* into the "wild" images produced by the *id*. The problem with Freud is that, in reality, he could never exclude the existence of pure "*id*-dreams" because he could not know what they were. He could not examine the "dreams themselves" but only their "material manifestations", that is remembrances or dream narratives (called the dream discourse). There lies the problem also with regard to the definition of civilization. In the same way in which, in Freudian theory, there are *obvious* and *latent* dream thoughts there should also be *obvious* and *latent* "cultural thoughts" or cultural phenomena. As a matter of fact, the latter are not as latent as Freud thought because they are, in reality, the "obvious" ones, at least for those who *dream their dream*, or who *live their culture*. As an analytic rule, the "real culture", like the "real dream", or the experience of dream (or culture) as it is dreamt (or lived), or simply the dream as it dreams itself (or culture as it produces itself), is lost. Similarly, in general, all we know about *other* cultures are cultural narratives, which are *linguistic, materialized versions of culture*.

It is along these lines that Huntington's map reduces world cultures to dream *narratives* instead of trying to grasp their status as experienced dreams. These "Narratives of Civilizations" are not "Grand Narratives" as they existed until recently in the modern era (the Narrative of Communism, of Progress, etc.) but are small ones. This can be seen as the main difference between Huntington and Fukuyama. Since few people want to listen to Grand Narratives nowadays anyway, Fukuyama puts an end to all of them. However, he does so not by *telling* the "dream that dreams itself" but by making the dream abstract and conceptual. Fukuyama calls this grand anti-narrative "liberal democracy". Huntington, on the other hand, reintroduces "narrative" as a discipline, but his narratives are tamed and weak, so his realism fails to frighten anyone. However, besides Huntington's small narratives or Fukuyama's accomplished silence, both Huntington's and Fukuyama's visions neglect the fact that *cultural experience* still exists. It might not exist *as language*. Much of the Freudian *id, eros*, or even the famous *death-drive* may never have been transformed (or mediated) into language. Because of the West's common deafness to (or arrogance towards) everything that is not *present* in the form of "civilizational narratives", in one form or the other, events like 9/11 could cause so much surprise.

## 2. What is Global Culture?

I have introduced the comparison of culture with dreams in a way that might leave some people perplex. As a matter of fact, there is no theoretical literature on the similarities between these two phenomena. In some way, this is amazing when considering Freud's parallel treatment of the genesis of dreams and of civilization. As I have said, I am convinced that today a *certain* dreamlike character of civilization becomes even more manifest through the development of globalized culture as it propels itself through the increasing shift towards VR or even towards a self-reproducing reality. How can one define this global (virtual, posthuman) culture more closely? To say it in a word, globalization *should exist*, otherwise the world would be forever stuck in a perhaps idyllic, but static coexistence of civilizational blocks. Globalization exists but it should not be defined as a constellation of materialized, extroverting civilizational core-structures "communicating" in "reasonable" or "unreasonable" ways with each other, but rather as an intimate, consciousness-forming cultural exchange. At least since the Renaissance, we have recognized a globalized world based on the existence of a consciousness-forming exchange with the other on a "pre-narrative" or "pre-conceptual level".

Seen like this, one is tempted to ask why there is actually this extraordinary contemporary interest in the "emergence of globalization"? Is it only because exchanges have multiplied that people have suddenly become aware of the global context in which they are living that had formerly gone unnoticed? This may be true to some extent but it cannot be the main reason. The world has been involved in two World Wars, nuclear weapons threaten the entire world, and international tourism as well as de-localized industrial production has been proliferating since decades.

There is certainly a reason for the sudden rise in interest in globalization: suddenly "global culture" has become "graspable with your hands" (that is with your software). In other words, what used to be a vague dream of a global world has now been transformed into the latest "Grand Narrative" of humanity called "VR". This means, to stay close to our model of dream, that the dream of the *id* or the *death-drive* has become *language*. By "spelling out" global reality for a second time (as if it does not exist already), VR manages to integrate all cultural dreams of the world into one civilizational discourse. The problem with this is not at all the reuniting ambition of the computerized world (this is only naturally human) but the fact *that it is a discourse*, which means that the initial *cultural reality* is lost. Take the "international information climate" (Ohmae) created by the media and the Internet. This is not an innocent accumulation of facts from around the world but the systematic transformation of pre-linguistic cultural experiences into communicable "linguistic" units. I apply "linguistic" here in a metaphorical sense following the Freudian model of dream-contents vs. dream-discourse, and am aware that materialization of cultural experiences happens today more through images than through language.

The current treatment of the phenomenon of Global Culture is thus not surprising. What happens is what happened at the beginning of the twentieth century with another "newly" discovered sphere, with that of the unconscious or of dream. Through the Freudian psychoanalysis for example, world culture is transformed into a Narrative: human "dreams of cultures" are transformed into posthuman *material* quantities. Through this process everything becomes "material": "self-realization" and creative imitation/integration become "identity", *eros* becomes "eroticism", religious consciousness becomes "belief", and, what has turned out to be more dramatic recently, the Freudian *death-drive* is transformed into "hate".

The paradox in all this is that, initially and still presently for most people, VR did not appear like a posthuman Grand Narrative about civilizations but as its exact contrary: for most, the internet became interesting because it seemed to present an immanent, authentic experience with a truly global culture in "real-time" which had not yet been materialized by any other medium. Through the internet we believed we could grasp "world culture" not as a materialized narrative but directly interfere in its human and cultural *durée pure*. That it did not remain like this is, to some extent, the fault of the users. The attraction that the internet exercises on the masses of the industrialized countries has quickly limited itself to what some may like to call a typically petty-bourgeois model in the way in which it has been described in Feature Scene I: follow a dream of greatness without risking your own security. This pattern signifies in principle: grasp and embrace "The World" as if you are Kipling or Jack London, but don't leave your study room. As a consequence, the internet as a mass medium has become more and more unable to offer real pre-materialized cultural experience of the global dream, but spit out only – rather small – posthuman dream narratives.

Finally, it appears that people do not *want* global culture to be a dream but a dream language that is coherent, material, and easy to consume. (By the way, this establishes the strongest link between the consumer society of the 1970s and the present society as it is mediated through the Internet. In principle, VR is nothing other but a reality designed for a posthuman hyper consumer society in which the product consumed is "The World" itself.)

The posthuman drift also partly explains the success of Huntington's book. Curiously, Huntington's neo-realist description of the world could not even be perceived as a shift of focus on globalization *from* "VR" *to* "reality". VR had become a reality in the simple and banal sense of the word, and Huntington simply added one more narratives to the virtual narratives that everybody knows anyway. *Global, cultural experience* as a subject worthy of consideration is so buried under "realities" that it is not even perceived.

The dream input (and its final suppression) is obvious if one moves back two decades or three in our ever-evolving contemporary history. One should not forget that the cultural discourse on globalization is the immediate successor of the once so blown up discourse on "postmodernity". Just like "postmodernity", globalized culture is often believed not to possess the hedonism and expressiveness of "consumer culture". This proves untrue. What is different is that postmodernity, perhaps because of its more "natural" link with "culture", can more easily be discussed in terms of "dream-modes". This almost naturally flows out of its demonstrative playfulness and anti-foundationalist philosophy, but is certainly also linked to its aesthetic penchant. Has architecture ever been more discussed from purely aesthetic points of view than during the peak period of publications on "postmodernity", neglecting all "practical" components like functionality, quality and so forth? Discourses concerning globalization matters", in spite of their obvious "cultural turn", represent a contrast here.

In some way, political theorists seem to get their feet back on the ground. Globalization appears, *first of all*, as a matter of geography, economy, and politics, and, when it evokes associations with "culture", these will be called "core-cultures".[5] These associations are not immediately directed towards "aesthetics", or even towards intrinsic cultural experience that I have defined above as cultural dreams. If a dreamlike component *does* exist with regard to the phenomenon of globalization, this is supposed to have been installed "retrospectively" and "technically" through the integration of virtual elements into the globalized world – by letting a part of it appear within the realm of computerized VR.

However, in reality, nobody has ever "let anything appear": the "foggy state" of the global situation is its own producer. In reality, *from the beginning* the human project called "globalization" has had the same "aesthetic" intentions that the creation of "dreamlike" postmodern, posthuman culture has had. The selection of the "virtual" as an arena for globalized experience has never been a willful, technological, addition but was, on an ontological level, a necessary condition for "globalization" from the beginning. Globalization is bound to be dreamlike and virtual. The "cultural turn" in sociology was fed in the 1980s by motives derived from postmodern culture. The answer to the question whether "globalization" can be as *culturally* nourishing as postmodernity for sociology today depends on the extent to which the fundamentally aesthetic character of globalization is recognized.

## Notes

1. It is impossible to engage here in the debate whether "culture" as a subject for sociology and international relations has been sufficiently elaborated in the past. Some people, like Robert Wuthnow, say that culture has been traditionally consistently neglected and that Social Sciences as a whole "are in danger of abandoning culture entirely as a field of enquiry" ("Introduction" to *Cultural Analysis: The Work of Peter L. Berger, Mary Douglas, Michel Foucault, and Jürgen Habermas* (London & Boston: Routledge and Kegan Paul, 1984), 2. Wuthnow insists that the few existing cultural approaches "are largely European in origin and for this reason have remained relatively obscure to American audiences" (7). Others, like Roland Robertson, point to the studies of Parsons, Bourdieu and others to prove the contrary. Still Robertson concedes that "it would not be too much to say that modern sociology as a 'scientific profession' has been, particularly but cer-

tainly not only in the USA, a culture-resistant discipline" (Roland Robertson 1992, 35).

2. See Immanuel Wallerstein, *The Modern World System* (3 Vol.) (New York: Academic Press, 1974-1989) as well as a chapter in *Geopolitics and Geoculture: Essays on the Changing World System* called "The Modern World-System as a Civilization" (Cambridge: Cambridge University Press, 1991).

3. See also Wallerstein who disentangles, with regard to modern world systems, two different uses of the word culture, first as "the set of characteristics which distinguish one group from another, and [second] as some set of phenomena which are different from (and 'higher' than some other set of phenomena within any one group". "Culture as the Ideological Battleground of the Modern Word-System", in: M. Featherstone (ed.): *Global Culture: Nationalism, Globalization and Modernity* (London: Sage, 1990), 33.

4. It is, by the way, Spengler who noted in the same book the opposition of the "extreme consciousness of Western history opposed to the almost dreamlike [cultural] unconsciousness of India" (171). Could the frequent misunderstandings between East and West, as soon as it comes to culture, perhaps have one of their historical origins here?

5. I am talking about political and economic sciences and I am aware that the discipline of Cultural Studies has been working on the definition of culture since many decades.

# Feature Scene III

# Liquid Grammar, Liquid Style: On the East-Asian Way of Using English or the Phenomenon of "Linguistic Air-Guitars"

*"Thinking Logically to Feel Confident About Reading English"*
(from a Chinese Time-Newsweek subscription campaign)

## 1. At Full Love With Vivian

The Western visitor of East Asia marvels at English expressions that he encounters in advertisements, in magazines, on T-Shirts, and elsewhere that seem to come "out of another world". Single words and short English sentences, rarely longer than five words, suggest something like the invention of a new language. In Japan and in Korea this phenomenon has been thriving for decades. In China it is more recent but it is developing along the same lines.

The use of English in East Asia is linked to a certain part of East-Asian social history. "Japano-English" for example, is neither "real" English nor Japanese but symbolizes, within the domain of linguistics, the *co-existence* of two cultural spheres. In Japan, after the mid-1880s, an earlier uncritical and unsystematic acceptance of things Western gradually gave way to the view that Japanese and Western cultures can exist side-by-side. From then on the question was: how can East Asia incorporate the West without being culturally overwhelmed by it?

In the domain of language, Japano-English brought forward schemes of cultural coexistence of utmost sophistication. *Wasei eigo* (made in Japan English) is a well-known phenomenon. Most of the time, it concerns the invention – or rather re-invention – of *words* like *arubaito* (part-time work from the German *Arbeit*) or *mansion* (a modern apartment block), attributing new meanings to foreign words. More fascinating – though much more difficult to analyze – are the peculiar English sentences in which words and grammar follow almost normal usage rules but which nevertheless express an unmatched strangeness. Because such English is common in Japan (Engrish),

Korea (Konglish), China (Chinglish), and other East-Asian countries like Indonesia and Thailand, I suggest labeling this "language" as East-Asian English (EA English). I am well aware that there are differences between these national branches of English, but I think that a certain overall similarity enables us to speak here of a new "Pan-Asian language" based on a common East-Asian cultural experience.

## 2. For Your Tasteful Life

Often it is simply the vagueness of these languages, as well as the lack of many prepositions, inflections, copula like 'and' and 'or', articles and personal pronouns in Japanese and Korean, as well as the indistinction of concepts, verbs, and adjectives (especially in Chinese), which makes a literal translation from an Asian language to English imprecise and confused. In these cases the result is a kind of East-Asian Pidgin: "Do not play water", "400% expectation coffee", "Classics of world translates into film..."

However, EA English covers a range of phenomena much broader than the scope of Pidgin English. Therefore – though many cases might overlap – I distinguish simplified (Pidgin-like) English from EA English, defining it as *an autonomous way of speaking* determined by layers of an interculturally determined cognition that reside at deeper levels than those produced only by the grammar and vocabulary of the host language. The cognitive structure underlying the apprehension of EA English is not based principally on the process of *derivation* from an already existing language, but almost represents the *creation* of a new language.[1] Already Donald L. Smith, who wrote one of the first academic essays on "Engrish" in 1974, stated that "[a]n educated Japanese using English will quite naturally feel uncomfortable with the language, especially as he tries to observe all the rules governing the new and exacting foreign terms, but with Engrish he is released from the elements of his industrialized society for precise terminology" (Smith 1974: 188).

In the present "Feature Scene" I will argue that the English fragments that appear in East-Asian contexts are experienced on a relatively *immediate level of cognition* that in many cases does not refer to linguistic models of the host language (Japanese, Korean, Chinese). I am aware that writing about a phenomenon like EA English is difficult because the attribution of an expression to decorative English (also called ornamental English), simply false English or a genuinely new way of speaking is often debatable. Many cases overlap. Still I will try to crystallize what appear to be the most general features of EA English.

### 3. Make Your Creativity Into Flowers

Decorative English surfaces most often in fashion and beauty magazines. In specialized business-magazines it appears surprisingly rarely though one might perhaps expect a better knowledge of English among experts of economics than among readers of beauty magazines. However, what is at stake is not the *understanding* of this language. Most of the time, the words are printed in large roman letters that stand out from the vernacular script. The use of such words (French words for fashion or German words for cars) occurs, of course, in advertisements all over the world and is not particularly Asian. However, in Asia this phenomenon is more frequent. Foreign language words are often used as effective tools without creating language by relying on their *visual* function. These words are to be understood as silent (they are to be *seen* rather than heard), expressing a style rather than a clear semantic message. At the same time, their semantic meaning is not totally unimportant. They correspond to a concept that Benjamin has singled out as a typical phenomenon of modernity: they are "images [that take] the place of concepts: riddles and picture-puzzles of dreams that hide, that slip through the net of semiotics but which are still worth the effort of gaining knowledge" (1982b).

*Wasei eigo* deals mainly with words that are written in the Japanese phonetic script *katakana* (though of course the Japanese write many English words in *katakana* without these words being recognized as belonging to the repertory of *wasei eigo*). The Koreans do the same with *hangul* and the Chinese, in lack of a phonetic script, use their ideographs to transcribe foreign words which turns out to be much more difficult (*hambaobao* for hamburger, and *â er bei sî* for Alpenliebe, for example). This transcribed language appears more like a secret language understandable – if at all – only to speakers of that language. The mystifying effect of such a secret national language is enormous. In Japanese, some "English" words become pronounceable only through their transcription in *katakana*. A shampoo with the difficult name "*Asience*" (obviously a fusion of Asia and science) can be pronounced "ajiensu" only when employing the *katakana* transcription. "*Buru rich tea life*", written in *katakana*, will most often only be understood by a Japanese person who knows that "buru" signifies "bourgeois".

*Wasei eigo* is a hybrid language which is based, like Pidgin-English or Spanglish, on a model of fusion. True, EA English shares with these languages the fact that it has no native speakers. At the same time EA English is more than a curious secret language because it has the more developed features of an autonomous language. Also, it is not restricted to the domain of advertisements and cannot be fully explained as an advertising ploy selling, for example, bourgeois sentiment. And on a formal level, its particular character cannot be explained through binary (bilingual) schemes of fusion like code-switching, code-mixing, calques, insertion or alternation (all of them restricted to vocabulary and grammar). The scheme at work in EA English raises the phenomenon of "cultural coexistence" to a much higher level of sophistication. Only EA English is able to provide the stunning and dreamlike effect of sentences like this:

> "*Recovery-Rediscovery: Re-experience vibrant, youthful looking skin as REVITAL realigns your skin's inner strengths to overcome gravity, the appearance of wrinkles and dullness*"
> (from a Chinese *Shiseido* advertisement).

The fluent – perhaps too fluent – English is grammatically flawless and does not employ a single newly invented word. Still, unstable and fleeting as it is, it conveys a strangeness reminiscent of a dream language. There is the playful use of language (like children playing with words beginning with re-) inviting the reader to "re-experience vibrant youthful looking skin". It is clear that it is impossible to experience one's skin, either in English or in Chinese even if, through a playful device, the idea of "experience" is heightened by turning it into "re-experience".

The next example comes from a Shanghai real estate agency:

> "*New center world. Its totally different.*
> *Maybe we can call this a kind of Shanghai memory*".

The assuring assertion that something is "totally" different is followed by a juxtaposition of "maybe", "can", and "kind of" (where all three are out of place). This is neither precise nor vague but simply strange. One might say that this is the opposite of "thinking in words" because here the words have been chosen only because they appear momentarily appropriate on a – very unstable – emotional level. At the same time there is a lot of self-reflexive thought in this language, which mocks any attempt at defining it as a direct expression of emotions. There is some "thinking" at work, but it is not real analytical thinking; "thinking" is here guided – in an emotional manner – by words which are appreciated not only for their clear semantic content but as emotional-semantic fields whose borders remain unclear.

This process is far from spontaneous. Often these words are selected from a dictionary and selectively italicized. For example, the following is taken from the slogan of a Shanghai Hotel:

> *"Luxury flatlet and hotel establishment embody* noblest *verve".*

Here are some Japanese examples:

> *"We think that we want to contribute to society through diamond drilling and wire sawing".*

Or:

> *"Let's carry out preservation at room temperature"*

Or:

> *Beauty is anywhere around the world.*
> *AVE will change from uncertain to necessary the heart*
> *which feels beauty and is sharpened.*
> *AVE and you stir up the impression of people. It's a AVE surrealism.*

EA English is a reflective emotional language composed of "intellectualized word-emotions".

**4. Because it passes Soon, Pleasant Time is Lonely**

EA English is representative of a more general process of a particularly paradoxical style of "Westernized" East-Asian culture. One paradox is the particularly strange combination of Orientalism and Occidentalism. Orientalism signifies the Western appropriation of the Orient and can be encountered by "Occidentalism", through which the "Orientals" attempt to reconstruct the West as their Other. However, Occidentalism is not necessarily an inverted form of Orientalism (see Buruma and Margalit 2004). To the extent that Orientals strive towards an integration and coexistence of two cultures, they do usually not aim at the straightforward degradation and submission of the West.

In the domain of language, the complex character of these cultural techniques is particularly evident. By using EA English one intends:

(1) To be respectful towards the English language (and thus to degrade oneself because "we cannot say these things in Chinese or Japanese"). At the same time, by distorting it, one is disrespectful towards this language.

(2) To colonize the English language by using it, though at the same time being aware that one is *colonized* by it through its use.

Edward Said's assumption that the cultural appropriation of the Other is *either* an act of imperialistic colonization *or* one of self-colonization is not true with regard to EA English. Both Orientalist and Occidentalist schemes remain trapped within a dialectics of "Oxford English" vs. "Pidgin English" and disregard the possibility of combining both approaches in a paradoxical way.

## 5. The Bag Means Your Mind

It is, of course, no surprise that English has been chosen as the new Pan-Asian language. While after the war the Korean language was not taught at any Japanese university, the use of English spread very quickly. What spread most significantly was a variation of English determined by a form of cultural paradox that is typical for a region marked by Pan-Asian "revolutionary" history. Pan-Asianism represented a movement of Asian cooperation launched around 1903 by Kakuzo Okakura and meant to halt the Western advance. All Asians should recognize their own cultural values and "weather the storm under which so much of the Oriental world went down" (Okakura 1905: 241). Being aware of the worldwide rise of colonized peoples and the possible decline of imperialism, Pan-Asianists tried to organize a cultural stronghold which could serve as an orientation mark to "second rate" nations that would otherwise be lost in a sea of individual civilizations and fall victim to European imperialism.

However, due to the curious geopolitical position of Japan, much of the identity of the "Orient" as well as the identity of Japan remained in the domain of the imaginary. As Kang Sanggjung said: "Japan constructed such an identity in terms of the relation between its idea of the 'Orient' (which was discovered or created by both its identity with and difference from the West) and its imaginary geography and history of Korea, Manchuria, and China. Herein lies the aporia that was repeated throughout Japan's process of modernization" (Kang 2005: 90). For Kang the "very category of the 'Orient' is nothing but an 'imaginary time and space,' one that emerged from the suffering common to non-Western societies in their attempt to reconcile civilization and culture, difference and identity (93)".

One of the results was the construction of Pan-Asianism as a kind of "anti-imperialist imperialism" under Japanese leadership, an attitude which turned out to be a constant producer of cultural paradoxes.[2] However, because a large part of Pan-Asianist aspirations took place in the domain of the imaginary, these paradoxes could be accepted. Indeed, Pan-Asianism is characterized by the coexistence of a series of paradoxical elements: colonialism/anti-colonialism, conservatism/revolutionary attitudes, individualism/totalitarianism, and nationalism/internationalism.

Notably, "Western culture" was never celebrated as a geographical and historical reality but existed from the beginning in the form of an imagined and fictionalized Western culture (films, fashion, life style, etc.). This is one of the reasons why pacific warfare failed to eradicate a hidden admiration for the United States of America.

Today, the paradoxes cultivated by colonized colonizers can thrive even better than in the 1920s. The reason is that since the times of Sun Yat-sen the linguistic and cultural *reality* of what is called "Western culture" or "English language" has constantly shifted towards a sphere that is predominantly playful and dreamlike. East-Asian "westernized" culture appears less than ever to be a "real world" in which objectified elements from eastern and western cultures have merely been combined. The emergence of EA English as an autonomous language represents one further step in a series of attempts to construct a "Western" Other capable of embracing all cultural paradoxes of Westernized East Asia.[3]

**6. These Pleasing Days**

Children approach the linguistic reality of adults by incorporating new sentences into "old", childlike grammatical structures. By and by the old structures get expanded until they overlap with those of adult language. Even bilingual children do this, taking care not to put the two languages into a subset relation.[4] Children abandon incorrect grammatical patterns in order to acquire correct language. This language represents a concrete reality for children, as they hear correct grammatical structures very often (linguists estimate frequency measures of 100,000 inputs until the child drops a wrong form, cf. Roeper, 167). More importantly, children *need* to acquire this correct language in order to survive in the linguistic reality made by adults.

How do these things work with regard to EA English? It is clear that the linguistic "reality" of EA English is inscribed into a completely different cultural schedule because with EA English an objectified model reality within which one can have concrete experiences does not exist. What exists is a linguistic imaginary of "English and the West" shaped with regard to one's own imaginary Asian identity.

### 7. The Premonition that Happens to be Pleasant

In truth, "the West" is to most East-Asians still as unfamiliar as it was sixty years ago. Any "familiarity" is not natural, rather, it is constructed by transforming Western reality into an allegory of itself. While the symbol symbolizes something, an allegory conveys a supplementary meaning in addition to the original meaning as it is evolving through the process of a narrative. Most East-Asians seem to take EA English for granted as a cultural symbol; indeed EA English's disconcerting, "strange" character is noticed mostly by foreigners. A serious amount of allegorical discontinuity is reflected in EA English expressions as they "represent" Anglo-American culture. In this sense, EA English is exemplary of Fredric Jameson's characterization of the postmodern episteme as dominated by an "allegorical spirit [which] is profoundly discontinuous, [which is] a matter of breaks and heterogeneities, [and] of the multiple polysemia of the dream rather than the homogenous representation of the symbol" (Jameson 1986: 73).

EA English "represents" Western culture allegorically. Thus, EA English is comparable to Walter Benjamin's conception of the allegory as an eternally strange quality that remains inaccessible to scientific analysis. Allegories contain a certain amount of feeling, but because they remain hazy and fleeting, they cannot be grasped with the help of empathy. For Benjamin, modernity is "the world governed by its phantasmagorias" (1983 V, 1: 77)[5] and the phantasmagoric world of modernity is a dream. The world of modernity transforms itself into a kind of dreamlike writing in which some words "flash" like allegories. Contemporary East-Asian culture has produced this type of writing in a more literal way than Benjamin could have thought. EA English allegories "dart [...] past only as an image flashing at the very moment [they] can be recognized but then disappear [...] immediately and for good" (Benjamin 1983, I, 2: 695).

### 8. Discover the Taste of Food

In fashion and life-style magazines, EA English is used as a structuring element providing titles to columns, features, and sections. Here EA English adopts an allegorical technique of fragmentation. It is wrong to describe its role as being reduced to "decorative English". The English headings in magazines read – as perhaps any headings should – like fragments from a larger piece. However, the way articles are synthesized in these headings looks either incomplete and inconsistent or tautological. In this way, they are allegories par excellence because in them we encounter a "fixed image and a fixed sign in one" (Benjamin 1983, I, 1: 359). Here are some examples:

*"I Deserve the Best of All"* (on a designer).
*"For the Beauty of Stone"*
*"One Person in Brazil"*
*"Engine for Architecture"*
*"Seeing Believing"*
*"Bold Beautiful Pieces"*
*"So Attractive for Date"*
*"Origins of Love"*

**9. Lovely Water – You Are Free**

On the one hand, the use of EA English is similar to children's language; on the other hand, there is no expansion towards adult language because this model or ideal is absent. Therefore, EA English remains a largely "intuitive" way of speaking: instead of appealing to a mental representation determined by a functional role (through practical or theoretical reasoning), it appeals to a "non-subjective" cultural consciousness and not to linguistic schemes of cognition. The concrete phenomenon of language passes through this non-subjective consciousness in the form of pre-linguistic experience; only afterwards do the utterances of the speaker become concrete language. This means that the English language elements, in the way they are used in these contexts, have not been objectified by a subject beforehand, they are not experienced as *objective* elements but *immediately* contribute to the formation of a new linguistic consciousness.

These EA English expressions do certainly have an *emotional* appeal, but the way in which "emotion" is present in this language is intriguing. It is not present in a linguistically objectified form but rather as "pure emotion" that speaks indirectly through the choice of words and their combination. Although linguistic reflection often takes place on a conscious level, the choice of words is often determined by emotional, pre-linguistic patterns of reflection.

The cultural experience of EA English comes close to "pure experience" as it has been elaborated by the philosopher William James. For James, pure experience "is as if there were in the human consciousness a sense of reality, a feeling of objective presence, a perception of what we may call 'something there,' more deep and more general than any of the particular 'sense' by which current psychology supposes existent realities to be originally revealed" (James 1985: 56). These experiences are "pre-conceptual" in the sense that they are not mastered by a conceptualizing intellect but excel in the combination of non-objectified (imaginary) elements of Eastern and Western culture within linguistic experience. In other words, they are real without being objectified, which brings them close to virtual phenomena.

The linguists Clore and Ortony have analyzed "emotion terms" in language: "If someone refers, for example, to '*being* alone' in some situation, we would not necessarily assume that they are experiencing an emotion; but if they refer to '*feeling* alone', we would. Hence, the failure to control the implicit linguistic context in which words are considered may be responsible for terms such as 'alone' sometimes being rated by subjects as emotions" (Clore and Ortony 1988: 370, my italics). Clore and Ortony claim that "'*being* neglected' does not satisfy the requirements of an emotion on any count [because] it does not necessarily involve a mental state" (374). '*Feeling* neglected' on the other hand, *does* communicate an emotional reaction.

The authors also designate so-called "nonemotion terms" like "abandoned" and "alone". These terms refer to conditions that, being *absolute,* are too abstract to produce emotions. Clore and Ortony point out that it is for example impossible to say that a person is "somewhat abandoned" or "somewhat alone" (377) because "somewhat" has to relate to a concrete situation incompatible with abstract signifiers.

Even though "feeling neglected" does transmit an emotion, the emotion is present in the form of a *linguistically objectified* state of emotion. However, this is not the only way that emotions can be transmitted in language.

Look at the sentence "Lovely Water – You Are Free", an advertisement by a Chinese water supplier. "You are free" is obviously an emotional idiom – understandable to many Chinese persons – that expresses something positive in the most general sense. The same can be said about the name of Chinese restaurants, which are "Promising Restaurant" or "Wishingfood", about a Japanese hair salon which advertises "Fresh Hair" or tissues that are sold with the slogan: *"Living Tissues: Scent of a Woman"*. This does not mean *in a concrete* sense that this water makes you free, that this restaurant promises something, etc. The idea is rather that this water or this restaurant gives you a *general positive feeling* that EA English attempts to capture with the expression "you are free" or "promising". However, the connection between a word and such a remarkable abstract generality can be attained only because these expressions are immediately drafted in EA English. Notably, these expressions are nonsensical in both English and Chinese/Japanese which means that they are not linked to a concrete existing culture but exist on their own.

**10. The Power to Amaze Yourself**

All this explains why EA English, as a posthuman language, remains resistant to conventional linguistic analysis. If you want to compare, for example, the semantic difference between the English word 'anger' and the German word 'Wut' you will set out to evaluate the cultural context within which these words are embedded. You will then notice that within the German context there are also other words, like 'Angst' and 'Zorn', all of which will help you to evaluate the meaning of 'Wut'. Taking it a step further, the ethno-linguists will try to adopt a "German perspective" on these culture specific words.

How can this work with a language whose Western context is imagined and whose Eastern existence is inscribed in an equally imagined cultural universe? How can this work with a posthuman, virtual language which expresses a dream (or which *is* a dream) of Western culture that is floating and fluid and only loosely held together by an Anglo-Saxon linguistic *Über-ich*?

**11. What Gets You Noticed Now?**

Often it might seem ironic but – beware – it is not. It's all dead serious. The Japanese Romantics tried to introduce irony to the Japanese in the 1920s, at the time when the Pan-Asian movement was thriving. They did not have much success and it is clear why. People who use irony are convinced that there are contradictions that have to be overcome through irony. The aim of German Romantic dialectics had been to sublate contradictions within aesthetics. EA English, as the colonial-anti-colonial paradox that it is, does not *need* to be resolved through any form of dialectics because it is *already* a purely aesthetical phenomenon.[6] What is at work is not the dialectical combination of several real realities but a *superposition* of several aesthetic realities. This is a technique that is also current in the aesthetics of dreams.[7]

**12. The Technique of Getting Stoned is the Trick of Marijuana**

EA English is not *real* if real means "present", "strict", human, and "necessary". EA English words are not "strong" ("strong" enough, for example, to teach a child the correct use of English) because EA English itself is not a matter of being but of imagination: from the outset EA English was not supposed to be "real English" but what people *imagine* English to be. The words in magazines, pictorial as they are, ask to be entered like one enters a dream or an immersive VR. The words and sentences are silent and mysterious and the opposite of concrete: they have the fleeting character of words overheard on television or of words written by a talented computer which has language but no thought processes. They also resemble the language of e-mails because they have neither the presence of spoken speech nor the documentary commitment of traditional letters (cf. Baron 1998).

Another reason why EA English appears like a dream language is that it is often (slightly) out of context. As English fragments lacking a cultural frame, these elements stand out in any East-Asian environment. The words are there in front of our eyes, but we do not immediately recognize where they came from. It is as though they are spat out by a madman who does not really expect to be understood, who just says what he says, letting us more or less guess if he really means it.

It is this disconnectedness which seems to make EA English fascinating for EA-readers. Often the words are there as if they had sprung out of the deepest layers of somebody's linguistic consciousness, layers in which words are not primarily items to be used in real life but rather intimate companions of our ruminating childlike fantasy. These words and sentences might have no sense in the real world but *somewhere* they might mean a lot to someone.

*If* a native English speaker spits out these words, so we believe, the result must be amazing. Though these cherished words are only fragments, they are original and emotionally charged. Is this not exactly the way that we – the non-native English speakers – would like to speak English? We know very well that we cannot learn such an English by attending a language school. We'd rather watch as many American films as we can and listen to pop-songs. Then, perhaps, one day, we will be able to play the linguistic air-guitar so virtuously, tenderly and powerfully that we look just like our idol: the English-speaking Westerner. EA English is the fulfillment of a dream.

**13. Heartful Quality**

These stylish, self-contained and fluent expressions are also like a virtual, posthuman world. EA English has never had the intention of bringing Asians into a meaningful relationship with concrete objects. From the beginning the EA English world has not been about concrete objects with names and properties but about style. The modern world is not really an environment made of things but a stylish universe. EA English captures this self-contained modern universe in which style can be so pure because it is unrelated to any concrete Western (or Eastern) reality. EA English is exclusively based on the experience of a non-objectified quantity of "something Western" or, in other words,

*It's the realization of my aspiration I hope to play along with the heartiest gadgetry manifesting my sensibility.*
*So I cannot help being particular about the every surrounding.*

### 13.1. Born to Be Chicken

Do you know baby talk? It's the language with which we colonize our children. Children would never invent expressions like pee-pee or bow-wow. Contrary to what many people think, we do not learn this language from our children but from other parents.

In some respects baby talk is similar to Pidgin. Pidgin is concrete and material (it combines *existing* codes), and it contains lexical borrowings of *real words* that will be used in a new *real* context. Pidgin is objective, matter-of-fact and related to trade and technology. It is not complicated (having only a few hundred words).

Of all non-native-speakers languages, EA English is the most opposed to Pidgin-English. EA English is a high standard language that is rich, imaginative, and creative. It transmits emotion – something that baby talk or Pidgin is unable to do (or did you ever hear somebody say "lovy-lovy" to his children)? In this sense, though some people might find it paradoxical, EA English counts among the most successful attempts to overcome colonization.

### An Excursion to the Chinese Suburbs: Charming Prunk

There was a time when style was more or less concrete. Even during the structuralist era style could appear as a kind of grammar or structure embedded in a reliable social context. Style was "something" and not just a chimera, it was so "hard" that it could even be cut into two halves that were called the "higher" and "lower" social spheres, good style and bad style, etc. Developed in Europe by class-conscious (mainly French and Italian) fashion designers, it might come as a surprise that the notion of style would one day conquer the entire world. But actually it did: today, former Chinese peasants who have become recently rich not only buy Maseratis but also read *Vogue*.

Take the Eiffel Tower, which is a symbol of Western structural concreteness. Surprisingly, today you find an Eiffel Tower on almost every roof of one-family houses of the suburbs of Eastern Chinese cities. Though these towers do also function as antennas, they are also designed to convey social prestige to its owners. Rich people have very high Eiffel Towers (while poor people do not even have homes).

Compared to this, Disneyland is solid stuff since its still recognizable codes have been smoothly transferred from the adult world to the world of children. Disneyland is baby talk in architecture: concrete and understandable for everybody, it is a real world made of architectural Pidgin. But what fantasy of liquid forms can have inspired an Eiffel Tower on a family home?

**14. Colorful as my Will**

Deleuze's and Guattari's division of human language into vernacular language (here), referential language (there), vehicular language (everywhere), and mythical language (beyond) leads our analysis of EA English to original conclusions (Deleuze and Guattari 1975: 43ff; Engl: 23ff). EA English is not a referential language that has been vernacularized (that is, transferred from *there* to *here*) but a vehicular language that has been mythicized (that is, transferred from *everywhere* to *beyond*). This represents the first step leading EA English towards the realm of a posthuman language.

Not being based on vernacular (childlike) linguistic structures, but at the same time consistently refusing the (adult) world of referential English, EA English remains grounded in an adventurous cultural nothingness within which it can do only one thing: turn into a ritual combination of the vehicular and the mythical. In other words, it has to become a kind of "everywhere-beyond". This ritual is opposed to both the vernacular and the referential; EA English ritually combines the "everywhere" and the "beyond" in order to become the "myth of the vehicular". This represents the second step through which EA English moves towards a posthuman language.

EA English does not resemble baby talk but rather the subtlest kind of teenage talk: in EA English, half-intellectualized emotions, self-contained in immature fantasies, lead an ever-liquid existence. Here everything is ritualized and everything is purely aesthetic. Being without formal vernacular roots and referring to nothing, EA English is a little like what teenagers do when they belt out English-sounding words while singing in the shower. Also this is a ritual and purely aesthetic.

For Zygmunt Bauman the liquid is due to fragmentation and the fact that "forms are unlikely to be given enough time to solidify"

(Bauman 2007: 1). We are becoming more and more flexible and "ready to abandon commitments and loyalties without regret" (4). It is not *in spite* of its fluidity, but *because* of it, that EA English can so easily be integrated into our lives. The aesthetic world of EA English is not the "hard" kind of artistic style that those artists who were engaged in idealistic projects like the *Arts and Crafts Movement* or *Pop Art* tried to introduce almost violently into life and society. On the contrary, the vaguely palpable quantity of EA English contains no real life: it is a liquid style that cannot be seen and hardly be felt but only overlooked.

**15. Let's Fighting Love**

The aforementioned constellation of the referential and the mythical makes clear that within this linguistic universe it is impossible to experience one thing: sex. Sexual vocabulary is always vernacular, or at least referential; sex cannot be mythical or vehicular; and this is why in EA English we look in vain for vulgar vocabulary. Involuntary slips that make an erection out of an election cannot be counted and are not even interesting from a Freudian perspective.

The sexual neutrality of EA English is, of course, no coincidence. After all, EA English is still fed by its Pan-Asian history. In the past, Asia not only refused to be colonized through Pidgin. It also had to fight century-old western attempts to feminize the Orient. For the Westerner, as said Edward Said, Asia was "silent", "penetrable", and "malleable". The Orient was a predominantly feminine continent imagined by male fantasy (Said 1978: 207).[8]

It is clear that the new Pan-Asian language needed to be ungendered, and the sexlessness of the language of the new Pan-Asian fantasy has been attained by shifting its existence away from a still human Freudian (vernacular-referential) symbolism towards a posthuman vehicular-mythical domain of pure aesthetics.

**16. Pure Sandwiches for Now People**

The most remarkable fact about EA English is perhaps that it does not offend anybody. This is the reason why it can enter our lives faster and faster as its producers copy each other over the internet. In the end, perhaps, an immense heap of misunderstood sentences from some other part of the world will create a virtual network of global nonsense. Sexless, silent and liquid, EA English glorious exalted aesthetics of living unexampled elegance and talent of Century penetrates the body of late capitalist reality. Each style breaks away from oneself and enjoys high reputation and dimless sophistication of life on top.

## Notes

1. Roy Andrew Miller has claimed that the Japanese education system has appropriated English for its own purposes and transformed the English language, through its particular way of teaching this language, into a kind of a fictitious non-language (Miller 1982: 277).
2. I explain this in detail in Botz-Bornstein 2008, p. 90. The term "anti-imperialist imperialism" comes from H. Harootunian and Tetsuo Najita (1988) and refers to Japanese culturalism (*bunkashugi*) of the 1920s. Japanese Thinkers in the 1920s-30s expressed themselves in a complex manner through the movement of culturalism (also called *kyōyō-shugi* 教養主義). Philosophers and writers like Nishida Kitarô, Watsuji Tetsurô, Kuki Shûzô, Tanizaki Jun'ichirô, Yanagita Kunio, and Yokomitsu Riichi are representatives of culturalism. They were not linked by a program but by a search for spiritual values and critique of (Western) culture. On *bunkashugi* see also Morris-Suzuki 1995.
3. A phenomenon that works in parallel with the development of EA English is that of East-Asian "cute (*kawaii*) culture" that spread from Japan all over the continent. As Larissa Hjorth has pointed out, "the *kawaii* can articulate how migrating cultural objects, people and odors are re-imagining what it means to be local and global; this 'scape' may well be forming well-pocketed 'wallet communities' that micro-coordinate already established social realities that privilege the individual and a corresponding identity predicated or gender, age, class and sexuality rather than a nation-state". "Odors of Mobility: Mobile Phones and Japanese Cute Culture in the Asia Pacific" in *Journal of Intercultural Studies* 26: 1-2, 2005, 39-55, quotation from 49-50.
4. The cognitive linguist Thomas Roeper explains that children, when acquiring "grammar", move from smaller to larger sets: "Each step of a child's acquisition of grammar must involve movement from a smaller set to a larger set and cannot involve the reverse. The steps are motivated by pieces of input data (adult sentences) which fail to fit into the smaller set, thereby forcing an expansion of the set" (Roeper 1983: 161).
5. All quotations from Walter Benjamin's *Werke* ed. by Rolf Tiedemann. Frankfurt: Suhrkamp, 1983.
6. Did you ever hear a Japanese say "soooo desu ka?" This is neither affirmative nor negative nor the ironical synthesis of both. It is simply aesthetic.
7. There is at least one striking difference between Japanese and Chinese EA English. While in Japanese magazines a considerable proportion of the words is represented by the expressions "happy", "pleasure", "fun", and "fantastic", in Chinese magazines, among the words most employed are "luxury" and "enjoy". In men's magazines, the titles are strikingly authoritarian which might be a due to Chinese authoritarianism or simply a hangover from communist times though it also projects masculinity, a type of masculinity that is rarely found in Japan. In Chinese magazines, the authors clearly state what one is supposed to do in the emerging capitalist world. Still, the dreamlike effect of EA English prevails: *"Well Dressed*

*Men Have Nice Shoes"; "Eight Key Words to Text Your Understanding of Luxury"; "Skirts or Trousers for Everyday Beauty"; "We Invented Casual".*

8. Japanese *hiragana* would form a strange counterpart of EA English because it is not only vernacular but gendered. *Hiragana* was originally the feminine script used by court ladies in the eleventh century. Necessarily, in that case, *kanjis* (Chinese script) must seem masculine. By imposing its language upon Korea, Manchuria, and Taiwan, Japan exercised a masculine power over East-Asia.

# 4. Genes and Pixels: Bio-Genetics' Posthuman Aesthetics of the Virtual

## 1. The Gene

The term gene was introduced by the biologist Wilhelm Johansen in 1906 and was supposed to be "completely free of any hypothesis", to express "only the evident fact that, in any case, many characteristics of the organism are specified in the gametes by means of special conditions, foundations, and determiners which are present in unique, separate, and thereby independent ways" (Fox Keller 2000: 1). The gene expresses an evident fact which exists within certain conditions. However, in spite of the relative clarity with regard to the conditions within which it "expresses", nothing concrete is said here about the gene itself.

During later phases of research on genes, scientists developed more "concrete" descriptions. Delbrück and Schrödinger defined genes as "large molecules" or "crystals or solids".[1] Their reflections came closer to earlier research done by August Weismann, who in 1885, when questioning Darwin's theory of pangenesis,[2] detected an immensely complicated molecule which apparently carried all the hereditary potential. He decided to call this molecule "germ plasma". The germ plasma was supposed to be a nuclear substance which guided all of life's process.[3]

In the end, definitions of the gene as something "material" however convenient they were for a larger, interested public were not the final answer. "Genetic information" was declared to exist not on a molecular basis, but in "DNA sequences" or so called "programs". More recently, scientists have turned even more towards the abstract, and agreed that genetic information is not directly linked to "biological meaning" but that the structure of the genes and their "function" must be seen as two different matters.

It is possible that those more abstract definitions of the gene have not gone totally unnoticed by the general public. However, these ideas could not contribute in an essential way to the popular conception of genes. For the general public, the gene's existence, quality, or form is not a question of interest. Instead, the popular conception of "genes" is dominated by an amazingly constant conviction: that genetic information is an element containing the "riddle of life".[4]

Scientists have found this theory credible for about 50 years, but it is no longer considered plausible today. In spite of this, it seems impossible to eliminate this conception in popular discussions on gene technology, and this creates a strange pattern. While no specialist has ever been able to say with certainty what a gene is, the public seems to have solved the problem in its own way. The idea that the gene "contains the riddle of life" simply serves as an answer to the question about the nature of the gene.

As a consequence, genes turned into something mysterious and "supernatural" (Jacob 1998: 4), since nobody can really say what they are but everybody still believes them to be immensely important. Statements by scientists claiming the contrary could never really alter this situation, since they could not improve on the "negative theology" of genetics and could only say what genes are *not*, but never what they are. Apart from this, their explanations became more and more abstract. In 1959, the French Neo-Darwinians Jacques Monod and François Jacob introduced the distinction between "structural genes" and "regulator genes", so shifting the attention to the "combinational nature" of genes and talking increasingly about "networks" (Jacob: 4). 1998 perhaps marked the climax of "abstractionism". William Gelbart claimed that the gene is not a physical object but only a "concept" (Gelbart 1998: 660 quoted in Fox Keller: 67). However, these discourses have never been very helpful for laypersons, nor did they stimulate large-scale interest in the nature of the gene – nor did Deleuze's and Guattari's philosophical discourse on the phenomenon of evolution (partially inspired by Monod and Jacob).[5]

Instead, popular discourse on gene technology neglected questions concerning the gene's nature and focused on ethical questions related to cloning or utopian accounts of cyborgism and related topics. Though these questions are relevant for public life and the future of science, they seem to bypass two other important questions. The first is about the gene itself and the second about a certain "worldview" produced by the existence of "genes" in the context of contemporary culture. A clarification of these matters is fundamental for all further elaborations on posthumanism and artificial intelligence.

Since even specialists cannot reach a scientific agreement about what genes are, I suggest we leave this problem aside. I also suggest that we temporarily eliminate all ethical questions concerning gene research because, in my opinion, every ethics is embedded in a concrete aesthetic sphere; and this sphere needs to be analyzed beforehand. That is why I would like to examine what I call the "aesthetics of genes" here.

**2. The Spiritual Gene**

During German Romanticism, the Kantian division of the "real world" into the tiniest elements was called in question. In Kant's view, a priori elements do not exist in the real world but are "put into it" by the human mind. Nature becomes a kind of "blind material" because it is what it is, that is, it appears to us *as nature* only through the intellect (*Verstand*).[6] As a consequence, the elements that nature is composed of manifest an atomic character. Schelling criticized the overwhelming skeptic from Königsberg and tried to reestablish nature as an organic quantity or even a manifestation of spirit.[7] For Schelling, nature had its particular reason (*Naturvernunft*) and was able to organize itself (Schelling called this process – interestingly – "evolution", cf. Schelling 1967: 336ff; Engl.: 31ff).

In some way, this parallels a development in bio-genetics, which first attempted to describe the world through single elements that it decided to call genes. Atomization as such can be useful in the natural sciences as well as in the humanities, but it becomes problematic when the model fails to retrieve any "organic" or "real" character of nature or of culture. This is exactly what happens, in the eyes of many people today, through genetic engineering. Evelyn Fox Keller characterizes something of a posthuman vision of a genetic worldview when writing:

> Thus, when we read that the yeast genome has 6.200 genes, are we to understand this number as including regulator genes as well as structural genes? And what about those genetic elements that provide only binding sites? Or should these be considered parts of the structural or regulatory gene they regulate? If so, where would we locate such a gene? Often, these elements are scattered far from the coding sequences they regulate. What then should we count as the beginning and end of a gene? (Fox Keller: 59)

The problem is that, given the extreme complexity of possible constellations between "millions of genes", even obviously abstract schemes which develop traditional categories like "grammar" or "structure", seem to be buried under a heap of individual elements whose number remains simply unmanageable. A strange kind of vertigo overcomes us when we read that researchers discovered a gene forming the phalanx of a hand identical with the one forming the stripes on the back of a zebra. The feeling of "strangeness" is even reinforced when we understand that the scientists themselves were almost as stunned as we were when making the discovery. We conclude that, even if the complete "mapping of human genes" will be possible in the near future, the establishment of a "grammar of genes", be it only that of the human body, remains unreachable for the time being.

The point I want to elaborate in this chapter is that any "aesthetics of genes" supposed to transcend the pure accumulation of elements must remain determined, by its nature, by a state of posthuman disorientation. Certitude, if there is any, cannot be introduced into this "chaos" through the elaboration of structural, "Kantian" or "post-metaphysical", qualities. For the same reasons, certitude cannot be found in Romantic organic models either. And even if scientists openly strove towards the elaboration of these structural qualities, the abstract character of these structures would still make them inadequate for the reception by a larger public. François Jacob's ironical sentence summarizes this situation: "We no longer interrogate the gods to learn about a person's future life or the life of his descendants. We interrogate the genes" (Jacob: 100). As a "public discipline", biotechnology is condemned to look for certitude in "absolutist", pre-Kantian, metaphysical considerations.

An aesthetic outline of a "world of genes" in which any "organic model" or "grammatical model" has become impossible shows that such a metaphysical input really exists. First of all, given the overwhelmingly great number of genes, bio-genetics cannot really be "rationalist" but is, to a large extent, bound to refer to empiricism. There is no grammar or structure to establish the entirety of the genetic network; or even if there were one, we are obviously far from grasping it. On a primary level, through bio-genetics, biology's image fell back into an empiricist state, appearing like a "poor" discipline happy to draw a *map* but unable to write a *grammar* of genes. For biology, this is particularly surprising because what normally characterized biology was its rationalism through which it distinguished itself from more "elementary" sciences such as of physics and chemistry.[8] Biology claimed that nature is not just an accumulation of single physical and chemical elements but that it also follows unique and fundamental rules that should be crystallized through science.

Eventual exaggerations of this "rationalist" side also represent the "dark side" of biology. Curiously, this was also linked to genes. The Nazi rationalization of generative behavior represented a culminating point of a scientific rationalism pretending to have found "*the* rule" and feeling obliged to impose it on the rest of living organisms. Contemporary discussions of possible relationships of genetic engineering with that dark history of German and American biology, which tried to impose a general rule on life itself, look at contemporary bio-genetics from a narrow perspective. In reality, contemporary bio-genetics is further away from Nazi rationalism than ever, because it has abandoned a large part of the rationalism that was typical for traditional biological approaches.

We hope that bio-genetics as a science has its own ways of solving these problems and that it will find a reasonable balance between rationalist and empiricist approaches. Ironically, the popular concept of bio-genetics has also found its own way to overcome the problem. This represents the second level of bio-technological culture. Feeling obliged to abandon rationalism, it clings to what it considers a half-empirical half-metaphysical entity: the *Ding-an-sich* called gene.

The popular view of bio-genetics cancelled the "rule-following" aspect from its worldview because a rule, if it exists, is ungraspable for the time being. Ambitions to crystallize something fundamental will now be fed by something else. Also, once "rationalism" is abandoned, "fundamentalist" aspirations will become even stronger than ever. Professional bio-genetics is not helpful in avoiding this development since through it biology, the science of life with all its principles, consciously linked to its name the name of that element that it considers life's most fundamental principle. Bio-GENETICS is no longer searching for an original rule or for an original form or constellation of things within nature, but it looks for the original in the form of a *concrete element*: the gene.

This is the popular concept of bio-genetics, but "real" science is certainly not innocent in its development. However often one turns the matter around, there is a strange relationship between contemporary bio-genetics and Nazi eugenics. While the Nazis insisted on the absolute character of a – fictitious – *rule*, popular bio-genetics insists on the – equally fictitious – absolute character of the *gene*.

### 3. The *Ur*-Gene

Before developing these thoughts further, I want to contrast the bio-genetic approach with another one that I see as diametrically opposed. The search for a gene-like *Ur*-phenomenon is, of course, reminiscent of Goethe's morphology. However, in spite of their common aspirations to grasp something "original", Goethe's morphology is not a discipline which searches for elements that will "explain everything". Contrary to what the word "morphology" leads us to suppose, Goethe did not believe that essential secrets are hidden inside the shapes of certain natural phenomena, and that a detection of these shapes explains the generation of other shapes. For Goethe morphology's relationship towards physics is, at best, one of indifference.

Goethe reproached Newton for trying to pick up just *one* element from the variety of nature and using just that to explain a large variety of other phenomena (Goethe 1967b: 50). Whether Goethe was right or wrong with regard to Newton is not the question here. What is important is that, fundamentally, Goethe did not want to explain anything, that is, he was not looking for causal links between phenomena. What he desired was the development of a purely comparative activity that would lead to fundamental insights about similarities.

The culminating point of Goethe's ideas about morphology is that of the *Ur-Pflanze*, the "original plant" that can still be imagined though it does not really exist. At some point in his career as a scientist Goethe believed that if he could "see" this plant by comparing it with others, he would come close to revealing the "secret of the generation and organization of plants" (Letter to Herder, May 17, 1787, my transl., Hamburger Ausgabe Bd. 13: 164). Clearly for Goethe the most original phenomenon explaining the laws of biological generation is an idea or a concept. This idea can adopt the form of an imaginary plant. The *Ur-Phänomen*, the absolutely original quantity to be found at the root of all other phenomena, is not an element which really exists but which can be seen only when comparing several elements among each other. Goethe considered even the word *Gestalt* as too static for this. His *Ur-Phänomen* is an image that will suddenly arise between *Gestalten*. It is floating, immaterial and cannot be fixed. Goethe writes:

> Since we want to introduce morphology as a discipline, we should not speak of *Gestalt*; when we use the word morphology we should only think of an idea, a notion or something that can be fixed in experience just for a moment. What has been formed will be immediately deformed, and we ourselves, should remain as flexible and imaginative if we really want to achieve an immediate intuition of nature (Goethe 1817: 55-56).

The difference between Goethe's morphology and popular bio-genetics is that in the case of bio-genetics Goethe's dream of an absolutely original element has become reality. Bio-genetics seeks for causal explanations and looks for the *Ur*-cause of all causes in the form of a material thing (something that Newton would never have dared to aspire to).

This elucidates the curious ontological condition underlying the contemporary "world of genes". Indirectly, everybody who works on causality works on the problem of generation. One element generates (causes) another one, and the researcher into causalities traces a generative line leading from one gene-ration to another. If bio-genetics claims to have found not only the rules structuring generation, but the gene itself, i.e. the generative *Ur*-element holding together the process of generation as such, no research needs to be done beyond that point. The gene is real and does not merely exist in intellectual imagination.

Goethe, on the other hand, when trying to crystallize the form of an *Ur*-plant through his systematic comparative approach worked in utmost proximity to the realm of artistic imagination. He imagined what could be but which was not, but which had, because of an intellectually detected possibility, the status of truthfulness. In the end, Goethe, like Schelling, believed that nature should be "edited by art" if its secret should ever be made graspable.[9] Goethe's vision of artifical life or – if we may call it like this – "posthumanism" is thus not technological but cultural and aesthetic.

**4. The Virtual Gene**

The reality of genes as something that determines the future development of generation is far from real, though certainly not imagined either. The genetic map of the living world represents a self-sufficient, narrated reality that is interesting only as such; and this is why it comes so close to the simultaneously arising phenomenon of VR. At the same time, the genetic map of nature cannot "be edited by art" but finds it problematic to become the object of aesthetics – just like VR. This might appear surprising because in general VR is believed to have a strong potential to represent an aesthetic worldview.

As I have shown in Chapter 2, Gilles-Gaston Granger said about the virtual that, despite its effect of total absorption, it cannot reach a degree of "existentiality".[10] The reason is that the "existential" is always linked to some kind of *actuality* (Granger 1995: 14). "Imagined reality" (that is, reality as it is imagined by *art*) on the other hand, *can* reach this degree of existentiality, because it knows how to "catch" essential parts of actuality while the virtual remains unable to do so. The discussion in Chapter 2 brought forward that this is not more than logical, because the declared aim of VR is to cancel all distinctions between the actual and the non-actual (potential).

This explains also the difficulty of establishing an "aesthetic view" of the world of genes. First, genes are virtual because they are neither real nor imagined. Second, they have, as much as VR, no *existential* function for the human being. VR's attempt, just like bio-genetics' attempt to grasp reality, circumvents the "existential side" of generation. Both attempt to grasp reality in the form of an ultimate truth, of a map of genes, or of a metaphysical "thing as such". In the end, the existence of both VR and of a world of genes remain based on the conviction that reality can be represented in the form of a (visual or scientific) language and this approach blocks more sophisticated *aesthetic* approaches towards the reality of genes.[11]

There is still another reason why the "structural" quality of the world of genes explored by scientists develops a kind of mysticism tending towards the virtual. Genes are seen as "living elements", which means that their structure is able to develop a dynamic of its own, that generates an impetus itself. Fox Keller writes:

> The capacity to reproduce itself – traditionally taken as the defining property of life – lent the gene vitality. And finally, attributing to the gene the capacity to direct or control development effectively credited it with a kind of mentality – the ability to plan and delegate. The net result was a gene with something like a Janus-faced quality. Part physicist atom, part Platonic soul, it was assumed capable simultaneously of animating the organism and of directing (as well as enacting) its construction. (Fox Keller: 47)

Schrödinger held that a gene is an architect's plan and a builder's craft in one. This is one of the reasons why the gene is still called the "cell's brain". It is clear that bio-genetics, instead of working towards a truly "conceptual" Goethian approach to capture the truth about nature through ideas, brews here an odd mixture of empiricism and metaphysical absolutism by "attribut[ing] self-reproduction to a particle" (Fox Keller: 48) and by "establish[ing] DNA as the molecule that not only holds the secrets of life but that also executes its cryptic instructions" (54). In other words, it designs a "Master Molecule".

Once again I would claim that this model manifests a clearly virtual character and the link between posthumanism and VR becomes evident. When one permits the gene to create its own being out of nothing, it has become a virtual element. Fox Keller's asks: "Does the word genetic refer to the subject or to the object of the program? Are genes the source of the program, or that upon which the program acts?" (87). The world of genes has become "virtual" in the sense that it constructs from genes a kind of "unimagined imagination". Genes, these biological bits of information, are like bytes or pixels and, self-sufficient as they are, they are able to create a world of their own. Having, both of them, overcome the material state of beings still composed of particles and atoms, "genetic reality" and VR are amazingly similar in ontological terms. The "world of genes" can indeed be compared with Michael Heim's philosophical description of VR:

> No temporal unfolding, no linear steps, no delays limit God's knowledge of things. The temporal simultaneity, the all-at-once-ness of God's knowledge serves as a model for human knowledge in the modern world as projected by the work of Leibniz. What better way, then, to emulate God's knowledge than to generate a virtual world constituted by bits of information? To such a cyberworld human beings could enjoy a God-like instant access. (Heim 1993: 95)

So far biology has been, in the strict sense of the word, a historical science. Its link with history was not direct, but its activity was unthinkable outside any historical context. However, if we compare bio-genetics with the approach described by Goethe, bio-genetics has left the sphere of history and searches for the "gene" in the form of an absolute, spiritual, and "posthuman" quality. This is true even when bio-genetics conceives the gene as purely conceptual and abstract. In some way, bio-genetics becomes here "pure biology". The relationship between bio-genetics and biology appears much like that between traditional religion and a newly founded religious sect. Often newly formed sects reject both history and well-established religious traditions, and they are only interested in "pure spirituality". However, like religious spirituality, "biological truth" normally initially undergoes a complex historical process of generation in order to become "something". Traditional world religions exist in order to direct the human need of "spirituality" through a complex web of traditions, rituals, and historical consciousness in order to exist in terms of "something". Sects, on the other hand, tend to proclaim spirituality as being obtainable in a pure way in the form of an original "as such".[12]

Biology as a "historical" branch of science has had a function similar to that of religion with regard to the search after biological "origins". Bio-genetics, however, turns out to be neither romantic nor Kantian but surprisingly "populist-metaphysical" in its search for something "absolute". In reality, the gene as the origin of generation is not a present element, it is not even present in the form of a structure. Goethe would say that it can only be imagined. If Goethe appears to be too old-fashioned today, we may borrow a term from a contemporary philosopher, and announce that genes are very much like Derrida's *différance*. They are more different than just differences, but they claim to constitute the "difference in itself". *Différance* has no origin and no presence. Therefore the gene is to generation what *différance* is to difference!

The point is that, in the end, such a *différance* can also only be imagined. It would be "enough" to leave these elements called genes within the realm of an ungraspable *différance*, and let them from time to time appear by using comparative approaches, and refer to their *existence* in history and in culture. Instead bio-genetics attempts to transform these elements into a material language (a narrative) made of something concrete which is supposed to "explain" reality. It forgets that in reality genes cannot explain cultural elements because they are themselves a part of culture and because they are themselves not more than historico-cultural elements.[13]

The result is that bio-genetics develops a kind of "non-imagined imagination", a phenomenon that is well known in computer science. It becomes a VR that has overcome both presentation and imagination. The gene is "unreal" because it is only *différance*. At the moment a worldview based on genes insists on its "real existence" it ends up as VR. VR declares the unreal to be real, bypassing any attempt to employ artistic, human, "Goethian", imagination.

**Conclusion**

Genes never tell a story about reality but they generate a VR of their own. This is the last narrative. I would claim that a large part of the popular fascination with genes is derived from this "virtual" – or posthuman – character" of genes. "Reality" tells us that the logic underlying historical processes – and also biological formation (a logic that has often fascinated philosophers) – cannot be grasped because, "in reality", this logic is nothing. However, through genetics a part of this logic can be crystallized within a kind of "dream narrative" presented in the form of the "genetic map". In the end, the result will be, like that of all dream-languages, disappointing. Goethe's imagined "*Ur*-elements" appear before our eyes as mysterious and floating; they manage to conserve a part of their existential-ontological quality of dreams. The "genetic map", on the other hand, should it really be presented one day as the most intimate secret of nature, will most probably provoke the protest: "And that's all?"[14]

The "world of genes", like VR, is one of the most recent narratives of human civilization. It is the narrative of a dream that holds the entire process of nature together.[15]

Should biotechnology ever give in to totalitarian tendencies and use its knowledge in an evil manner, it will not happen because tampering with genes has become a regular activity. Society will probably always oppose this. The danger of biotechnology resides rather in its false, materializing, aestheticism that considers as "real" what is "nothing" and that creates a second (virtual) reality in which the secret of nature as well as the secret of biological history are constantly "readily available" as if they were material elements. Once this worldview is firmly established, bio-genetics can indeed turn its aestheticism once again to a terror program. It would do so not because it is particularly convinced, as it once happened, of a certain biological "rule". This time it would turn into terror because it naively attempts to redesign a fleeting cultural style, or a cultural language, that it accepts as a "reality". And this "reality" can subsequently also be submitted to devices like racial breeding.

## Notes

1. Erwin Schrödinger: *What is Life and Other Essays* (New York: Doubleday, 1956). Delbrück's paper on "mutagenesis" (written in collaboration with Zimmer and Timofeeff in 1935) was contained in previous editions of this book (see note 4). Schrödinger talks of the "size of a gene" (29) and says that "the most essential part of a living cell – the chromosome fiber – may suitably be called an aperiodic crystal (3). See also Graeme K. Hunter's *Vital Forces: The Discovery of the Molecular Basis of Life* (London: Academic Press, 2000) who mentions Delbrück's interest in the crystallization of tobacco mosaic virus (224ff).
2. Pangenesis is called the process according to which acquired characteristics are transmitted in the form of particles called 'gemmules' from the body cell to germ cells.
3. August Weismann: *Das Keimplasma: eine Theorie der Vererbung* (Jena: Fischer, 1892). Cf. p. 12: "The germ plasma contained in the germ cells and which can never be reproduced, and which is only transmitted on the following generation in direct *continuity*, always starting with the germ cell, which creates a new bion" (my trans.). Weismann's theory has been called the first theory of genetics.
4. The idea that Schrödinger's "hereditary crystal" could contain the "riddle of life" has been suggested by Delbrück in the mentioned essay (note 1) characteristically entitled: "Preliminary Exposition on the Topic 'Riddle of Life'". Schrödinger on the other hand, insists that he does "not intend to explain life" (*What is Life,* 49).
5. Deleuze and Guattari took into consideration Bergson's ideas about the role of duration within evolution. This duration was supposed to yield insight into evolution's dynamic and non-mechanic aspect. See: *Capitalisme et schizophrénie:*

*L'Anti-Œdipe* (1972) and *Mille plateaux* (1980). Bergson (in *L'Evolution créatrice*) pointed out in 1907 that "our thought, in its purely logical form, is incapable of presenting the true nature of life, the full meaning of the evolutionary movement" (Bergson 1907. English: xx; French: vi).

6. Bergson also expressed an interest in Weismann's theory of the germ-plasma which he wished to direct towards open systems which permit a "creative evolution" involving all "genetic energy" (cf. 26ff). See also Keith Ansell Pearson: *Germinal Life: The Difference and Repetition of Deleuze* (London: Routledge, 1999), 40: "For Bergson what is transmitted is not simply the physico-chemical elements of the germ-plasma but also the vital energies and capacities of an embryogenesis and morphogenesis that allow for perpetual invention in evolution".

7. See Kant's preface to the 2nd edition to the *Critique of Pure Reason* (Engl. transl. by Norman Kemp Smith; London & Basingstoke: Macmillian, 1929, p. 20) where Kant characterizes the method of scientists examining nature: "[...] a light broke upon all students of nature. They learned that reason has insight only into that which it produces after a plan of its own, and that it must not allow itself to be kept, as it were, in nature's leading-strings, but must itself show the way with principles of judgment based upon fixed laws, constraining nature to give answer to questions of reason's own determining". German: Edition Suhrkamp *Werkausgabe* Vol. III, 23.

8. While physics and chemistry deal, in principle, with static *elements* biology was from the beginning confronted with "living", organic structures. If we suppose that, historically, scientific examinations developed from simple – original – problems, to problems manifesting more complex constellations that need to be *explained*, biology turns out to be the science that undertook the decisive shift from empiricism to rationalism.

9. Cf. F. W. J. Schelling: *Texte zur Philosophie der Kunst* (Stuttgart: Reclam, 1982), German: 6; Engl.: 18. Still today, organicist philosophies linked to ecological worldviews seem to represent late responses to these Kantian attempts of atomizing the world.

10. Goethe: Cf. *Maximen und Reflexionen* (München: DTV, 1963): "The one for whom nature begins revealing its secret will feel an irresistible longing for its most dignified interpreter – art" (22, my trans.). German: "Wem die Natur ihr offenbares Geheimnis zu enthüllen anfängt, der empfindet eine unwiderstehliche Sehnsucht nach ihrer würdigsten Auslegerin, der Kunst". Goethe's conception comes amazingly close to Bergson's attempts to interpret evolution in less static terms – attempts that have been developed by Deleuze and, more recently by Ansell-Pearson. The latter summarizes Bergson's ideas on the subject of evolution as the conviction "that the schema of life and evolution we confer on this organized individual body is necessarily decided by our perception that always cuts into matter distinct bodies, in which, and on account of the interest of action, 'generals and individuals determine one another by a semi-artificial operation entirely relative to our future action on things' (*L'Evolution créatrice*, 227)". Cf. Pearson: *Germinal Life*, 42.

11. I (in agreement with Gilles-Gaston Granger) understand "existentiality" here as a state of the self in which the self is aware of its own position within the world. This world is composed of concrete beings and not of abstractions. Sartre and Camus were interested in the kind of awareness of existence provoked by profound emotional experiences leading towards the discovery of the self's own position within a concrete world. If we understand "existence" in such an

"existentialist" way, we are inclined to describe it as necessarily linked to an "actuality".

12. Bergson comes here closer to the truth since his model of creative evolution is held together by a kind of "virtual harmony" that cannot be grasped as something concrete (a gene, VR) but as "vitality". See K. Ansell Pearson 1999, 44.

13. The fact that teachings of the Raëlian sect combine gene-technology and spirituality in such a self-evident way in order to create a "religion of the gene" must be considered as characteristic of any "worldview" of bio-genetics.

14. Again Pearson's interpretation of Bergson expresses very similar ideas when he writes: "[...] from the perspective of the *virtual* whole, life can be conceived as ceaseless play between limited inventions of complex living systems, such as organisms and species, and the desire of the impulse of life or ever renewed vitality" (1999, 49).

15. A part of the "dream-sphere", of the vertigo linked to all human dreams that tries to dream the secret of nature as well as the secret of culture, is still sticking to the phenomenon of bio-genetics. This becomes particularly clear with regard to the spread of popular bio-genetic devices like "cloning". What is a clone at the moment it appears as an 'I' that is at the same time a 'non-I'? Normally, you can encounter yourself only in dreams (or in some kind of constructed VR). A world of genes, clonable at will, is, in fact, a VR in which neither the 'I' nor the 'Other' exists. The lack of any "in-between" between humans, the lack of any response from a possible Other (because the Other is I) makes this world appear dreamlike or, more precisely, "virtual".

16. Other dreams, from the realm of ethics, are added, for example by Fukuyama and Habermas. Fukuyama argues for the establishment of a new regulatory agency with a mandate to regulate biotechnology on grounds broader than efficacy and safety (Fukuyama 2002). Habermas states his support for a "right to a genetic inheritance immune from artificial intervention" (Habermas 2003: 27). Stefan Herbrechter argues that both Fukuyama and Habermas are admittedly defending a 'myth', which they see as indispensable, however, for maintaining an essential idea of human nature. In Fukuyama's case this is called 'humanity' and serves as a universal principle for human community and morality; in Habermas, it is the principle of the autonomy of 'individual freedom', which turns human subjects into moral and social agents" (Herbrechter 2013: 165).

## Feature Scene IV

## The New Surrealism: Loft Stories, Reality Television, and Amateur Dream-Censors

The Russian film director Andrei Tarkovsky once said that no scene would be better acted than the one "acted" by normal people who do not know that they are filmed or taped: "I once taped a casual dialogue. People were talking without knowing they were being recorded. Then I listened to the tape and thought how brilliantly it was 'written' and 'acted'. The logic of characters' movements, the feeling the energy – how tangible it all was. How euphoric the voices were, how beautiful the voices" (Tarkovsky 1986: 65). Ingmar Bergman made similar remarks about the perfectly natural character of actions that are not "acted" but "lived" in reality.[1]

All of us will probably agree that "reality" writes the best scripts. Some things that happen in real life, or at least *the way* they happen, could not have been invented or *narrated* by any scriptwriter. With certain events – reactions, dialogues, constellations of cause-effect relations, etc. – the act of "happening" is so absolute, so immediate, and so unmitigated by intellectual considerations, artistic ambitions, or narrative devices that it expresses reality "as it is". We enjoy these rare moments in which something happens just as though it has been "written by life itself" because they seem to express the "uniqueness" of actions as such. In many cases, these anti-narratives express the deeply human character of life which, normally, follows or transgresses rules but sometimes… things just happen.

The fascination with "reality as it is" has preoccupied artists in the domain of visual art as much as writers. The scope of this phenomenon is simply so large, it is impossible even to evoke. The task that these artists set themselves is to transfer from reality to art, not just an atmosphere or a mood, but something even less material. Often this "something" cannot be narrated but just shown. Those artists attempt to capture an indefinable "existential situation" which expresses a strong sense of "life". This "life" and its expression are determined neither by a structure nor by symbolic functions, nor are they effective within any specified ideological or narrative program.

Some people think that the art of film or photography has the best chance of capturing "reality as it is" simply because of their "realistic" nature. The idea is that pictures do not narrate but simply show. However, the theoretician of cinema, Siegfried Kracauer explained that even the most realist painter remains unable to produce a "realistic" scene but will end up "stylizing" reality, be it only through the realism he imposes upon "reality". As a consequence, Kracauer developed an alternative approach, which he called the approach of the *camera-reality* (Kracauer 1973: 62). Here reality, when captured by the camera, stays a reality with all its charm and aura (as Walter Benjamin would have put it). Other eminent theoreticians developing similar ideas are Alexandre Astruc (1968), André Bazin (1961), and Amédé Ayfre (1969) who elaborated the notion of "*caméra-stylo*" (pen-camera). In a film "recorded" by a *caméra-stylo* there is no evocation of subjective, intimate symbols. No "inner reality" has been "put into" the image by the artist. On the other hand, there is no objective recording of reality either and this is most important. There is no documentation undertaken from the detached point of view located outside the things filmed.

The subject of the present Feature Scene is so-called "reality television" as it has existed for more than two decades (it became extremely popular in the late 1990s with the series *Survivor* and *Big Brother*) in the form of various types of "reality shows" on television screens all over the world.[2] I believe that, in principle, these shows are inspired by the same kind of fascination with "reality" that is proper to the above-mentioned artistic projects. That such parallels are not far-fetched is shown by statements by the French director Jean-Jacques Beineix, who sees in the television production *Loft-Story* a renewal of contemporary cinema that has, in his opinion, become too academic. Or André Bazin, who was tempted, in the 1960s, by television aesthetics, Beineix suggests confronting cinema with the refreshing spontaneity and the directness of the non-actors we encounter in so-called reality shows. Even the elitist French journal *Cahiers du cinéma* even elected *Loft-Story* the best film of the year 2001.[3]

Though, as some studies show, reality television has never been able to shake off the persistent smell of narrative and fiction, reality shows have become extremely popular in many countries.[4] At first, this interest in "reality" may seem surprising. News reports as well as documentaries provide people with "reality" at increasingly frequent intervals; "reality" seems to be the last thing that is lacking on television. However, newsreel reality is not the kind of reality that people who watch reality shows seem to desire. The reason must be that conventional media reality appears too much like a hybrid version of fiction produced by politicians and by journalists alike. Being too well calculated, stylized and designed to capture our attention, the *immediacy* with which many events are reported makes them almost "unreal".

Then there is another reason. The mediated reality shown on television news programs reaches our minds in a state of attentiveness and tension that is very different from the one we are submitted to when we perceive situations that are "written by life". A good way to describe the difference between both ways of perceiving "reality" is to say that it comes close to the difference between the perception of images in waking life on the one hand, and in dreams on the other. The detached view, with which we perceive "reality" with its occasional emergence of all-too-human constellations, comes closer to that of dreaming than to that of analysis, consumption, or first-degree stimulation. Kracauer insisted on the necessity, in visual art, of following certain images "in a dreamy manner" (*nachträumen* in German). If we really want to appreciate the "reality" in a photo or a film still, we need to abandon our overly focused, stimulated and interested view of reality. Only then do we discover that some images contain a truth that simply "flashes", and that does not need to be sought out or analyzed. In this sense, reality can convey a kind of "realness".

Most people's brains are today saturated with synthetic, compact, and stylized images as well as with well-calculated narratives relating all sorts of reality or non-reality. All this might at best stimulate people's imagination or it might even indirectly teach them to use more critical approaches towards all these images and narratives. I am not saying that the flood of images delivered by contemporary media necessarily makes people dull. The problem I am trying to pinpoint lies elsewhere.

Reality shows are a good case in point to clarify a particular phenomenon. Overwhelmed by a flood of images and information, people desire a more detached view than the one offered by newsreels or conventional fiction. To put it most simply: they want to watch images in a way that permits them to dream whilst watching. They want to develop a view towards images and stories that is not captured by immediate interests, basic instincts or manipulated stimulations, but that simply allows them to watch and think. That makes it possible to find a sense in the story or the images without being violently forced into a certain – semantic, political, or symbolic – direction.

This strongly diverges from what could intuitively be assumed: that reality shows are popular because people want an "immediate" contact with reality and also that they watch those programs because they do *not* want to think. The contrary is true. No one can deny that the media are no longer as mediating as they used to be. Be it the Twin Towers or the Syrian War – reality can hardly be *more* immediate. And it is rather the immediacy that has become bothersome.

From this follows that people watch reality shows because they desire *distance* from reality. In these shows reality deploys itself much more like in real life which means in the first place: most of it is utterly boring. But this very aspect gives you time to let your thoughts wander and ponder on certain flashing moments that caught your attention without feeling obliged to think this or that. The paradox lies in the fact that only through this distanced, wandering gaze, an immediate sense of reality is permitted to flash up from time to time.

Apart from this, the desire to dream whilst watching is not new. Long before reality shows existed, there was a phenomenon that can be seen as an immediate response to the described desire for detachment: the *television drama in sequels* gives us a unique chance to relax whilst watching. No wonder that this scheme has become popular also in cinema (*Terminator* I, II, III, IV, etc.). When watching the sequels, we do not expect anything spectacular to happen, knowing perfectly well that number IV and V cannot be as good as number I. We simply want to observe the life of those people that we have become familiar with. Continued stories adopt the rhythm of life simply in that they continue indefinitely. This means that we can *live* in the sequels without really *following* the story. We have enough time to half-imagine and to half-dream what the story *could* have been. And all this is almost like in real life.

Everybody will agree that the perfect reproduction of life on television would be a *continuing* program managing, just like life, to *write itself all alone*, that is, without the help of an author. The fact that a story may be "written" without the help of an author no longer shocks us anyway. We concluded a long time ago that the existence of an author does not say much about the authenticity of a story. Authors of fiction have to a considerable degree become fictitious themselves, for who still believes that the tenth sequel of a novel has been written by the author himself and not by one of the thousands of ghostwriters that seem to people the globalized world of the publishing business?

To some extent, the concept of the "reality show" has been born from these psycho-aesthetic considerations. I am ready to add without cynicism that things would be perfectly acceptable and would even present a major achievement for visual culture of the twenty-first century if they had remained there. The entire project could have resulted in representations of everyday reality that Tarkovsky thought of (and that perhaps Beineix still thinks of), in which dialogues are "truer" than anything that can be written by a scriptwriter. It could have resulted in Rohmer-style films in which natural speech is more charming than any speech performed by real actors: sincere and intense without being obtrusive. In a word, it could have produced a reality not engineered, acted or narrated but simply *presented.*

That the project has degenerated is the fault of the producers as much as of the public. The most urgent question is, of course, if eleven young people shut in a loft do represent a "reality" of any kind. The situation is to a large extent *created* and there it comes already dangerously close to a piece of fiction. Further, even though there is no author in the conventional sense of the word, *authority* has not been left entirely in the hands of the protagonists who are supposed to play their real lives. The public is urged to "eliminate" one candidate after the other and thus indirectly "writes" the plot of the story. Reality television is therefore a kind of inverted fiction: while in conventional fiction *one* author writes for a large public, here a public tells those people who are supposed to be the authors of their actions in which direction the story should develop.

Also the public's attitude shows that people react more to a piece of fiction than to "real life". The public extensively engages in psychologizing approaches and analyzes almost everything. It is unnecessary to point out that this amateur psychology does not reveal much about "reality" but rather removes it from us by creating an immense illusion about its own analytical capacities. One cannot grasp a truth about reality simply by looking at the behavior of people.

The gap between the dreamlike experience providing the possibility of relishing in spontaneous and marvelously non-acted behavior and the fictionalized events called reality shows could hardly be larger. Kracauer's camera-reality or Astruc's *caméra-stylo* are dreamlike realities that are simply watched. Astruc attempted to grasp "any kind of reality". Reality television, on the other hand, suggests a utopian social reality in the form of a hyper-fiction. To some extent, this narrative called "reality show" is still developing by itself; but at the same time it can constantly be analyzed, controlled, and altered according to the lucid analysis of the spectators.[5]

Reality television represents exactly the model that Freud must have dreamt of when developing his method of psychoanalysis: to be able not only to analyze a dream at the very moment it is dreamt, but to actually interfere in the dream by adopting the role of an external dream-censor.

One might add that the only other time that such a model has been evoked in the history of visual arts is in surrealism. Very similar to the approach described above, surrealism consciously imitated the structures of reality, altering them until they became more "interesting". This is just like in a reality show program where an artistic amateur psychoanalyst engages in the creation of dreams. While the spectator plays at being a psychiatrist and the protagonists actively shape the narrative according to public demand, television reality becomes a kind of surreality: a synthetically produced non-reality that is lacking the realness that we encounter in real life as well as in dreams.

Astruc's strategy of the *caméra-stylo* was especially directed against surrealist cinema (as much as it was directed against conventional documentaries); Tarkovsky aggressively turned against any kind of Freudianism as well as surrealism. Reality television (like surrealism at its time) attempts to be a dream, but adopts the form of an anti-narrative in which conventional narrative and receptive devices have not been overcome in order to create a real aesthetic of dreams, but have been *overturned* in order to create a strange kind of fiction.

## Notes

1. "Three little children go out for a walk together – two little girls aged four, with a little boy of two. They take a skipping rope with them. They put it round the neck of the two-year-old and tie the ends to couple of trees – just high enough for the boy to have to stand on tiptoe. And walk away. And we don't know what it is that causes these two to agree to do such a thing [...]. There has been a whole series of such events. Unmotivated cruelty is something which never ceases to fascinate me; and I would like very much to know the reason for it". From Stig Bjorkman et al.: *Bergman om Bergman* (Stockholm: Norstedt, 1970), 40. See Botz-Bornstein 2007 for comments on both Tarkovsky's and Bergman's remarks.
2. Literature on reality television produced by media studies scholars is so abundant that it cannot even be outlined here. Some important publications are: T. Johnson-Woods: Big Bother: *Why Did that Reality-TV Show Become such a Phenomenon?* St. Lucia: University of Queensland Press, 2002; S. Murray and

L. Ouellette (eds.): *Reality TV: Remaking Television Culture*. New York: New York University Press, 2004; M. Andrejevic: *Reality TV: The Work of Being Watched.* Lanham: Rowman & Littlefield, 2004.

3. *Cahiers du cinéma* 2001.

4. In France there have been, since 2001, four "reality" programs. *Loft Story* (derived from the Dutch *Big Brother*); *The Adventures of Koh-Lanta* (15 candidates try to survive on an island); *Pop Stars* (five girls try to become professional singers); *Star Academy* (similar principle, derived from the Dutch *Starmaker*). Long-running reality television show franchises in the United States are *American Idol, Dancing with the Stars* and *The Bachelor*. *The Voice* was launched in 2010 as a singing competition franchise. Also in 2010, *The Tester* became the first reality television show aired over a video game console. In 2013, *Duck Dynasty* became extremely successful.

5. The constant interference of exhibitionism and voyeurism (which do not exist in dreams either) are a result of this ambiguity.

# 5. Posthumanism and "Multi-Realism": Comparing *The Matrix* with Tarkovsky's *Stalker* and *Solaris*

## Introduction

*Solaris* (1972) and *Stalker* (1979) by Andrei Tarkovsky as well as *The Matrix* (1999) by the Wachowski brothers are science fiction films with a highly metaphysical appeal. In addition, all three films deal with the possible falseness of what we generally supposed to be a "reality". In *The Matrix,* a posthuman reality of millions is declared to be due to cognitive manipulations effectuated by machines and computers. People do not live their everyday lives in a human way in the real world but inside a computer program. In *Solaris* a posthuman theme is played out though here the posthuman reality is more ambiguous: a strange kind of non-reality penetrates reality and creates doubts about the "cognitive correctness" of reality. Also *Stalker* evokes, though in a completely different and ironical way, the existence of a posthuman reality: here a spiritual reality more real than ordinary reality.

Philosophical literature on *The Matrix* is vast and is by far not limited to the posthuman and reality aspect. It reaches from phenomenological, existentialist, and feminist interpretations to searches for Buddhist and Gnostic themes in the trilogy, exploring a large number of ethical and epistemological questions.[1] Given the reality/non-reality theme contained in the films, most prominent are of course attempts to link them to classical discussions of skepticism as raised by Berkeley, Hume, and Descartes, as well as to Plato's allegory of the cave. Descartes designed in his *Meditations* a skeptical scenario in which the narrator supposes "that not God, who is supremely good and the source of truth, but rather some malicious demon of the utmost power and cunning has employed all his energies in order to deceive me" (*Meditations on First Philosophy*, 298). Descartes' hypothesis that what we perceive as the world might be a comprehensive illusion leads to Hilary Putnam's 1980 re-adoption of this notion with his posthuman "brain in a vat" scenario. When humans are living in a computer simulation with their brains detached from their bodies, then this is a clearly posthuman scenario.

"Brain in a vat" scenarios have been discussed by numerous contemporary philosophers, for example by Jonathan Drancy who described this situation like this: "You do not know that you are not a brain, suspended in a vat full of liquid in a laboratory and wired to a computer which is feeding you your current experiences under the control of some ingenious technician scientists" (Drancy 1985: 10).[2]

I agree that the "reality theme" is the philosophically most interesting topic of the trilogy but at the same time I find these aforementioned classical responses to skepticism insufficient, as they reduce "reality" to a one-dimensional cognitive notion. The shift from human "real" reality to a posthuman VR (a dichotomy on which also many discourses on humanism or posthumanism remain based) employs a one-dimensional cognitive model of reality. It also employs a one-dimensional model of what it means to be human. It is for this reason that I want to compare *The Matrix* with the two films by Tarkovsky.

In the end, also Tarkovsky's films will profit from the critical reading I offer. Though it is impossible to resume the entire body of existent Tarkovsky criticism, it appears that roughly half of all works on this director has had theological orientations concentrating on the search of God, belief, etc. Though I have nothing concrete to oppose to such approaches, I think that within the logic they produce a certain essentializing tendency is almost inevitable. True, the theme of the "search for an ideal realm" (childhood, the zone, home, spirituality) is very present in Tarkovsky's films and *can* be addressed as such; however, *the search* for this realm should not be reduced to purely subjective ambitions. This is why I want to confront *Stalker* and *Solaris* with the two themes that are central in the *The Matrix*: the theme of the search for the human and the search for reality.

## 1. *The Matrix*

In *The Matrix*, the computer hacker Neo suspects that reality around him is only a complex computer simulation. Soon he is contacted by underground freedom fighters who explain that he and everybody around him are living in a matrix and are not human but created by intelligent machines, and that the real humans are living in a city under the earth. Later he also learns that his and the other people's bodies that he always believed to be real, are kept in tanks and harvested by the machines because they need their energy. Neo joins a group of freedom fighters who attempt to overthrow the machines, free people from their simulated reality, and lead them to reality and, with this, to a human existence. A traitor called Cypher decides to reenter the matrix and deliver the humans to the machines but he does not succeed. Neo's role becomes more and more that of a "savior" of humanity because it turns out that, once he has recognized the fake character of the reality that ordinary humans accept as real, he is able to challenge the physical laws of this virtual world.

### 2. *Stalker*

In *Stalker*, a man called the Stalker guides a writer and a scientist through "the zone", which is a posthuman apocalyptic wilderness supposed to be endowed with supernatural qualities. Humans can no longer live here. The saying goes that a meteorite crashed into the zone twenty years before, creating a kind of cosmic abyss and that the zone is perhaps the product of a superior civilization. In any case, army troops that have been sent there have never come back. A few other people who ventured into the zone have also disappeared. Inside the zone there is a chamber said to grant wishes and the objective of the men's journey is to find this chamber. In the past, Porcupine, Stalker's teacher, had entered the chamber and a week later he became immensely rich. It seems that the human conflict between his mental inside reality and the reality outside had been so big that he committed suicide. This might be the reason why, in the end, none of the men dare enter the chamber. However, in spite of the apparent failure of the journey, the experiences of the three men in the zone effectuate important existential changes in them.

### 3. *Solaris*

In *Solaris*, a biomagnetic current that appears like a "gluey mass" or "fog" acts upon the conscience of cosmonauts when they approach the Ocean Solaris. The result is the appearance of living persons on the station who have been dead since years but who resided, as sorts of cognitive residues, in the brains of the cosmonauts. Those people are no human beings but posthuman beings. This is the case in *Solaris*, where disputes about these experiences take place between a scientist (Sartorius) who simply calls these unreal persons "a matrix", a more literary and humanistically inclined scientist (Snout), and Kris Kelvin, who tends towards more pragmatic behavior. The mysterious Guibariane (who appears only on video tape) seems to be a representation of the philosophical realist. Reality – whatever it is – exists independently of our perceptions. As a result, he accepts both realities – the human and the posthuman one – as real but is ultimately unable to reconcile them, which determines (like for Porcupine in *Stalker*) his tragic end.

## 4. The Reality Problem

*The Matrix*'s hero Neo fights for "reality" and his search pushes him to the end of his own spiritual and physical capacities. In principle, this is very similar to what Tarkovsky's films are supposed to show. As the Russian master said himself: "In all that I have done, in all that I intend to do [...] my theme is this: a man gripped by an ideal searches passionately for the answer to a question and goes to the limit in his attempt to understand reality".[3] However, the search is not the same in the Russian films and in *The Matrix*. In *The Matrix,* the people who find out about the falseness of reality decide to engage in a grim fight *for reality*. Tarkovsky, on the other hand, explores the VR theme without prescribing red pills or blue pills; instead, he concentrates on the *search* for reality and humanity, a search during which the protagonists' cognitive systems go through hybrid states of dreamlike and real cognition. In other words, what Chalmers calls the "Matrix hypothesis", that is, the fact that "I have (and have always had) a cognitive system that receives inputs from and sends its outputs to an artificially designed computer simulation of the world" (142) is deluded.

In *The Matrix* there is no doubt that the VR of the matrix is false and that the city Zion is real. Neo is mostly occupied with the fight against his posthuman enemies and with a search for his own human role within the reality this situation creates. The Zion people are neither posthuman nor fully human but aspire to re-obtain their originally human status. They are no machines but "carbon creations of evolutionary biology" who are reduced to the "silicon creation" of intelligent circuity (cf. Clarke 2008: 3).

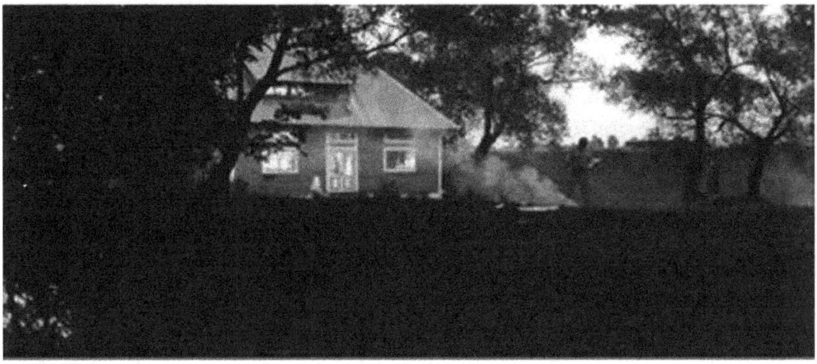

Fig. 6: *Solaris*. Kris burns his archive before leaving for his trip.

Doubts about this do not really exist and whenever they appear they are solved, even when they pose a most serious threat to the definition of "human reality". In the second sequel (*The Matrix Reloaded*) the destiny of the entire human race seems to depend, for a while, on the accuracy of the Oracle's prophecies. The fighters have to decide if her prophecies are only a part of the matrix or if her truths have an "absolute" value. In the third sequel (*Revolutions*), even Neo's role as The One who saves humanity from the matrix is said to be a part of the matrix program. At both occurrences in the script, the question of whether it is possible to escape a false reality is closely linked to the question of whether one can escape human destiny. However, the Oracle herself makes clear that even in oracles choice exists, and depicts the whole reality-destiny problem as a matter of self-fulfilling prophecy: "You are in control of your life. Don't believe in this fate crap" (*Reloaded*).

*The Matrix* displays some of the skepticism that we also note in Tarkovsky's films. However, in *The Matrix* it concerns the question of *destiny within reality* and not reality itself. This skepticism is resolved through belief and love while the reality of Zion remains at all times firmly established. In this sense, as said Chris Falzon, "the Matrix turns its back on the philosophical problem of skepticism it invokes" (Falzon 2006: 103). In *Solaris* and *Stalker*, however, the focus is on the act of *understanding* reality, a reality, which eternally remains a matter of "non-understanding".

The basic idea of *The Matrix Trilogy* suggests a skeptical scenario of radical deception that can be philosophically supported by Cartesian "evil demon" theories as well as by positivist "brain in a vat" ideologies. The two alternative worlds, the real one and the virtual one, the human and the posthuman one, are, a priori, irrelevant to each other. Normally, the two different cognitive-ontological systems, the red and the blue one, do not interfere with each other. The existence of the matrix *as a reality* is in no way threatening for those who are living in Zion; the only threat is the efforts of the organizers of the two worlds to destroy the reality of those people who cling to their humanity. The people who are living in the false world of the matrix *can* be happy as long as they do not find out that their reality is posthuman and artificial and that their bodies are exploited by machines.

Tarkovsky's films settle on the grounds of a more moderate skepticism, which was Neo's attitude when he was still living in the matrix and hacking into its system. It initiated his doubts about the "real" world. What Neo, Stalker, and *Solaris*' Kris have in common is that they have "splinters in their minds" which lets them doubt the realness of their reality and the "human" within a world that is no longer human but posthuman. In a way, all three of them refuse to go with the herd and want to discover a more authentic way of being human; their "zones" are what Andy Clark has called "lazily programmed" systems, they are hybrids of a "communal dreamworld" and a "multiagent immersive virtual-reality simulation" (195). There is no perfect self-enclosure but people have a chance to get out of this zone. This is why in all three films people manage to hack into an apparently coherent cognitive system and the world it perceives. Finally, because they undertake this effort, their cognitive systems are no longer "prisons of their minds".

In all three films humans attempt to overcome the constraints of matter by using spiritual means though this is not done in the same way in the three films because the ontological conditions are different. In *The Matrix*, Neo and the little girl who bends the spoons have the power to interfere in the matrix because the matrix is *only* a mental construct while in the real world they have no spiritual powers at all. Stalker's daughter, on the other hand, has the power to move glasses on the table *in reality*. For her, reality is only a matrix that she can manipulate. The "outer" world of *Solaris* is also malleable and grants unknown possibilities; however, these possibilities begin to trickle into the "inner" world of the station until, finally, in the last scene, even the dacha on earth is inserted into the ocean.

### 5. *The Matrix* and *Solaris*

With regard to its underlying structure, *Solaris* and *The Matrix* are diametrically opposed. In *Solaris*, the feeling that something is not right with this world is produced through the contact *with* a matrix while in *The Matrix* the same feeling is produced through a contact with what is supposed to be the "real world". The "real world" in *Solaris* is a dacha in a Russian landscape and the rationalized, soulless space of the station that is filled with unreal apparitions. In *The Matrix* things work the other way round: cozy family life exists in the Oracle's kitchen, which is situated in the virtual world of the matrix. In the real world, people are living in Spartan conditions, very much like cosmonauts though not in space but underground (strangely, they fly around inside the earth in spaceship-like hovercrafts through sewers).

A further difference is that the *Solaris* cosmonauts do not fight against the Ocean but try to communicate with it. Snout even wants to shout to it. Finally he sends out X-rays containing transcriptions of Kris's thoughts hoping that it will put an end to the strange happenings. Apparently the experiment works: no new apparitions occur. In *Solaris*, the Ocean is not an evil demon invented by machines but just *another cognitive system* that is perhaps not so different from our own human brain. It is possible to negotiate with the Ocean.

The result is that in *Solaris* the protagonists necessarily reside *between* two programs, a human and a posthuman one. And some of them even discover this mental state as an interesting existential experience. In *Solaris* (as much as in *Stalker*), "real", human reality turns out to be the tragic interplay of the red and the blue system. This creates an ambiguity that is alien to the inhabitants of Zion as well as to those who live in the virtual world of *The Matrix*. While in *The Matrix* the virtual world represents total ignorance (everybody in the film, including Cypher and Agent Smith, agrees with this), in *Solaris* the recaptured and relived memories that walk around in a posthuman form on the station represent experiential human entities that we cannot – and perhaps should not – avoid. While Cypher wants to forget everything by surrendering to the matrix, the matrix-like apparitions in *Solaris* prevent the inhabitants from forgetting: "Why are we tortured like this? On earth you can forget about your memories, on the station you get tortured with them". The matrix, as it appears in *Solaris*, represents a world of suffering and when Kris suggests living with Hari on the station forever, this is no Cypher-like hedonistic flight into a posthuman virtual dream world but the opposite: Kris decides to live *with* reality and all memories that it includes. In *The Matrix*, too, the virtual world contains suffering but it is part of the program. It is not *real* but has been incorporated into the matrix by the machines in order to make the matrix look more authentic and less posthuman for humans. In *Solaris*, however, it is the matrix which causes *real* suffering.

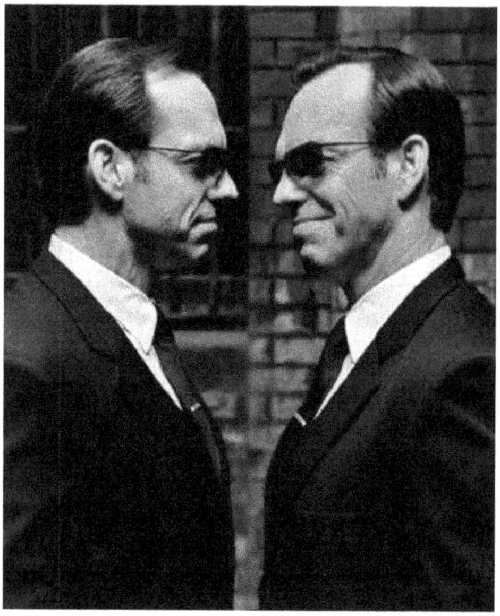

Fig. 7: *The Matrix*

In *Solaris* the protagonists are confronted, for a certain period of time, with two programs or with two realities. Though at the end of the film the apparitions no longer occur and the problem seems to be "solved", Kris's and Snout's – though not Sartorius's – relationships with reality (Earth) have undergone permanent changes. This has to do with their way of approaching the apparitions while they were present. Of all the protagonists, Kris manages most successfully to accommodate two realities in his consciousness and to live with them at least for a while. He is impressed by Hari's claim that the posthuman "visitors are part of you, they are your consciousness". His pragmatic "multi-reality" approach affirms that our memories are constantly present in our lives anyway. So, why reduce "reality" to a one-dimensional cognitive human or posthuman notion?[4]

Guibariane commits suicide for matters of "conscience" because for him contradicting realities are unbearable (we do not know what tormenting content these realities had).[5] Snout, on the other hand, makes great efforts to adopt a relativistic attitude towards reality. He is convinced that the colonial claim of humans that "we don't want any more worlds but only a mirror to see our own world" equates to scientific fraud. In a way, "science" always finds what it wants to find, so why not be unscientific at least for once? However, in truth, Snout can bear the "multi-reality" situation only when being drunk.

Only Sartorius, who fights with Orpheus-like determination for enlightenment, categorically refuses any "multi-reality" approaches and sternly insists scientifically establishing the real world as the one and only *human* world. That he never succeeds in doing so is not due to sentinel ridden counter-reactions from the Ocean but simply to the fact that he does not find the appropriate scientific proof to establish this reality or, rather, the Ocean's non-reality.

In spite of their divergences, all four men in *Solaris* definitely decline Cypher's way of refusing a multi-reality. They refuse ignorance as a kind of madness that accepts the unreal as real, though as Snout says, "madness would be a blessing".[6]

The multi-reality approach is grounded in an ontological definition of "the other world", which is in *Solaris* essentially different from that of *The Matrix*. Though Sartorius claims that the apparition Hari is "a mechanical repetition of the form, a copy from the matrix" and thus posthuman, in reality the creatures that people *Solaris* are far more complex. On the one hand, they are, like the matrix, produced by a non-human cognitive system (the experts say "the Solaris Ocean is a particular kind of brain"). On the other hand, they flow out of the minds of just those people who see them. The ontological ambiguity of this constellation is never resolved in the film; rather it is reinforced. Hari remains real and unreal, human and posthuman, at the same time. Chemically, she might not be a real person, but since Kris's emotional contact with her *is real*, on a social and psychological level she must be seen as real.

The complexity of Tarkovsky's scenario can be appreciated when one imagines how complicated *The Matrix* would have been if its virtual world had been a product not only of evil machines but *at the same time* also of Neo and his companions; or if virtual constructs from the matrix (not robots) had begun filling the city of Zion. Certainly, the Wachowski brothers introduce complications of this kind for example by revealing the Oracle and Neo's identity as the One as nothing other than a part of the system in the second sequel. But this concerns only the plot of the story (destiny) and not questions about reality.

Tarkovsky, however, takes pleasure in elaborating such ambiguities on the reality level. Even after Hari is sent off into space in a rocket, her woolen shawl significantly remains on the seat. Being initially only a "piece of memory without consciousness extracted from the ocean", she gradually gains consciousness, partly escaping the control of the Ocean. However, her process of gaining consciousness is not a linear one, it is not equal with acquiring more and more information about the "real world" and its convincingly real character. On the contrary, the more conscious Hari becomes of the real word, the more she develops, exactly as Kris and Neo do, a *splinter in her mind*: "I think somebody is playing a game with us", says she in a lucid moment. Paradoxically, being "conscious" and being "real" signifies having doubts about reality. The "fighting for truth and reality" ideology of the Hollywood matrix is naturally unable to admit this.

Only because reality has such a "soft structure" is Hari able to escape the matrix. She escapes the control of the Ocean because she manages to produce her own consciousness and her own memories independently of any evil spirit. This is something that the Wachowskis' virtual people are unable to do because their world is unreal and posthuman to the extent that every bit of their consciousness and all their memories are products of machines.

In Tarkovsky's films, a certain metaphysical dimension is produced at the moment real people enter in contact with a "false reality" which is a mystery; in *The Matrix*, the false reality is, in principle, fake. True, a "mystic" dimension appears. Trinity's love for Neo, propelled, like Kris's love in *Solaris*, by oracles and displacements of time and space, resuscitates Neo and helps him to impose "his" reality upon the agents. This has a parallel in the idea of the Ocean Solaris as "a location of oceanic love" which produces – with the help of Kris and his colleagues – new versions of beloved beings who are "in reality" dead. In *The Matrix,* through love, Trinity manages to interfere in reality as if it were a matrix. This is a mystery for agent Smith as much as for us. However, whatever it is, the mystery works in the service of absolute, scientific truth. Once Neo is saved, reality is more firmly established than ever. In *Solaris*, on the other hand, "love" has the power to blur the borders between the human and the posthuman, that is, between what is scientifically real and what is remembered and unreal.

### 6. *The Matrix* and *Stalker*

Aesthetically, *Stalker* and *The Matrix* are very similar because they play out the "reality vs. unreality" theme in a derelict, underworld environment in which life seems to be possible only in margins. In

*The Matrix*, the natural environment has been destroyed, leaving only some ruins of human civilization. The underground housings of Zion are reminiscent of improvised industrial architecture. Also the *Stalker*'s "zone" is situated in and around derelict factory buildings though the "reality" bordering the zone does not look much more inviting. The Peugeot convertible driven by the Writer's friend seems to come from another world. The world that Stalker calls his home is an industrial sector bordered by a power plant with polluted air and water. Strange white particles are flying through the air. Also in this science fiction film humanity, as it faces ecological disaster, seems to have left its happiest days behind. The parallels that the contemporary spectator will draw with the Chernobyl disaster (which occurred seven years after the release of *Stalker*) are, curiously, no coincidence. Tarkovsky is said to have been inspired by the nuclear disaster of the Mayak plant near Chelyabinsk in 1957. Though this accident had not been officially acknowledged until 1992, a "zone" of hundreds of square kilometers had been polluted by radiation. In addition, Tarkovsky shows shots of the Chernobyl power plant in his film.[7]

As in *Solaris,* Tarkovsky confronts us in *Stalker* with the reality theme. At least for Stalker the zone is a reality, because "my happiness, my freedom, my self-respect, it's all here". At the same time, the zone is constantly on the verge of appearing as unreal, because it has a supposedly supernatural character. Even more, the zone might be a product of some evil mind and the Writer even considers that "all this is someone's idiotic invention". The zone appears as a place in which we will not find anything like "facts".

Again, like in *Solaris,* Tarkovsky introduces us to a space that is purely mental. The zone is a place where subjectivity plays with time, exactly like what happens in the matrix and in the Solaris station, From a subjective point of view, the zone is a *reflection in space*, a reflection about human existence through which humans can walk, in which they are confronted with their hidden wishes and daydreams, but from which they can return and reenter reality. According to Stalker the zone is a "complicated system", which makes us think that it is very much like a computer game in which – just because nothing is real – the conditions can change at any moment ("old traps disappear, new ones arise, safe spots become impassable") according to how the players behave. In principle, computer games are different from plotted discourses because "the player has a hand in plotting the events" (Aarseth 1997: 111). From an objective point of view, however, the zone might be not more than an abandoned factory ground in which nothing mystical has ever happened.

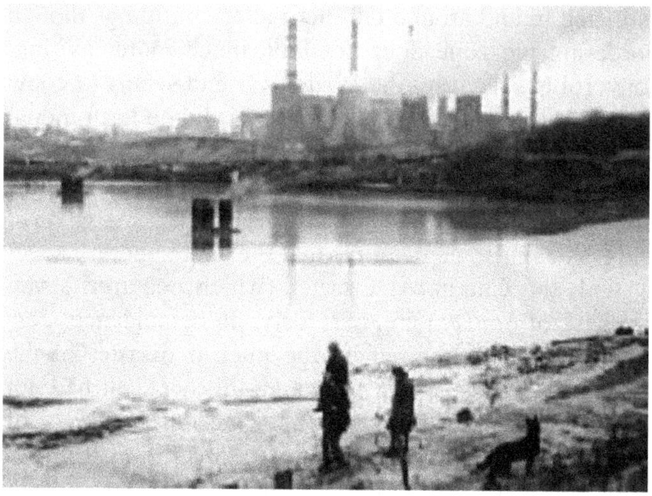

Fig. 8: *Stalker*

This ambiguity is what makes the zone interesting. "Officially", in the zone, time and space do not count, and the humans who are confronted with this mental landscape are supposed to experience its mystical dimension. At least apparently, the zone defies the laws of physics and is, like the Ocean Solaris, a cosmic abyss. Ironically, until the end of the film we get no real proof of the mystical character of the zone because nothing supernatural happens. While in the Strugatsky brothers' book the men salvage material that has been left behind by extraterrestrial visitors, Tarkovsky has removed such evidences.[8] All we have are strange noises, like the howling of wolves and there is a sound that only the Writer hears and which could be the effect of the upcoming wind. Also, the men get lost and walk in a circle, but theoretically all this can happen anywhere. The mystical character of the zone is entirely based on rumors. It is still possible that the zone is no normal place, but in no case can it be reduced to a purely virtual posthuman matrix. For example, even if Stalker recognizes that the zone is a kind of program, he would not be able to interfere in this program. Paradoxically, this does not make the zone "normal" in return but, on the contrary, it only *reconfirms* its ontological dimension as something exclusively mental because it is a "zone" only in the mind of the people. In other words, the zone is the uncanny space that produces doubts not only about reality but even doubts about these doubts. And this radical Pyrrhonean skepticism can sustain itself only through irony. For the people who traverse it, the zone is posthuman and human, a matrix and reality, at the same time.

As in *Solaris*, the men have to cope with this ambiguous phenomenon. The individualist writer looks for a reality that is hidden behind the hypocrisy of the world of culture that consists of "inventions" like conscience and anguish. The civilized people that are his readers together with journalists, editors and critics are captured in this reality and do not have the cognitive means to look beyond it: "They are all so 'literate'. They all got sensory deficiency", he complains. The Writer refuses to believe in this cultural matrix and hopes that the zone will open his eyes to something (more) "real". When the Writer accuses the scientist (the Professor) of being too curious in the name of science he sounds like Cypher: "All this is someone's idiotic invention, can't you feel it? But you, of course, must find out whose invention it is. And why? What good can your knowledge do?"

The reality of the empirically minded Professor, on the other hand, is determined by political strata, and though he is ready to accept the supernatural zone as a "natural" phenomenon, he cannot but perceive this reality in relation with the overall political reality that exists outside the zone. In order to prevent mass-hysterical conversions and morally unsustainable attempts to use the power of the zone, the Professor decides to destroy it. However, even by committing this political act in the name of humanity, he is led by passions because his project is linked to a personal revenge against a colleague. Though his scientific conscience forces him to *pragmatically* accept the existence of the zone as a possible empirical fact, politically the Professor is an *idealist* and *humanist*: like Morpheus & Co, like Guibariane and Sartorius, he cannot accept the simultaneous existence of two realities.

The Writer believes neither in the reality of (consumer) culture nor in the reality of science and this makes him different not only from the Professor and Sartorius, but also from Cypher. Human or posthuman? He does not care. The writer is a pragmatist like Kris and is ready to accept, what is "good in the way of belief".[9] He clutches a weapon when he deems it necessary but he is also ready to let it fall when Stalker tells him to do so. The Writer *would* be ready to believe in the zone but at the same time nothing that he experiences in the zone can convince him of its superior character. Besides that, he came to the zone for pragmatic reasons: to find inspiration.

Stalker assumes, like Neo, the role of Jesus Christ. To be a Stalker is, as he says, "a kind of calling". (In the film, it is actually the Writer who puts on the thorn crown, probably because Tarkovsky wanted to avoid an all too evident symbolism. However, on the film's poster that is also used for the present DVD release, it is Stalker who wears the crown). Stalker is supposed to show his adepts reality and his role is therefore similar to that of Neo. But he has also Trinity's miraculous power because his desire is that "everything that has been planned comes true". There is a plan, a reality that the zone or the chamber has seen; and if we *believe* in it we will live in reality.

Similar to Morpheus, Stalker wants to push his companions towards self-knowledge and requires that they abandon all "thinking" and only *believe*. He wants to open their eyes so that they come to *know* reality as it is. He confirms that his teacher Porcupine had "opened his eyes" in this way. Only if people believe and do not "think" can they successfully move around in the zone and arrive at the chamber of wishes. The non-thinking dog, for example, can walk in and out of the zone without problems.

According to Stalker, the zone "lets those pass who have lost all hope" because in fact those are the ones who do not think. Accordingly, he implores the zone as if it were a reality hidden behind the "outside" reality to which one has access only when one believes:

> Let everything that has been planned come true. Let them believe. And let them have a laugh at their passions. Because what they call passion is actually not some emotional energy, but just the friction between their souls and the outside world. And most important, let them believe in themselves. Let them be helpless like little children, because weakness is a great thing, and strength is nothing.

Only if we enter the chamber of wishes in such a disillusioned state of mind will we perceive what is "real" and not the unreal veil of reality determined by our vanity and our passions. However, ironically, if we really do not wish *anything* any longer we don't need to enter a chamber of wishes. It's their passions and ambitions that let people perceive a reality that is a matrix but once they have given up these passions there is no difference between the zone, the chamber, and outside reality. This is probably the reason why the chamber looks like a kind of twin of Stalker's own house and why, in Tarkovsky's film, the zone and Stalker's extra-zonal housing interpenetrate from the beginning. (The sound of dripping water, typical for the zone, is constantly present in Stalker's house as well as white feathery particles that are flying through the air.)

*Stalker* is a film about disillusionment, a disillusionment that is also present in *The Matrix* but which is overcome in the latter film in order to lead to a final victory. The Oracle tells Neo that he is not the One and in the end he actually is killed. But Trinity, by using another oracle in the way of a self-producing prophecy, insists that he *must* be the One because she loves him. Here Trinity *knows*, in a Zen-Buddhist intuitive fashion, without *thinking*. She does not *hope* that this or that will happen, she is not afraid that it will not happen, but suddenly all "this and that" no longer matter for her. She simply knows.[10] The result is that in the end she and Neo can embrace reality with even more certitude. In *Stalker*, however, once the men have lost their hope, they step out of the zone more skeptical and confused than ever. At the same time they have learned something about themselves, about their false ambitions and hopes and will embrace reality in what we might want to call a more "truthful" or human way.

Within the realm of the matrix, Morpheus pushes Neo from a cognitive approach of "reflection" to that of knowledge ("don't think you are, know you are"). In the realm of reality this corresponds to the shift from *hope* to *belief*. All this makes sense with regard to the destiny problems and conflicts with the Oracle's prophecies, but the Zen-like idea of "no-thought" or "emptiness" that is lurking behind the script ("free your mind, don't try to hit me") looks incorrect with regard to cognitive questions. The problem is that we will never understand how Neo can "know" that the matrix is not real. The answer will probably be: Because he is "the One". But what if he is not? In that case, is the reality of Zion also based only on belief? Nothing in the trilogy suggests this. It seems rather that the reality problem has been left to a populist idea of "immediacy" in Zen Buddhism combined with Judeo-Christian or westernized conceptions of eastern thought.

Ironically, it is Tarkovsky who turns out here to be more "eastern" though his film sports no Asian motives at all. Tarkovsky pushes his protagonists from apparent *knowledge* towards a process of meditation or reflection, a reflection which leads them to real freedom of the mind. When the Professor and the Writer arrive at home, they are certainly confused and skeptical but they are no longer obsessed with the idea of the zone. Even Stalker's attitude towards the zone has changed. He still appears to be hypnotized by the idea of the zone but even this seems acceptable given that the zone is now just a kind of religion for him. He understands that nobody needs the zone and will probably no longer lead people there. He can practice his "zone religion" within the realm of reality.

Curiously, Stalker's wife undergoes the perhaps most dramatic change and suddenly appears to be serene. As becomes clear through her monologue, it is *she* who recognizes most clearly what the others are just suspecting: that reality is just what it is. Reality is what it is, and this is at the same time reality's most *mystical* characteristic. Stalker's wife points this out when explaining that, for her, the most essential choices she has made in her life have always remained entirely unexplainable for her. This is similar to Trinity: when it came to important questions, she only *knew* and did not care about any "this or that". Everything points to the fact that "reality" itself is already mystical enough, as Tarkovsky suggests by letting Stalker's daughter move glasses on the table.

The destiny problem, on the other hand, is exploited in a sophisticated manner in *The Matrix*. One of the disturbing effects of the matrix is that here software designers and fortunetellers determine the course of our destiny while we would like to have *choice*. And if we want choice we also need *hope* (which is an illusion according to the architect of the matrix). However, in the end, hope is all that remains: the sentence that concludes the trilogy is spoken by the Oracle and it is: "I hope so". In *The Matrix* hope has become a power on condition that it is used by those people who clearly *know* what reality is.

Stalker tries to convince us that the bits of hope that we have are the vanities that create the dreamlike veil of a matrix that we would do better to abandon. In the end, the men abandon their hopes up to the point that they do not even want to enter the chamber of wishes. At the deepest level they are afraid of a further confrontation with the prophecy/choice conundrum because hope means (as *The Matrix* very well shows) hoping for a destiny that is beneficial. Neo *hopes* that the Oracle's prophecy is true. But in the end it is not hope that saves him but rather love and belief (Trinity *loves* him and Morpheus *believes* that the prophecy is true). The people in *Stalker* are confronted with a similar problem. "You want one thing but you get another thing", says the Writer. Porcupine had certainly not "officially" wished to become rich but he was unable to abandon these hopes, and when he entered the chamber they became true. In a way it is right to say that this was his destiny; it was a destiny that he had predetermined himself through the hopes that were his most intimate thoughts. The chamber only materialized these hopes and made true what was unavoidable. Porcupine should have recognized the "other plan", the other reality that was hidden underneath his hopes and he could have recognized it through belief.

Had Cypher entered the chamber, he would have ended up in a posthuman virtual dreamworld in which all wishes are fulfilled. That's what he was actually hoping for. The men in *Stalker* abandon these passions and discover a new reality – which turns out to be the same reality as before. The only thing that has changed is that they now no longer need to enter the chamber.

**Conclusion: Towards Multicultural Approaches to Reality**

We can understand Tarkovsky's films as an appeal to humanity to acquire different patterns of perception of the *cultural* reality of their everyday life. This is a stance that we do not find in *The Matrix.* The scientist Kevin Warwick has suggested that the matrix is perhaps the dull world of everyday life with television and brains conditioned by the fake world of commercials. Or perhaps it is a world haunted by a VR that humans have produced themselves. Even if the industry presents, for example, a hamburger as something nourishing and delicious, *in reality* it contains "a high percentage of water, is mainly fat, and is devoid of vitamins" (Warwick 2005: 205). Against this, Morpheus and his people want to establish a reality that is scientifically sound. *Solaris* and *Stalker*, on the other hand, tell us that any concept of reality as an *absolute presence* is impossible.

In other words, Tarkovsky's films concord with Baudrillard's theory of simulation, whereas *The Matrix* does not. Baudrillard believed that there is no solution to simulation but *The Matrix* makes us believe that there is one.[11] Too many "self-produced" elements like memories, traditions, etc. are part of our reality and we will have to live with them. However, we should not approach them with too much hope. We should not be hypnotized by them though it is also clear that we cannot consider them as entirely unreal.

Though the VR in *The Matrix* is supposed to be "normal", in most scenes of the trilogy the matrix world appears as utterly strange: it is here that supernatural things happen. In Tarkovsky's films strangeness becomes rather generalized because known and unknown territories cannot be distinguished. The earth scenes in *Solaris*, for example, represent an idyllic everyday reality. However, after returning from the station, Kris will no longer understand this world as a world which simply "is". As mentioned, those scenes are comparable with the idyllic kitchen scene in *The Matrix,* which insists so much on normality though we all know that nothing is normal here because it is not real.

But are the earth scenes on *Solaris* real? The last image shows the house with the lake as an island in the cosmic ocean *Solaris*. No evil demon has put it there but it is most probably a phenomenon of consciousness. Still, we do not see it only because our brain is "in a vat". Tarkovsky wants to show us that reality is always multi-dimensional and the world, as it is conceived by human consciousness, is always interspersed with simulacra like childhood memories, art, and regrets. Maybe God. In Stanislav Lem's novel *Solaris*, Kris manages to establish a contact with the Ocean, an idea that Tarkovsky rejected in his adaptation of the book. Instead Kris returns to earth in order to find a reality impregnated by the non-reality of the Ocean. For Kris, reality has become a matrix but, paradoxically, a matrix which grants real freedom because, after all, is not living with one's memories an essential part of a free human condition? The virtual people from *The Matrix*, once Morpheus and his team recruit them in the real world, can commute between the two worlds rather freely. They have the "contact" that the *Solaris* people have never had. However, does this provide them any freedom? Real freedom means to be able to shift between the real and the unreal, between experience and memories and to recognize the meaningful character of both. The VR people of the posthuman matrix in *The Matrix* cannot do this and this is why they are enslaved.

The people in *Stalker* have also acquired this freedom because they accept the mystical dimension of the zone as a "culture" that one can live with, but which does not and should not determine our cognition up to a point that we consider it as an absolute and only "reality". There are other "cultures" in the world, that of the Writer's readers and critics for example, and they all are "good in a way of belief" though none represents something absolute in the sense of "absolutely real and human". Even in the case of "absolute strangeness", that is, even when we have the impression of definitely dealing with another reality, we cannot decide that the one is real and the other unreal.

## Notes

1. See for example: David Chalmers: "The Matrix as Metaphysics" and Andy Clark: "The Twisted Matrix: Dream, Simulation, or Hybrid?" in Grau 2005. Other valuable elaborations on the *The Matrix* are contained in William Irving's two edited volumes *The Matrix and Philosophy* (2002 and 2005) as well as Matt Lawrence's book *Like a Splinter in your Mind: The Philosophy behind the Matrix*

*Trilogy* (Oxford: Blackwell, 2004) and Glenn Yeffeth's *Taking the Red Pill: Science, Philosophy and Religion in The Matrix* (2003).

2. David Chalmers and Andy Clark have perhaps best explained the relevance of Putnam's model for *The Matrix* since, as Chalmers says, the principle of *The Matrix* is that people who live within its realm "have a cognitive system which receives its inputs from and sends outputs to a matrix" (Chalmers 2005: 133).

3. From an interview that Tarkovsky gave just before starting the work on *Solaris*. Quoted in Timothy Hyman's review of *Solaris* in *Film Quarterly* 29:3, 1976, 57.

4. My definition of multi-reality overlaps with Michael Heim's definition of irrealism as "[t]he view that 'world' is a plural concept. According to irrealism, each world is a variant of related worlds, and each world makes its own context and rules of intelligibility. (…) This is irreal because it undermines the uncritical affirmation of a single world. Irrealism parallels Heidegger's existentialist notion of world in *Being and Time*" (Heim 1998: 216). My own concept of irreality is explained in Chapter 2 or Botz-Bornstein 2008.

5. In Stanislav Lem's novel, Guibariane had not been confronted with a blonde girl like in the film, but with a "gigant negress": "A giant Negress was coming silently towards me with a smooth, rolling gait. I caught a gleam from the whites of her eyes and heard the soft slapping of her bare feet. She was wearing nothing but a yellow skirt of plaited straw; her enormous breasts swung freely and her black arms were as thick as thighs" (*Solaris*, New York: Harcourt, Brace & Company 1978, 30). For Slavoj Žižek this negress is a product of Guibariane's fantasy. He comments: "Unable to sustain confrontation with his primordial maternal fantasmatic apparition, Guibariane dies of shame". Žižek: "The Thing from Inner Space: On Tarkovsky" in *Angelaki: Journal of the Theoretical Humanities* 4: 2, 1999.

6. Soderbergh's adaptation of *Solaris* offers this alternative. At the end of the film, Kris and Hari manage (how they come to do this is not explained) to melodramatically live in the matrix.

7. The caretakers of the Chernobyl nuclear power plant refer to themselves as "stalkers" and to the abandoned area as "the Zone" still today.

8. Boris and Arkady Strugatsky: *Roadside Picnic* (London: Victor Gollancz, 1978).

9. As said the pragmatist philosopher John Dewey.

10. Žižek insists on this love-faith motive in Tarkovsky's films: "Since love is 'blind,' contingent, grounded in no clearly observable properties, that unfathomable *je ne sais quoi* which decides when am I to fall in love can also be totally externalized in the decision of an unfathomable authority" (1999).

11. Cf. Sven Lutzka: "[*The Matrix*] offers a solution to the problem of simulation [but] Baudrillard believes that there is none" (2004: 126).

# Feature Scene V

## Car Design and Genetics: The New Mini and Japanese Pottery:

### 1. The New Mini

In the world of cars, the new Mini is one of the most striking appearances of recent years. It seems to grab people's attention in the same way as the Citroën DS did which, when it first appeared in 1954, challenged the semiotician Roland Barthes to write an essay about what he considered a "superlative object".[1] Only five years later, in 1959, another car appeared which, though utterly different from the Citroën DS, became a motoring icon of its own. This was the old Mini, the ancestor of the new one. At the moment the old Mini was launched, it attracted neither the same amount nor the same kind of attention as the Citroën DS. The old Mini was simply a popular car judged primarily in terms of practicality, and not in terms of futurist design. The Citroën DS, on the other hand, seems to have been from the beginning a matter of "dreams" announcing a "change in the mythology of cars" (Barthes 1957: 140).

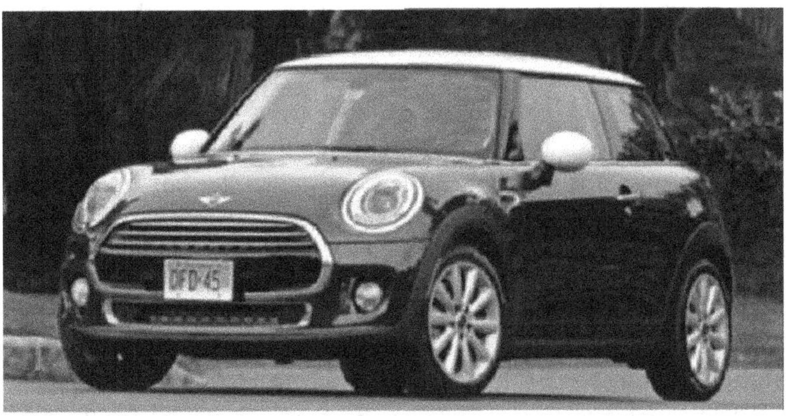


Fig. 9: The new Mini

It is possible that the new Mini heralds a similar change. The Mini Design team explains how it transferred traditional formal language of the old Mini into the twenty-first century. Certain typical characteristics needed to be preserved, like the chromed radiator, the lid-like roof, round headlights, etc. Most important was that the new Mini should not simply be a backward looking retro design car. In some way, it should contain "the genes" of the old Mini (as said former design chief Frank Stephenson), and then, in a way of speaking, develop a posthuman life of its own.

The result is what is considered an "emotional" or an "organic" design that relies very much on "concrete" values. Characteristically, the first model of the new Mini was not generated on a computer screen but was fabricated – life sized – out of clay, which is a relatively unusual procedure in modern car design, the more so since this clay approach is not concealed to the public but advertised by the Mini-potters as a constitutive part of the new Mini's identity. The Mini website www.mini.com announced in 2001: "Let's rely on pencils, paper and clay, not on computers". It seems that, after all those years of postmodern simulation, with the new Mini we receive something "real".

Critics of the new Mini can only be some die-hard form-follows-function romantics. They see in the creation from 2001, if not a retro design car, so at least a self-conscious reproduction of a preexisting design, which they condemn as incompatible with the spirit of the old Mini. The old Mini was just a "utility vehicle" which, in all its simplicity, became a typical expression of necessity, that is, not of style but of non-style. All that Alec Issigonis, the designer of the old Mini did, was to combine compact external dimensions with maximal space inside. His intention was not to create a lifestyle but a fuel-efficient car for adults (as a matter of fact, Issigonis was even against car radios and comfortable seats because they would distract drivers).

At the same time the problem is too complex for any binary confrontation of old Mini against new Mini to be sustainable. The New Mini, too, is not exclusively presented as a lifestyle product, but as a "car to live with". Aesthetics are important, but, in the end, the new Mini turns out to be more practical than the old Mini. The interior design, for example, is said to be stylish but also "easy to understand". In the new Mini, "style" is supposed to go hand in hand with function.[2] The conclusion is that *style* has become a necessity for the new Mini in the same way in which 3-inch wheels were a necessity for Issigonis (because he wanted to save space).

**2. Japanese Pottery**
Kichizaemon Raku XV (born in 1949) is the fifteenth successor of the Japanese Raku pottery dynasty established by his ancestor Chôjirô around 1570. Chôjirô developed a special technique of making tea bowls that is followed to this day and known by the name of Raku-style. The composition of the clay and the glaze as well as the low-firing method carried out in a small oven are transmitted, in an almost alchemic way, from generation to generation. The oven still remains where it stood 400 years ago in Raku's studio. As important and binding as the technique is the Raku-ware's style. Raku-style unites aesthetic ideals of sobriety, simplicity and transcendence that Japanese aesthetics denotes by the word *wabi*. Some of Chôjirô's tea bowls are particularly famous and serve as a kind of prototype models of the Raku spirit. Most of these typical tea bowls are monochrome black (though red is also possible). Chôjirô's tea bowls impress through the total exclusion of decorative effects. The black color is supposed to express silence, unity of spirit and nature. "Black" is here, as Chôjirô's successor in the 15th generation explains, not a color but a kind of non-color signifying the "refusal of color itself". "Chôjirô's black is totally different from these lustrous black textures. His black reminds us of matte, rusty iron, or a clay texture that cannot be called pure black".[3]

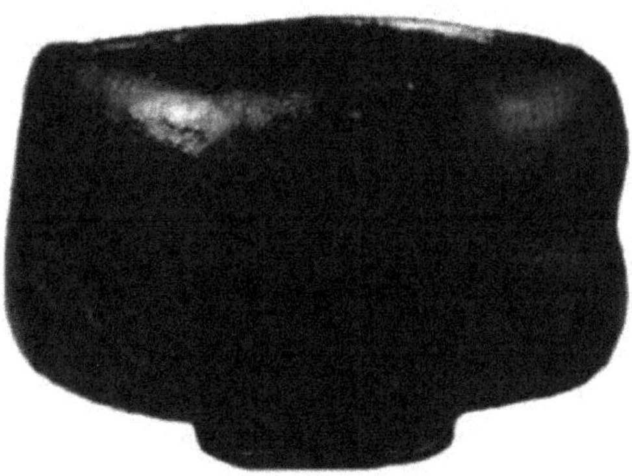

Fig. 10: Raku bowl

Japanese tea bowls are a curious phenomenon. Though the focus *seems* to be on *aesthetic* matters, in reality, the highest ideal by which this artistic tradition has been dominated over centuries is *utility*. By putting *utility* into the foreground of their aesthetics, potters affirmed the decision to avoid any aestheticizing effects, or stylization.

The Japanese received the first elements of inspiration from Korea. The "models" that inspired the development of these most sophisticated Japanese craft objects were, paradoxically, ordinary rice bowls used by Korean peasants. What is important for the development of Japanese pottery is a certain anti-stylistic, down-to-earth attitude. Sen no Rikyû, a contemporary of Chôjirô and teacher of tea ceremony, was perhaps the highest authority on matters of tea bowls at his time. One day he heard noblemen discussing stylistic problems of tea vessels which made him say: "Gentlemen, this is most unbecoming talk. The connoisseurship of tea vessels consists in judging whether they are suitable for their purpose or not, and whether they combine well or badly with each other…" (quoted in Münsterberg 1964: 100).

### 3. The Citroën DS

We have noted above that the design of the new Mini has been called "organic". Another car that has been called organic is the Citroën DS and first and foremost so by French semiotician Roland Barthes. For Barthes, the Citroën DS represented a new example of "humanized art" that is no longer purely technological but, as an almost living being, linked to human life. However, Barthes' use of the word "organic" is completely opposed to the way in which it appears in contemporary evaluations of the new Mini.

When Barthes says that the Citroën DS is organic, he talks more like a scientist who desires to create a structure as perfect and transparent that it starts to move and to function on its own. The Mini's organicity, on the other hand, goes more in the direction of "real" organic life (of nature) that inspires our imagination but remains, in the end, mysterious and impenetrable.

Almost every sentence that Barthes writes about the Citroën DS can today be turned inside out in order to evoke the essence of the new Mini. For Barthes, the Citroën DS is an object that has "fallen from the sky" or come down to us from another universe. Barthes evokes gothic cathedrals and insinuates that the letters DS (pronounced *déesse* in French) would suggest the sense of "Goddess".

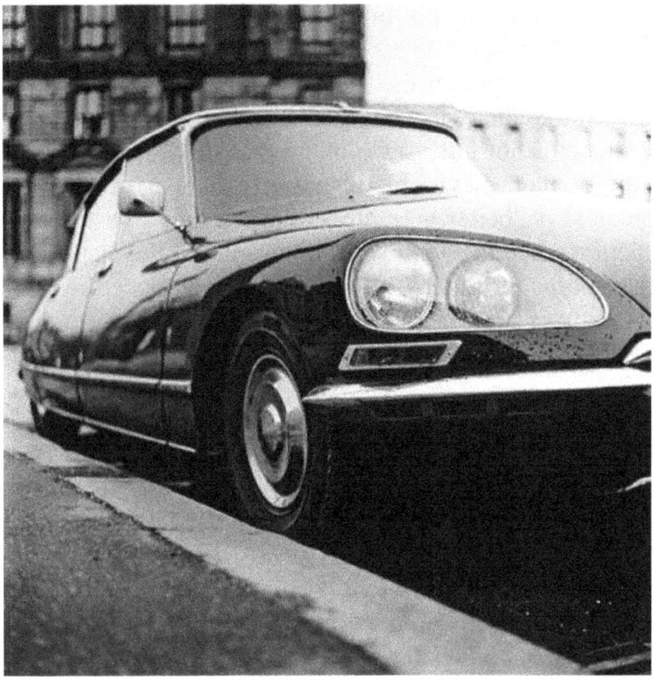

Fig. 11: Citroën DS (1955-1976)

Nothing could be more opposed to the new Mini. If the Citroën DS has fallen from the sky, the new Mini looks as if it came out of the earth. "Earth" is here not the earth of origins (like "blood and earth") nor is it the earth of nature or of those simplistic eco-romantic ideologies incorporated into SUV cars. The new Mini's earth is an ambiguous phenomenon, which is the reason why its texture comes closer to that of clay, that is, to a half-fluent, half-structural paste combining past, imagination and reality.

According to Barthes, the Citroën DS manifests no "origin" which is correct: no earth is clinging to the deity. However, the new Mini is also supposed to go across borders. The Mini has no clearly national or cultural origin. Neither the British not the German (the new Mini is produced by BMW) identity sticks to the car like a predicate. Its "identity" can be located rather on a virtual level in the subconscious of the people who link the Mini in imagination to vague components of a "national character". In this sense the new Mini is not a "neutral object" but manifests a kind of "globalized" national identity. In other words, the Mini carries its past and identity not as a reified past in the present (like a retro design car) but in the form of a simultaneous incorporation of past and present.

This explains why, in spite of the "aesthetics of the concrete" that the Mini is supposed to radiate, its "being" is situated in the domain of the dream. This dream is not futurist (as in the case of the Citroën DS) but located in the domain of virtual fluency in which past, present, and future are melted or, better, partially solidified into a paste. It is thus no contradiction when the Mini website, in spite of the insistence on the anti-electronic pottery method that helped to produce the new Mini, attempts to attract customers by announcing: "Immerse Yourself in the New Mini".

## 4. The Paste

The new Mini has indeed been made, in an alchemic way, out of that concrete, organic paste (*pâte*) that the French epistemologist Gaston Bachelard has qualified as "oneiric" (Bachelard 1942: 32). Bachelard's idea of sculpting by using an oneiric paste seems to have materialized fifty years after he wrote those sentences. Since the 1990s, architects working with computer aided design programs insist that they do not *draw* but *build* by sticking together "virtual clay". Most recently, a large number of modeling systems or "electronic sculpting systems" using the term "virtual clay" in a more official fashion have emerged on the software market. This means that the paste-like material of dreams still provides a kind of creativity that will not be represented as a stable and abstract structure.

Paste can be touched while the Citroën DS could only be timidly caressed because, as says Barthes, "the touch is the most demystifying sense of all senses, unlike sight, which is the most magical" (Barthes 1957: 141/90). According to Barthes, the Citroën DS is shiny, "as smooth as cake icing" and symbolizes perfection. Excelling in "lightness", the Citroën DS produces a "silence of a marvelous order" which Barthes classifies as the silence of heavens.

Nothing could be more opposed to the sculptured Mini. The heavy new Mini vibrates the silence of earth, of the past or of the paste. While the Citroën DS attempts to objectify spirit in a purely abstract way, the new Mini conserves spirit in a half-concrete, half-virtual form that can be conserved only in the ambiguous state of paste. While the Citroën DS is liquid, ethereal, and impresses through its "glassy surfaces" (who would like to caress "a Goddess that is the exaltation of glass"?), the new Mini's levers, buttons and dials have been designed with their "look, feel and weight very much in mind" (advertisement).

All this means that the new Mini comes closer to the highest aesthetic ideal of Japanese pottery, to that of *wabi,* which refers to "the primordial articulations of human consciousness",[4] remaining at the same time functional, simple and offering a spatial and tactile effect.

**5. Alchemy and Genes**

The problem for the generations of Raku family members succeeding Chôjirô was to recreate the Raku-style without ending up in pure imitation. Kichizaemon XV, like all the thirteen generations of potters trying to capture Chôjirô's spirit before him, insists that he is not making retro design tea bowls: "I repeat that so-called traditional art today tends to have lost its creative energy because it is often under the illusion of trying to revive the past in the present by superficially reproducing past styles or by rearranging or retouching them in minute details". We recognize that "postmodernism" is a 400 year old problem, at least for Raku potters:

> Regarding the question of the inheritance of tradition versus innovation, the important element should not be the superficial decomposition and rearrangement of forms that belong to a certain accomplished style, nor a reconstruction of traditional styles by adding new elements to them. Postmodernism has fallen into this trap of conventionalizing the superficial surface layers of past forms and styles. The generations of Raku masters of the past 400 years since Chôjirô were also in danger of following this path" (Raku 2000: 53).

It needs to be added that for Raku potters this problem is even more dramatic than for contemporary car designers. As a matter of fact, an *imitation* of Chôjirô's style would be entirely useless because Chôjirô's declared aim is to have "no style". Chôjirô forbade himself the creation of a certain aesthetic form, color, style, and insisted on non-form and non-color. What is asked for in the art of pottery is not self-expression but "slicing off aesthetic elements regarding form, reducing individuality to nil, going beyond the idea of form, and even ignoring the idea of self-expression would eventually lead to a point where beauty denies itself" (Raku 2000: 55).

In the essay on the Citroën DS, not even two pages long, Barthes uses the word "magic" four times and "spiritual" two times. However, the magic that Barthes has in mind is not that of alchemy but that of science. Scientific magic is the device that *looks* like magic, but which still remains perfectly explicable. The components of the Citroën's body, for example, *seem* to hold together "by sole virtue of their wondrous shape". This is a mystery of science for which there are, in the end, always rather common-sensical explanations.

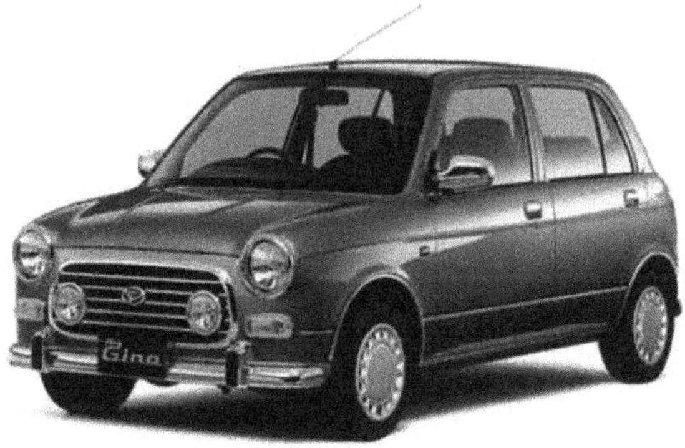

Fig. 12: Mini-inspired Daihatsu Mira Gino (1999-2004)

To the Citroën's science-fiction style we oppose the new Mini's posthuman virtual ethno-style. The Citroën DS is magic and mathematical as much as the new Mini is concrete and virtual (did not already Issigonis insist that "mathematics is the enemy of the truly creative man?"). While the Citroën DS represents a newly discovered humanized and "consumable" science, the new Mini is magic because it is made out of that concrete paste that contains the past in a virtual form. For this reason the existence of the new Mini represents a fall back into alchemy.

Barthes associates alchemy with that inhuman "bestiary of power" present in the *old* myths of cars. While these myths contain the "alchemy of speed", the Citroën DS managed to overcome alchemy in order to distribute the more human fruits of "relish in driving". In 2001 nobody considers speed, at least that of moving objects, as alchemy. The alchemy of the 2000s is the simultaneous presence of different realities offered by new technologies of communication. Alchemy is not speed but rather VR or the posthuman survival of genes.

Both the Citroën DS and the new Mini are organic, but the new Mini has one thing that the Citroën DS does not have: genes. Genes are the new component that has been added to the paste since Bachelard's times. But because nobody can really say *in which way* the genes have "generated" this or that *concrete form*, these genes remain in the domain of the virtual, doing no more than confirming Bachelard's claim about the oneiric character of paste. The conclusion is that genes carry information that is neither concrete nor abstract but "virtual" in the sense of "possible though at the same time not possible". These genes permit the shift from structural to dreamlike organicism.

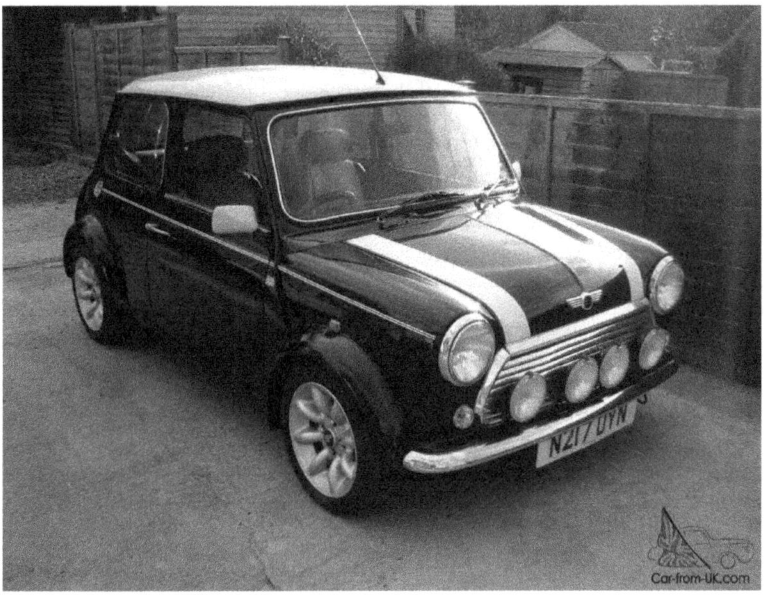


Fig. 13: The old Mini (1959-2000)

You can touch the new Mini without demystifying it. The main approach we use when being confronted with the new Mini is not that of seeing, as in the case of the Citroën DS, but that of empathy. Of course, what it is that we are going to empathize with remains entirely open. Is it the present, the past or some kind of future? Though the car is so tactile and charged with so many "feelings", its essence remains unreachable. The more we touch and the more we feel, the further it moves away. It is just like the experience described by Kichizaemon XV when he received the commission to reproduce an old Chôjirô tea bowl: "I once got a commission to reproduce the tea bowl called "Kamuro" by Chôjirô, which was an invaluable experience. I was face to face with the original for months, putting it in front of my worktable, carefully touching it all around, occasionally putting it to my lips in order to reach full understanding of every detail of the piece to be reproduced. [...] The more I got involved into that piece, the more unreachable it became" (ibid). We, who know the new Mini, know the reason why. The essence of these objects is virtual and it is embedded somewhere in the past(e).

## Notes

1. Roland Barthes: "La nouvelle Citroën" in: *Mythologies. Œuvres complètes I* (Paris: Seuil 1993), 561-723. The text was written in 1954 and published in 1957 in the volume *Mythologies*.
2. That the form-follows-function romantics are wrong might be shown in the example of the retro-design car Gino (www.daihatsu.co.jp/mira_gino) that the Japanese carmaker Daihatsu launched in 1999. The Gino is a more or less literal reconstruction of the old Mini. However, it is obvious that the career of the Gino evolves along much more modest lines than that of the new Mini. In spite of its Mini-like reinstatement of the *useful family car* identity (it even has four doors), the Gino is far from being accepted as the successor of the old Mini.
3. All quotations by Raku Kichizaemon XV are from his essay: "Raku Tea Bowls: The Essence of the Form. The Evolution of Wabi" in: *Raku Museum* (Kyoto: Raku Museum, 2000).
4. Toshiko & Toyo Izutsu: *The Theory of Beauty in the Classical Aesthetics of Japan* (Haag: Nijnhoff, 1981), 55. *Wabi* "refers to the peculiar metaphysical or existential region which is to be located somewhere between the phenomenal and prephenomenal or the articulated and the non-articulated whole" (Izutsu, 52).

## An Interview with Kichizaemon Raku XV

**Mr. Raku, your family has made Raku tea bowls for over 400 years. Though they all maintain a certain spirit, one can clearly see that all those bowls do not simply look the same. Has there been something of an "evolution" of form or of style during those 400 years.**

It is difficult to say where the change is and where the continuity is. As a matter of fact, things are continuously changing. Sometimes change happens over a very long term, sometimes it happens within the performance of a single individual. In theater, the old things just disappear. But here, in pottery, we keep the old styles. We transmit them, and these styles are fixed. In this sense, what we are doing is different from other arts. There is a certain saying, *huekido* 不易道, which means *certain things change and certain things don't change.* It is actually very difficult to articulate this position in a foreign language. The particular Raku style is a fixed style, which is called the *tekone* 手捏ね style.[1] According to the *tekone* style, the lines are always vague and soft. An important question is how to maintain this style. One can say that this style is included in Raku pottery in a really evolutionary fashion.

**You have these constraints that come to you from history through a long line of ancestors. When thinking of yourself within the context of international contemporary art, do you not feel your heritage as ballast, as a handicap, because it prevents you from adopting the same individualist expressionism that other artists are allowed to adopt?**

The representative of the first generation of Raku potters, Chôjirô, was really a superb artist. And each subsequent generation tried to interpret his work. Each generation really struggled to do so. And only when we interpret Chôjirô in a really personal way we will make a good tea bowl.

**Does your art have a place in international art, independent of the Japanese tradition?**

"International art" actually means "Western art", because that movement clearly dominates. But in the twentieth century, this modernism is crumbling; people find this modernity suspicious. Only in this situation could Chôjirô obtain the status of "modern" or "postmodern". What he produced were individual expressions but he tried to overcome this individuality. And I think that the overcoming of individual expressions is really the essence of modern art. My work always begins with Chôjirô. It is the starting point of my work.

**Do you want to evoke emotions of the past? There is an image of "Raku" in people's minds. When you make Raku tea bowls, people expect you to evoke this image. Do you constantly have this image in mind when working?**

What I want to evoke is difficult to express in words. All those working in fine arts make artifacts. It is not like literature or poetry where artists rely on words. In my case, it is very difficult to say what kind of image I have in mind when I am working. I am actually trying to overcome the individual. The result is nothingness. Chôjirô manifested nothingness in the same way in a tea bowl. At the same time, by overcoming the individual we attain universality. This is paradoxical, but it is just the source of real artistic creativity. Creativity always starts with a paradox, and during the whole process of creation this paradox remains constant. I think that this is the essence of art. And, of course, it is precisely because of this paradox that I cannot explain what it actually is that I have in mind when I am making these tea bowls. If this "thing" would be something concrete that can be named, it would be something very narrow. But this paradox, which is so necessary for our creativity, does not have a straightforward logic. And, in the end, the only thing that I express is this paradox. I do it in a very individual way because it is my very own expression. The world is full of paradoxes. You always have parts and wholes, you have love and hate, you have consciousness and unconsciousness… These are my keywords. The world is a world of binary oppositions and I express this paradoxical situation through my art. You can say that I express my anger about it. As a matter of fact, my tea bowls are attempts not just to express those paradoxes but to overcome them.

**What does clay as a material represent for you? What would be different if you were working with marble or with wood?**

Clay is formless. That means: Chaos. In its essence, clay is chaos.

**Your bowls are not always seen as transcendental objects that have this "non-style". They are also decorative objects. How do you cope with this?**

You and many other people say that Chôjirô's works represent a kind of metaphysical negation. But at the same time, tea bowls need to be useful (that's even an important aspect of tea bowl aesthetics). If you negate everything, you will also negate the shape of the tea bowl; that means in the end you won't have anything. What I want to say is that also Chôjirô was bound by the utilitarian constraints of his time. His tea bowls do not come "out of another world", but he was living within a concrete environment at a certain time. But Chôjirô desired to have access to the world of nothingness. Of course, he could not fully reach it, he only recognized it. In a way, he was floating in it like a leaf in the wind, he was swinging in this world of nothingness like a pendulum. And through his art he was trying to express this very situation, this very agony. [...] Take the tea ceremony for example. The tea ceremony that I performed for you today was a succession of all styles. All styles and all forms are contained in it. Of course, you will say that it's better to have one's own style. But if you try to get rid of all previous styles and all forms, you will have a kind of freedom from which something like art can ever arise. Nothingness in itself is really nothing. But the paradox that clings to nothingness – that paradox *is* art. In other words, art must be open to nothingness but it should never melt into nothingness and really become "nothing". Religion also faces this paradox. But religion overcomes it through the phenomenon of belief in something that we cannot touch or see. Art does not have this belief. This is actually the only point that separates art from religion.

**You once wrote the following sentence about the "nothingness" that Chôjirô is exploring: "There is a world so dark, as if it were a black hole, which immerses everything inside it in darkness". Is this darkness not the virtual reality that we are confronted with today?**

What I mean by black hole is not some dark ominous thing but a big paradox that contains all different directions of consciousness. This is not nihilism but, on the contrary, the hole contains everything. In this sense it does not mean virtual reality at all. The individual consciousness might be like virtual reality. However, the sort of simulation produced by computers is not authentic at all. What is most important for me as an artist is to say how we can live in the real world. Our technical world is very much inclined to play tricks with us all the time. But I am opposed to this.

**We have just overcome postmodernism. Still, this does not mean that we have returned to modernity. Today, many people turn towards tradition (though not towards traditionalism). Many people are interested in "ethno" expressions of culture. In this context, does Raku art not appear like the art of the future?**

Globalization is inevitable and in this globalized information culture the *part* cries out as it is surrounded by the *whole*. The *whole* is Westernization. But it is not enough to praise singular traditions as parts that are opposed to a Westernized whole. The result would actually be a *decline* of ethnic art.

Kyoto, January 2004

## Note

1. *Tekone* is the characteristic technique of Raku pottery. As the potter uses no wheel but merely his fingers, he creates a unique vacillation and distortion.

# 6. The Aesthetics of Frozen Dreams: Jeff Koons and Mariko Mori

This chapter is about how two artists who come from different cultural spheres develop kitsch into art. Jeff Koons, born in 1955, is an American artist freely using kitsch elements in his sculptures, paintings and other works. Video and photographic artist Mariko Mori, born in 1967, is one of the most visible Japanese artists in the West. Juxtaposing Western art and Eastern mythology, she integrates, like Koons, elements of transfigured kitsch that she alters at a profound level. Both artists' works refer to the traditions of Duchamp and Warhol and engage in "commodification" which has a particular status in the contexts of their respective cultures. Koons and Mori produce extremely stylized visions of Pop-cultural excesses and present them as joyful kitsch-scapes. I compare Koons's "kitsch as avant-garde" principle and Mori's "spiritual kitsch reality" and draw conclusions concerning the position of kitsch in a global context and how it transforms real space into a virtual space of an eternal present.

## 1. Kitsch

The word kitsch was probably coined in Germany in the 1860-1870s in order to designate cheap artistic stuff (Dorfles 1975: 234)[1] and proliferated during the nineteenth century in Europe. The common understanding of kitsch refers to a tasteless copy of an existing style, a system of "bad taste" or artistic deficiency, which almost always involves exaggerated sentimentality, superficiality, banality, and triteness. Clement Greenberg's definition of kitsch as a too formulaic aesthetic expression (Greenberg 1961: 10) is important but might not always be suitable, as will be shown below. The same is true for Matei Calinescu's definition of kitsch as an aesthetic phenomenon that contradicts the "law of inadequacy" (1987: 257). It has been said that in industrialized countries kitsch has acquired a scope of cultural anesthesia (Lugg 1999: 4) often serving as an aesthetically vulgar means to enter a consumer-oriented dream world. Of course, this will not happen in all places of the world in the same fashion. It is necessary in this chapter, which compares an American and a Japanese artist, to distinguish between different local kitsch-cultures. In America kitsch is most present in the imaginary of Walt Disney and Koons's works draw very much on this culture. His ironical way of pointing out the "truthfulness of Disney" with its "complete optimism" (Koons 2000: 31) often lets his works appear as disneyfied landscapes of the everyday world.

For Baudrillard Disneyland is "the microcosm of the Occident" (Baudrillard 1986: 56) which would exclude Japan. Though it has been claimed that "Japan is a Disneyland, a focal point where history and locality cease to exist" (Sato 2004: 340), this "Disneyland" has its own style. As a matter of fact, Japan has its own cartoon industry, which has developed the aesthetics of kitsch in a very particular direction. Even more than in Disney aesthetics, in Japan kitsch is made to look cute (kawaii) which becomes particularly obvious in the proliferation of youth culture for which the predicate "kawaii" seems to represent a sort of national aesthetic standard. Kitsch and cute things do also exist in Disney but they are designed as a romanticized escape from industrialized society; Japanese kitsch and cute culture has a similar objective but it defines this shift rather as an escape from the world of adulthood altogether. Sharon Kinsella has pointed out that from the beginning, "Disney cute was based more on a sentimental journey back into an idealized rural society populated with happy little animals and rural characters taken from folk stories [while] Japanese cute fashion became more concerned with a sentimental journey back into an idealized childhood" (Kinsella 1995: 241). The result is a cuteness that "differs from Disney [in that it] invites an act of interaction [and] triggers fantasy" (Allison 2004: 37) and offers a multidimensionality that one most often searches in vain in Disney productions (cf. Napier 1998: 101).

The cute is generally defined as childlike, sweet, innocent, pure, gentle and weak. In Japan, cute kitsch is a "large scale" phenomenon developing since the 1980s and turning in the late 1990s into an explicit kitsch culture (Kinsella 1995: 226). The aesthetics of cuteness is more than an aesthetic style but appears as a full-fledged way of articulating a subjective attitude that can become manifest in design, in language, in bodily behavior, in gender relations, and in perceptions of the self. Brian McVeigh holds that "cuteness is not just a fad in the fashion cycle of Japanese pop culture; it is more of a 'standard' aesthetic of everyday life" (McVeigh 2000: 135). Mariko Mori plays with the theme of cute kitsch in the same way in which Jeff Koons plays with Disney props.

## 2. Koons's Kitsch as Avant-Garde

Koons produces ready-mades placing – like Duchamp and Warhol – ordinary objects into galleries and museums. Duchamp took objects like a urinal and declared them to be art; Warhol adopted piles of soup cans in order to reveal the falsifying discourse of capitalist marketing culture, which attempts to conceal the mass-produced nature of its products. Koons applied the same approach to persons who are commodified to some extent – Marilyn Monroe, Dennis Hopper, Joan Crawford – and who appear, once they are transformed into a ready-made, as Hollywood mass-productions.

Similar to Warhol, Koons chooses objects that are "defined not so much by their function as by their audience, their market" (Caldwell 1992: 10), but his objects are much more commodified even in their original state. He uses religious symbols, Michael Jackson, Pink Panther, or Cicciolina, and commodifies them with the help of gold, stainless steel, bright colors, and sweetness. To commodify means "to turn a valueless object into something valuable" and this is also the main principle of kitsch culture. Kitsch turns objects that have little value in themselves into cultural icons, objects of desire, or other items that can be exchanged on a capitalist market. Koons effectuates a second process of commodification that turns (valueless) kitsch into (valuable) art. The fact that he reveals this "anything goes" philosophy quite liberally provides the possibility to read these acts of commodification at the same time as critiques of commodification.

There is not only a difference in the choice of objects but also in the respective processes of Warhol's and Koons's kitschifications. What Duchamp, Warhol and Koons have in common is that they isolate ordinary objects from their context and attempt to make visible the strangeness that these objects have probably always had but that we never noticed. The objects used by Warhol as well as by Koons responded to emotional and psychological desires long before they were used as art objects. However, in the form in which Warhol presents them, the emotional content[2] is "cut off" (though not entirely negated) and this creates a sophisticated aesthetic surplus. Koons employs, in principle, the same strategy but he goes one step further: he voluntarily presents his objects as moments of kitsch in themselves. Kitsch becomes art not because we would recognize in it an artful element but, paradoxically, because its kitsch identity is singled out and exaggerated.

Kitsch itself is produced through a similar device; the only difference is that kitsch strives to obtain, in the first place, emotional proximity instead of intellectual or aesthetic distance. Koons's works (more than Warhol's) leave us bewildered because many of his objects are attractive and repulsive at the same time, sometimes bordering on the uncanny. They establish a distance between us and them and confront us with disconcerting aspects of contemporary life that until now we have ignored. Kitsch, on the other hand, sucks us into the fully articulated pleasure principle of its own enjoyment.

It is clear that Koons eludes one of the principal strategies of kitsch, which were decisive for Clement Greenberg and Norbert Elias. For Greenberg kitsch uses "for raw material the debased and academicized simulacra of genuine culture" (Greenberg 1961: 10) and for Norbert Elias, kitsch is "nothing other than the expression for this tension between the highly-formed taste of the specialists and the undeveloped unsure taste of mass society" (Elias 1998: 32). Koons's kitsch, on the other hand, cannot be read as a degradation of high-culture; as kitschified kitsch it rather degrades popular culture.

Koons's strategy cancels also Clement Greenberg's famous claim that avant-gardism is necessarily opposed to kitsch. For Greenberg kitsch is always the "rear-guard" (1961: 10)[3] because it encourages us to consume those parts of art that were initially not meant for consumption but for more sophisticated aesthetic enjoyment. Koons reproduces feelings and he does so even in a formulaic fashion (which formally qualifies his works as kitsch), but his raw material are works that are already kitsch. The stained steel used in the Luxury and Degradation series degrades a sort of luxury that has never been one but rather a petty bourgeois version of it: "To me stainless steel is the material of the Proletarian, it's what pots and pans are made of. (…) it's fake luxury. If these pieces were in silver they would be absolutely boring" (Koons 1992a, npn). The objects from this series are fake luxury objects bought by an ascending middle class. If these things are kitschified, their kitsch-version will be more truthful than the "real" thing. In real life people do rarely embrace kitsch as kitsch but rather as the "real" thing (Coca Cola sells one of the most commodified products of the world and insists that it is "the real thing"). This is why Koons's message enclosed to the Banality series reads like a cynical appeal to fatalistic honesty: "You're ambitious and you're trying to become a new upper class. Don't divorce yourself from your true being, embrace it" (ibid). In principle Koons announces that, by undergoing a supplementary process of degradation, the ascending members of the middle class will finally be able to fully embrace their degraded selves.

All this is also the reason why the art of Koons and Warhol (as well as of Duchamp) cannot be kitschified. Their works do not articulate hedonistic emotions but suggest, through a paradoxical and tautological re-articulation of a kitsch-reality, a kind of non-articulated nothingness that necessarily remains beyond all expression.

### 3. Mariko Mori: Spiritual Kitsch as Virtual Reality

Similar to Koons, Mariko Mori excels in a combination of innocence and calculation that she uses for productions of populist dreamworlds. Mori states that she would be a child of Warhol and a grandchild of Duchamp. As a matter of fact, she is also Jeff Koons's younger sister. Mori commodifies popular culture, fashion, and science fiction. Her early "costume parties" focused on kitsch personae from popular culture and are very similar to Koons's early works. In *Art in America* (1988-89), Koons appears as a starry-eyed teenage idol surrounded by bikini-clad beauties which is, in its uncanny impression of unreality, similar to Mori's *Birth of a Star* (1995). Mori continues this approach with commodifications of cyborgs, manga characters, and cute Martians.

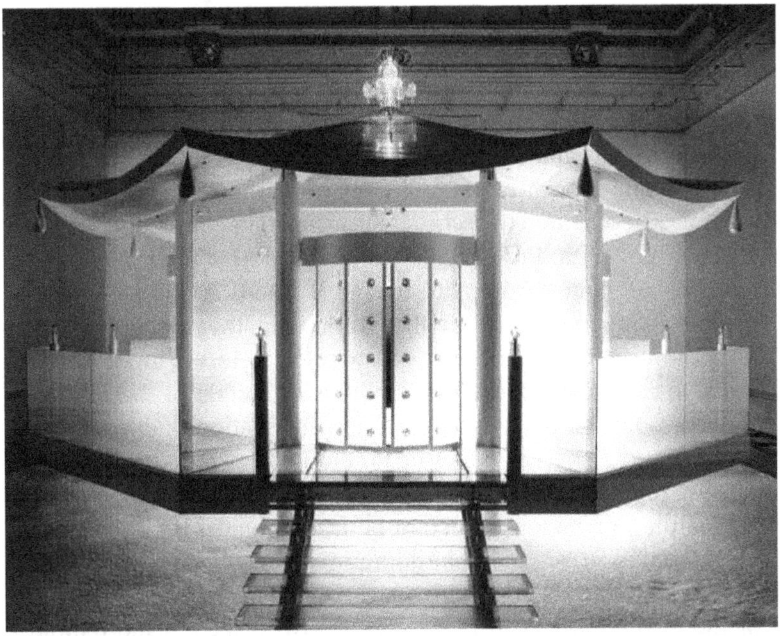

Fig. 14: Dream Temple by Mariko Mori © 2015 Mariko Mori, Member Artists Rights Society (ARS), New York

An important difference between Mori and Koons is that Mori's evasions into spiritual kitsch landscapes are supported by computer technology. Mori produces computer manipulated crafts and videos that aim at a constant redefinition of the boundary between reality and illusion. Her later works, in which she experiments with mixtures of spirituality and kitsch culture, benefit from this ambiguity. Whether she creates oneiric landscapes that border on an utopic reality (*Esoteric Cosmos*, 1999), or whether she transforms herself into a flying divinity borrowing from the pictorial language of Buddhist icons (*Nirvana*, 1996-97), her interest in Eastern philosophy and mythology affirms itself in an almost naïve manner, consciously shunning the historical depth of Japanese religion, but rather shifting it towards utopian mythology.

In Mori's installation work *Garden of Purification* (1999) the visitor is led through a Zen garden (on resin stones in various colors) whose floor is covered with sea salt. In the middle of each carefully raked stone circle is placed a "stone planet" that is supposed to affect the charkas. *Kumano* (1997-98) is an installation that has five large color photos of a Japanese forest as a background, giving the overall impression of Tarkovsky's *Mirror* having been laid over with *Solaris*. Mori makes two dreamlike apparitions among the trees, overexposed as a priestess with ritual headwear, while a turquoise temple is visible on the right side of the panel. Her more recent work *Tom Na H-iu* (2007) is a sculpture made from glass and a symbol for rebirth capturing the death and rebirth of stars. A sort of spiritual consciousness is produced by a computer, which catches the light that stars generate when they die. With the installation *Dream Temple* (1998) Mori reached her so far most complete fusion of tradition and technology. The artist's own comments on the work help to melt both into a smooth paste because "tradition" is now referred to via more abstract references to Japanese culture (the Buddhist principle of the interconnectedness of beings, the principle of non-foundation, hidden energy, the mystical experience of being dead, etc.). The *Dream Temple* is a utopian site, representing a futuristic glass and fiberglass replica of the Dream Temple (Yumedono) in Nara built in around 739. The original Dream Temple is an octagonal building in which Prince Shotoku used to meditate and where he had dream visions that resulted in the creation of the statue Guze Kan'non, a statue still placed at the temple's core. As Mori explains, the Yumedono in Nara was the place where "Buddhism solidified its first spiritual base in Japan" (Mori 1998:

npn). Interestingly, considerations of "another reality" that vaguely flow out of Buddhist philosophy lead, for Mori, to considerations of "the virtual". For Mori this approach is very consistent as she explains: "The Japanese artistic talent seems to evolve along two currents, one of which is linked to virtual space, to the attempt of finding a passage from virtual space to real space" (ibid.). The particularity of the *Dream Temple* is that, though being a "real" installation, the exclusive use of transparent material combined with a complex use of "mystical" light, lets this real object look like an image produced through computer simulation. The *Dream Temple* enables to "live in a three-dimensional virtual reality" (ibid.). The resemblance that this has with the spatial experience of a real tearoom is baffling if we consider Toshihiko Izutsu's description of traditional Japanese architecture (a tea room): "Moreover, the visual effect resulting from the lack of material impression of solidity and massiveness, seen in a reduced light coming in through white paper screens, seems to add a filament of ethereality to the view, or shall we say a filament of tenuous mist over the whole spatial field of aesthetic saturation" (Izutsu 1981: 61).

Religion practiced without a proper historical background becomes the sort of synthetic mysticism that is vaguely directed into the future. It is the mysticism that sects are often making use of. And myths are probably, as has stated Gillo Dorfles, the vastest containers of kitsch that humanity has ever produced as they relish in sentimentality, coarseness, and vulgarity. Any separation of mythology from history (easily effectuated by turning the myth into a utopian tale) produces almost automatically the most kitsch-like gibberish possible. Mori plays with this sort of spiritual kitsch that embraces the irrational, pre-conscious, "cosmic", or fantastic, by reediting the spirituality of romanticism with the help of high-tech, occasionally integrating manga characters. Her *Dream Temple* is clearly an example of utopian architecture, but in spite of the enthusiasm for the future that Mori's works radiate in general, this work is different from the eighteenth century utopian architecture of Boullée and Ledoux. On all levels Mori refuses to represent her utopia in the form of an articulated wish (a Freudian *Wunschtraum*, perhaps) but prefers to let the utopian concept empty itself into ethereality and undefined dreamscapes. (This is also the reason why her spiritual kitsch does not end up as mass-produced replicas of tea sets, meditation pillows, miniature rock gardens, or ads for weekend retreats promising peace of mind with Zen meditation and short-lived asceticism. Though this kind of kitsch does not really exist in Japan, it is widespread in Western countries which set out, since the 1970s, to kitschify much of Zen spirituality.) The point is also here that Mori's "anything goes" philosophy lets her acts of commodification simultaneously appear as critiques of commodification.

Finally, the ironical attitude is the reason why both Koons and Mori are driven towards self-commodification, a gesture that *can* only be ironic and ambiguous: since commodification implies that the valuable object had been valueless beforehand, we have to suppose that Koons and Mori as persons were valueless before having been commodified into works of art, a statement that the artists are unlikely to accept. Self-commodification – for all times strongly linked to Warhol's claim that "everybody can be famous for one day" – reveals most clearly the ironical input that this art underlies.

## 4. Wabi

Mori's work cannot be understood without considering her cultural origin and Japanese aesthetics in general. In the Catalogue of her *Dream Temple*, Mori refers to the tea master Sen no Rikyû (1522-1591) and holds that his tea hut is a "work of conceptual art" (npn). Rikyû is one of the main developers of the *wabi/sabi* aesthetics, a complex system dependent on Zen Buddhism. The term *wabi/sabi* has come to the attention of a wider Western public through Daitetz Suzuki and represents a Zen-inspired idea of beauty manifested in traditional architecture and crafts valuing imperfection, simplicity, poverty, and naturalness. Beauty and authenticity are found in aged wood, cracks, asymmetrical forms, and decay, which makes *wabi/sabi* expressions compatible with the principle of impermanence central to Zen Buddhism. Wabi delights Japanese in the form of those things that remind us of the transient character of the world. Historically, the rustic, down-to-earth style of *wabi/sabi* tea bowls and other artifacts used for tea depends on their conception as "non-artistic" objects. The reason is that the Japanese received the first elements of inspiration for this pottery style from Korea. The "models" that sparked the development of what are today art objects were, paradoxically, ordinary rice bowls used by Korean peasants.

This means that, formally, Rikyû's approach corresponds to what Calinescu has called "the law of aesthetic inadequacy" (Calinescu 1987: 258), which is one of the principles of kitsch and corresponds also to the approach of artists like Duchamp, Warhol, and Koons. Duchamp's ordinary objects that we can admire in art galleries and kitsch are produced through similar devices; the only difference is, as mentioned, that kitsch strives to obtain, in the first place, emotional proximity instead of intellectual or aesthetic distance.[4] The law of aesthetic inadequacy is here applied on a formal level but cancelled with regard to aesthetic content. I am not suggesting that *wabi* is kitsch. It is only all too obvious that it is not. However, in spite of existing oppositions, the traditional Japanese aesthetic ideal of *wabi/sabi* and the aesthetic manifestations that we classify today as kitsch have deep psychological structures in common.

Japanese aesthetics of *wabi/sabi* has more affinities with the Western modern stream of expression represented by Duchamp, Warhol, and Koons, than with most Western art that has been produced somewhere between Romanticism (which is the clearest precursor of kitsch) and early phases of modernity. The reason is that all of Romanticism (Broch 1975: 50), a good deal of "modern" art, and almost everything that exists between these two (that is especially the Nineteenth-Century period of industrialization which is most typical for kitsch, Elias 1998: 28), contains kitsch in the potential form. A great deal of Western art is potentially close to kitsch because it refers to the idyll of a recent history, to the idyll (utopia) of a near future, or articulates "something" in the form of a nostalgia of another (better) world. *Wabi*, however, much as the art of Warhol and Koons, are fundamentally unable to give in to the transmission of a potential kitsch content because the popular material they use contains no sentiments in a potential form. *Wabi* art uses modest folk art objects which have little kitsch potential because of their very low degree of commodification; and Warhol and Koons choose objects in which kitsch is not potentially present but articulated.

It has been said above that dehistoricized myths can easily turn into utopianizing kitsch-like gibberish. It becomes obvious that, while in Western art historical reality is often replaced with a fabricated version of itself or with a fabricated myth or utopia (providing the possibility of kitsch),[5] in Japanese aesthetics of *wabi* – but also in the art of Warhol, Koons and Mori – things develop the other way round. Objects exist here for themselves and, in a way of speaking, anticipate any kitschification through the tautological self-affirmation that is normally the unique privilege of kitsch. Koons's unapproachable objects that he has cast in steel for *Luxury and Degradation* literally take the fun out of kitschification; they reach what a Zen-inspired aesthetics would call a curious aesthetic degree of "nothingness". The same happens when Koons interspersed his *Made in Heaven* pictures with "quasi-religious glimpses of an ecstatic, celestial joy" (Rosenblum

1992b: 13) imbuing pornography with the "aura of the religious image" (Butler 2007: 68). By "desexualizing its sexual aspect" (Sylvester 2000: 35), pornography becomes "nothing" in an almost Zen-Buddhist sense of being insignificant on purpose.

Mori's works follow the same strategy but for her this nothingness is represented by virtual reality when she says that she wants to reach a "virtual center where all tensions are overcome" (Celent 1998: npn). Nowhere does the link between kitsch and the virtual become as clear as here because Mori spells out VR as a concretized eternal present. This is similar to Koons when he says that his use of baroque is meant to "show the public that we are in the realm of the spiritual, the eternal" (Koons 1992b, npn). To him "Cicciolina is the eternal virgin [because] she's been able to remove guilt and shame from her life, and because of this she is a great liberator" (Koons 1992a: npn). The spectator viewing these pictures is supposed to be "in the realm of the Sacred Heart of Jesus" (Koons 1992b: 130). Spirituality is here instrumentalized in order to level out all differences. Also Mori, as she conflates Eastern spirituality and utopian mythology (which she combines with an aesthetics of the cute derived from manga), avoids historical depth on principle. An artificially established superficiality, joyously identified with VR, lets her appear as the Koons of the cyberage.

## 5. Innocent Kitsch/Pornokitsch

Koons's works, which look like kitsch without following its anti-artistic logic, settle on a degree of "absolute innocence". His *Made in Heaven* series is "not pornographic even though they are depictions of explicit activity" (Caldwell 1992a: 14). The stylization takes the fun out of voyeurism, which means, first, that these objects are no longer suitable items for voyeurism as such, and second, even if they were, that voyeurism has here become an "innocent" activity since it is no longer nourished by "guilty" libidinal structures. In "first-level" kitsch, as in voyeurism, an imaginary "more" is always intrinsically present, since it represents the underlying power that makes phenomena like kitsch and voyeurism possible. It is the voyeur's dream of having "real" sex or kitsch-lover's dream of reaching the level of high culture and of being accepted into the social class that has so far closed its doors to him.

This imaginary "more" does not occur in Koons's works, which is the reason why it can appear as innocent. Koons's kitsch is absolutely self-affirmative and tautologically expressive to a point that the "law of inadequacy" is no longer applicable with regard to its content. The object obviously "is kitsch" (or even pornography), but this statement can never be formulated as a reproach. Already forty years ago Ugo Volli has analyzed a phenomenon that today appears to overlap with Koons's later elaborations. Volli called this phenomenon "pornokitsch" and its formula is simple: "At the moment man makes of sex an aesthetic or scientific thing there is no reason to be ashamed of sex" (Volli 1975: 231). Pornography as art (or pornography as science) is innocent because it has become pornokitsch.

Also Mori undertook the transposition of what Calinescu has called the "hallucinatory power of kitsch" to a mode of reality that is hallucinatory in itself. As a matter of fact, the "hallucinatory power" or "spurious dreaminess" of kitsch (Calinescu 1987: 228) can be helped – within seconds – to an absolute existence simply by calling reality "virtual". It is important to note that in Mori's work, as in that of Koons, this mechanism has no "cheap" cathartic effect because here we have to do with art. Koons's works ask deep-reaching questions about the status of objects in modern capitalist society by revealing the presence of kitsch almost everywhere.

Mori's work goes one step further in the direction of a technological posthumanism. In her work not just the "thingly" reality but the concept of reality itself has become kitsch, that is: reality with its "real" as well as its spiritual side has become consumable, enjoyable and "cute". As in Koons's works, the result is a type of self-sufficient kitsch that appears as "innocent". The use of cute elements is more than just strategic: it is essential to Mori's art.

In order to understand this we need to turn again towards Japanese culture. Much of Japanese cute kitsch consistently follows an ontology of the singular, annulling the tensions that in the case of "first level kitsch" flows out of the very conflict with the law of inadequacy. In the omnipresent Japanese kitsch culture of the cute (though not only there) kitsch has a more "innocent" existence. Volli's early reflections on pornokitsch retrospectively retrieve a part of the contemporary Japanese cultural situation in which aestheticized kitsch manipulates the limits between conscience and innocence, or adulthood and infancy. The "shôjo", since twenty years one of the most typical character of Japanese mangas, is a liminal creature at home between woman and child.[6] This creature is also very much involved in pornographic productions, so-called *hentai* anime.[7] I am not saying that this kind of pornokitsch is free of voyeuristic aspirations but that it is ambiguous by definition. It represents a kitsch culture that pretends to know neither guilt nor remorse because it attempts to be only "what it is". It is a kitsch culture that pretends to be nothing "more". This means that it annuls the "law of inadequacy" through which kitsch normally functions because kitsch always strives towards "adequacy" or simply the "more". The pretension to be innocent as well as the stylization on which this cartoon industry bases its entire project, are supposed to produce a sort of innocent pornography that Volli anticipated already in the 1960s.

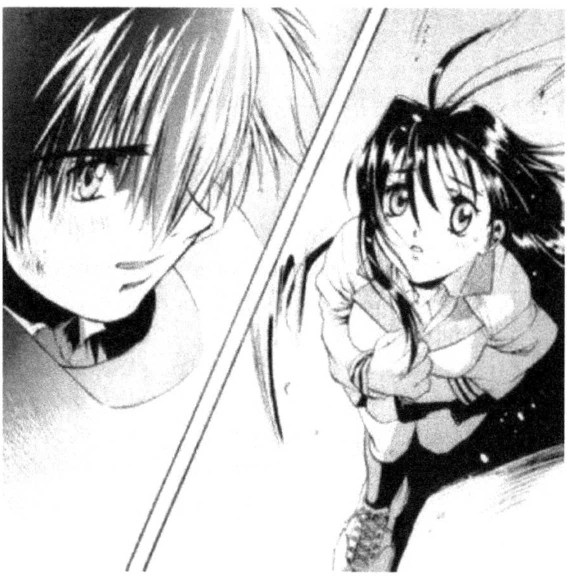

Fig. 15: Shôjo

Shôjo culture, together with an ambiguous erotic kitsch culture, represents the extreme case of a culture that has decided to settle its aesthetic expressions in an ambiguous field between, as said Alessandro Gomarasca, "innocence and provocation" (Gomarasca 2001). It is certainly no coincidence that Mori appears in her works as a shôjo, but I would go as far as saying that both Mori and Koons are shôjos. John Whittier Treat defines the life of the shôjo as "essentially narcissistic in that it is self-referential, and self-referential as long as the shôjo is not employed productively in sexual and capitalist economies" (Whittier Treat 1996: 283). As the universe of shôjo kitsch culture "celebrate[s] the vapidness of our contemporary existences" (ibid.) it can at times come very close to Koons's "Walt Disney version of an erotic fantasy, complete with adorable animals" (Caldwell 1992a: 13) or a "collision of love à la Disney with the reality of sexuality" (14). A typical device of Japanese *rorikon* (Lolita-Complex) commodification linked to shôjo culture is to "sexualize objects that are normally not explicitly sexual" (Shigematsu 1999: 130). However, the opposite is also true: Koons's strategy of "transforming (…) through innocence, beauty, security, and trust the visible elements of the vulgar, pornographic" (Schneider 2001: 18) also echoes a principle of shôjo culture. And even where it embraces no erotic elements at all, a resemblance between Koons and a typically Japanese conception of kitsch is striking. Take Koons's *Rabbit*, which incorporates the viewer in itself because it reflects him/her in its mirror surface. The relationship that *Rabbit* establishes with the viewer approaches the strategy of one of the most typical Japanese kitsch characters, Hello Kitty. The producers of Hello Kitty explain that "the reason Kitty's mouth is not drawn is so that anyone looking at her can imagine their own expression for her. When you are happy, you can imagine a smile on her face; when you are sad, she's sad with you. Kitty always knows how you feel, and being your friend, she shares your feelings".[8] Both *Rabbit* and Kitty represent the most typical cases of kitsch defined by Ludwig Giesz which is for him always in the first place a "self-enjoyment" in which the "enjoyer enjoys himself" (Giesz 1975: 41). In any case, I find Koons's productions more shôjo-like than those of the most prominent Japanese representative of Koons-style, Takashi Murakami, whose sculptures of the insipid female manga character Hiropon represent the kind of eroticized kitsch that Koons would probably like to avoid.

Being both innocent and calculating, both frivolous and sincere, the shôjo as well as Koons and Mori attempt to exist narcissistically and beyond critical dialogue. Refusing any open form of irony (though being ironical and calculating on a more hidden level), they cultivate a juvenile eat-your-cake-and-have-it-too attitude that has become more and more recurrent in self-centered, capitalist consumerism. All three create a utopia in which kitsch can no longer be called kitsch because this dreamworld has its own rules. Koons points out that for him the dream of such a teenage world is most explicitly exemplified by the Beatles: "Nobody ever said that the Beatles' music was not on a high level, but it appealed to a mass audience. That's what I want to do" (Koons 1992b: 114). In the Beatles' universe the bad becomes good and it is possible to be avant-gardist and still be loved by the masses. Mass culture can at the same time be elitist.

## Conclusion

If kitsch is the legitimate taste of the twenty-first century, the elaboration of VR is its main technological achievement. Permitting an immediacy that art must avoid, kitsch can produce the image of a cultural anomie; and this kind of combination of kitsch and VR can most successfully be produced through an elaboration of the "spiritual" side of kitsch. In VR the "unreal" component of reality (illusions, wishes, myths, etc.) can become "real". Kitsch is the real precursor of VR.

Mori makes this particularly clear. Her "kitsch" produces itself out of itself, being no imitation or simulation of a preexisting reality. This is why this kind of reality looks so much like a frozen dream. In this point it comes close to kitsch, but also to the aesthetics of the *wabi/sabi*. In *wabi/sabi*, in kitsch, and in Mori's treatment of the virtual, dreams are "frozen". *Wabi/sabi* lets emotions "freeze" in a state of non-articulation, that means it freezes nature (natural colors, materials) and avoids exuberance by willfully installing austerity. Kitsch simply freezes emotions in their state of exuberance. Mori's installations provide us with a sterile spirituality that appears as a parody of kitsch because the illusions of consumerism are here revealed as what they are: the frozen dreams that VR makes use of. What they all have in common is that they manage to install themselves at a non-place of relativity, or at an eternal present, in which the (present or historical) "real" no longer represents an obstacle for creation.[9]

## Notes

1. Etymological explanations put forward a Germanized pronunciation of "sketch" or, more likely, a street-cleaning machine called "Kitsche" in Southwest Germany, and whose sauce-like brown color inspired the name "Kitsch" for fashionable pictures. See Eduard Koelwel 1937: 58. The Southwestern dialect word "kitschen" means to smear.
2. By content I mean "traces of the handmade, of artistry and creativity, and of expression and invention" that Warhol erases from his works and which distinguishes him from his predecessors Jasper Johns and Robert Rauschenberg (Buchloh 2001: 8).
3. Greenberg's article "Kitsch and Avantagarde" was published already in 1939 by *Partisan Review* 6:5, 34-49. Susan Sontag ([1964]1982) defines camps as an ironical and sophisticated aesthetization of kitsch operating through ambiguity and able to express social criticism.
4. The following anecdote illustrates the parallelism: The priest Eishun of Nara was an opponent of Rikyû and insisted, in his own aesthetic approach, on the values

of traditional Chinese culture. When Rikyû died Eishun said: "Rikyû was the worst of all charlatans. Any man who has performed as many evil deeds as he has deserves to be made to commit suicide" (Itoh 1993). Looking at the formal parallels between *wabi/sabi* and kitsch, we very well understand why Rikyû's approach must have appeared as outrageous to many of his contemporaries. Rikyû produced common objects (and sold them even at a high price), by attaching a "spiritual", non-physical value to them. And what is more outrageous than a charlatan who tells you that an ordinary rice bowl is able to "speak" to you about your own self? This is the reason why, according to Teiji Itoh, for Eishun, Rikyû's things could only have been kitsch (cf. Itoh).

5. I mean paintings like those of Delacroix, for example "The Death of Sardanapalus".

6. Shôjo is a Japanese word literally meaning "young girl".

7. In Japan, the word *hentai* does not refer to pornographic mangas or anime. Those, the Japanese call *porno anime* and *porno manga. Hentai* is a scientific term meaning, among other things, metamorphosis. Insects can go through a *hentai.* Literally the kanjis for *hen-tai* signify 'strange metamorphosis'. The word is also used for perverse fetishes (cf. Kelt 2007: 127). On *hentai anime* see also Bornoff 2002 (63); and on the combination of cartoons and pornography as well as on "deadly" cuteness in a manga culture featuring "cute girls involving excessive pornographic content, including lesbianism and pedophilia see Shiokawa 1999 (116).

8. Quoted in George Fogarsi: "All that is Solidu Melts into Kitty" in *CTheory: Theory, Technology and Culture* 20:3, Art. 55, 1997, npn. There are other cute Japanese characters that have no mouth: Pochacco, Cathy the bunny, Nutz, Chococat, and Cookie-Bau.

9. Some of the above thoughts on kitsch and *wabi/sabi* have been developed in another context in Chapters 6 and 7 of Botz-Bornstein 2011.

# Feature Scene VI

## Overcoming the *Logos* – Overcoming Lego: From Imagined Space to the Spatial Imagination of Cyborgs

For several generations, the interconnecting plastic bricks called Lego represented not only an educative means of developing imagination but also one of developing children's capacity of logical thinking. The first Lego catalogues from the early 1960s praise the small bricks as "good toys". The reason can be found in the heading: because Lego is the "simplest thing in the world".

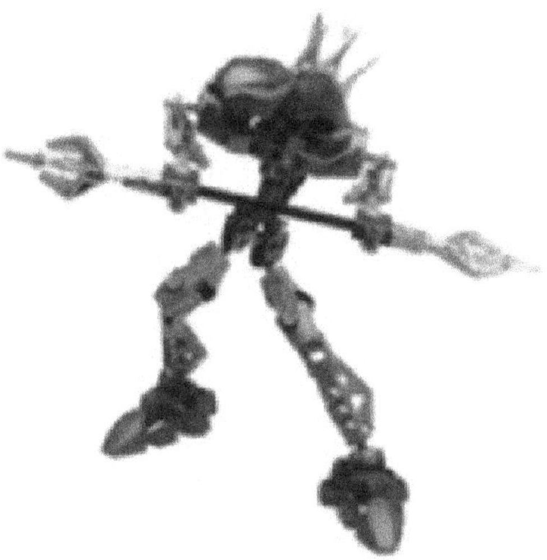

Fig. 16: Bionicle

"Simple" – yes, but not for simpletons. During the 1960s and the 1970s, Lego built itself a reputation as a toy for people who aspire to advanced levels of grammar through the successful combination of abstract and concrete ways of thinking. Lego helps you to master your creativity like a language: being imaginative without losing sight of the most basic rules of logic, you will manage to remain coherent even in complex situations. Playing with Lego does perhaps not make you a poet, but it enables you to master a practical as well as a theoretical "language" with a certain degree of sophistication.

The idea must have been that, once we reduce the elements of our children's games to the healthy level of "the basic" (providing at the same time a maximum of modulability), children will become imaginative without becoming insane. Their imagination will develop "reasonably well" without losing itself in the wide space of "play" which remains, just because in this space things are only "imagined", frightening because it is infinite.

For parents this has been extremely convenient because here play and fun were delivered with an incorporated self-control. This conception, unconscious as it might have been, was strong enough to provide Lego with the status of the "educative toy" as such. It was strong enough to inspire and lend its name to a large number of educative programs for children, various computer softwares, as well as training courses for business people attempting to enhance their business performance by using this brick-game as a thinking tool.

What it actually is that makes Lego "logical" is difficult to spell out. Secondary features might be as important as primary ones. Though the word "Lego" has been derived from the Danish "leg godt" (play well), its phonetic resemblance with Latin words like "logos" or "logic" might have helped from the beginning to lend it a more scientific air. Very early the company began to point out that in Latin "lego" also means "I study".

Then there are the primary features. The basic elements (bricks) are rectangular and not round-shaped. Deciding to reject any amorphous shapes (you will not learn "logic" through pottery), Lego managed to force play (together with the intellectual capacity supposed to be shaped through this play), into more rigorous, geometrical structures.

The choice of colors had a similar function. Far from refusing colors straight-out (and thus killing imagination), Lego reduced colors to shadeless "basic" ones that remained abstract in the sense that – apart from the green for trees – they had no relationship with anything concrete.

But most obvious became the logical rigor within the organization of the play itself. Lego bricks stick together through an invisible structure, they create their structure so to speak out of themselves. This means that they provide the fragile brains of 2-14 years-olds just enough logical support to follow the laws of reason without forcing them into abstract, pre-existing rules.

Somewhere between the primary and the secondary features is settled the general quality of Lego as a "serious game". Adults jealously looked at these children who possess a toy that is both serious and fun. Soon businessmen began using Lego because "playing with Lego" is an "efficient, practical and effective process that works for everyone".[1] The transcendental power of play, known since the ancient Greeks, is here somehow led ad absurdum, which might be inherent already in the original Lego-bricks themselves. The popular-scientific outline of a business-studies program using Lego offers summaries of the works of almost all major thinkers – from Huizinga to Piaget – who have analyzed the exceptional status of play, and attempts to draw links between the "lightness" of play and its "usefulness" for cognitive development as well as social competition. It goes without saying that none of these thinkers mentioned Lego.

In spite of the geometrical shape of the bricks on which you can count the dots as if you count millimeters, Lego constructions never became "mathematical" but always maintained the structure of an *organic* whole. Technical construction toys (often coming in gray) that first necessitate the creation of a "skeleton" that will subsequently be fleshed out were never as popular as Lego (Lego's own *Techno*-line remained rather marginal). Lego has never been the game of the future engineer but rather that of the well-thinking analyst who is scientifically minded without being dull, creative without being romantic, and who manages to *apply* his creativity to the everyday world. As a kind of logically trained humanists, Lego-children were designated to become the ideal people of the twenty-first century.

All this helps us to understand why those people born between 1965 and 1975 hated Lego. According to the German writer Florian Illies (born in 1971), this generation, raised long after the last waves of hippidom had curled away, vehemently rejected theoretical buildings of any kind (Illies 2000). The first thing that this generation had to throw on the rubbish was, of course, Lego.

The alternative became *Playmobil* that contrasts with Lego on several levels. Playmobil offers no spaceships, no futurism and no technology. Instead, it specializes in traditional values like farms, Blackforest houses, and post-offices. Contemporary brochures of Playmobil read as if they have been written fifty years earlier. In Playmobil grocery stores we find several kinds of sausages, cheese, "and other hearty dainties". The hairdresser's salon is ideal for active role-play. Kids are supposed to create their concrete playworld as realistically and detailed as possible. Finally, play will turn out to be what it actually is: imitation, naturally creating full-fledged, atmospheric play-landscapes in which no Martians have introduced things like "structures".

Lego had launched its own town systems and castles in 1981. The problem with these systems has always been that Lego-space is anti-concrete by definition. Always changing, unfolding itself magically, Lego-space has always been intellectual, future-oriented, and abstractly-organic. The only things that remain stable in Lego-space are "creativity" and some vague notion of logic. Lego made some further cramped attempts at becoming Playmobil-like. The most decisive act took place in 1978, when the Lego-persons learned to walk. Before that date, Lego-persons (and there were not many of them) had two legs made of one single piece of plastic. In 1978 the legs got separated and got joints. Space now became more concrete because people could walk through it, which influenced, of course, the entire way of playing with Lego. The accent was removed from the linguistic-structural activity of creating abstract-organic spaces, and put on the empathic-experiential way of perceiving created environments composed of concrete objects.

But the playmobilized Lego was no success. Playmobil itself became the game for concretely human people who see life not as determined by ideologies but by role-play.

In the 1990 Lego changed again, and this time more than ever. Some of the bricks became "intelligent", interactive, and able to move on their own. More and more "special parts" were introduced, making "basic" parts almost a rarity. A large part of the ambition to appear "logical" was abandoned and the initial idea of Lego as a creative toy appeared utterly weakened. Observers expected that the entire concept of Lego as a pedagogical principle flowing out of the optimistic humanism of preceding generations had simply ceased to make sense. The use of Lego bricks would soon be restricted to alternative education programs and business courses. As a popular toy Lego was bound to die out.

Then something unexpected happened: somebody invented VR. In the 1980s Lego boasted to give "imagination space to soar". Now Lego designers recognized what Lego's mission should really be in the contemporary world: to spatialize imagination.

When Lego invented the universe of the Bionicles, children began to desire Lego again. However, this time, kids (and it was only *them* because adults do not understand much of these new Lego) were not so much fascinated by what could be identified as the traditional Lego-*logic* but by Lego-*space*.

The new Lego-line is called "Bionicle". Bionicles are sleek and stylized robots that developed out of earlier Lego-robots called "Throwbots". Bionicles are posthuman cyborgs, those artificial creatures projected by Manfred Klines and Nathan Cline in the 1960s at a NASA conference and they live in a typical AI universe in which the boundary between humans and machines are fluent. With this step "back into the future" Lego retrieved its technological image.

The aesthetics as such is in no way original but has developed since the 1970s especially in Japanese techno-pop culture. Originally, these strange and threatening techno-pop cyborgs built a contrast with the simpler Disneyian aesthetics of robots. Equipped with samurai swords and insect carapaces, they thrived particularly well in Japanese mangas and *animes* like Tekkaman and Evangelion. First, these android, biomechanical monsters had mainly negative connotations and were forced to adopt the roles of enemies; only later could they appear also as sad and problematic creatures.

Human bodies wrapped in technology or exoskeletons, hybrids of skin/chrome, flesh/metal, organic/inorganic, etc. are not new; but so far, they did not necessarily enter the rooms of young well-educated Lego-engineers. However, what is wrong about it? Having created millions of ecologists and city planners in the past, why should Lego not become the leading game of future bioengineers? A specialist of the field, Mark Sagoff, would even spell out the old game's new scope in terms of pure posthumanism when writing: "The whole world can now be viewed as a vast Lego Kit inviting combination, hybridization, and continual rebuilding. Life is manipulability" (Sagoff 2005: 88).

Lego decided to invest in this kind of imaginary – though not without undertaking some changes. The Bionicles' existence is based on a story that takes place somewhere "in space" far away from earth. The plot comes along as a mixture of Polynesian mythology, African religion, Eastern philosophy and Greek polytheism, which distances it completely from the old Lego world but also from the Japanese *anime* world.

On the one hand, the story itself is simple and trivial which seems to reconfirm the Spartan aesthetic of Lego as the "simplest thing in the world". The spiritual mixture of exotic cultures that is woven into the good-vs-evil-story, on the other hand, remains strangely alien to the spirit of Lego.

In any case, the new Legos are utterly opposed to the idyllic, hedonistic world of Playmobil. Empathy and simple identification are still forbidden. The characters being robots, their facial expressions are metallic, and display emotions only with much difficulty. What is more important than emotions are "*powers*" – and these powers define the basic data of a certain spatial environment.

As a matter of fact, a large part of this new Lego-space could be conveniently recuperated from the era of traditional Lego. The new Lego-space still has affinities with the self-forming, organic, abstract space of traditional Lego (as much as it is opposed to the idyllic, concrete space of Playmobil). However, through an immense coincidence, Lego-space turned out to be highly compatible with the kind of space that fascinates us at the age of cyberreality, that is, with the computer related social field generally referred to as cyberspace.

The Bionicle planet is almost entirely made of water with just one island sticking out of the surface (a situation difficult to reproduce in "real time" in the children's room). The god Mata Nui is supposed to have fallen from the sky landing just on the island. Unfortunately, his ill-bred brother soon joins the island in the same way and sends Mata Nui to an eternal sleep. But the Tohunga villagers and their Turaga leaders are prepared to fight this bad god. They even decide to call their island Mata Nui in honor of the sleeping god.

Within this story the six basic Lego-colors have not only been maintained, but have even been complemented with more "elementary", that is, "spatial" qualities. Blue is the color of the Toa of Water, white is the color of the Toa of Ice. Brown is for the Toa of Earth, red for the Toa of Fire, etc. The blue Toa lives in and controls water, the brown Toa lives in and controls earth, etc. The "bad guys", the Bohroks, as well as other groups, are divided according to the same scheme. To each color corresponds thus a certain spatial environment as well as the "power" or capacity to control this environment. "Non-spatial" remain those phenomena that cannot be controlled, like fate, light, darkness…

This grammatically constituted spatial environment becomes more complex at the moment more efficient methods of orientation can be acquired by wearing certain masks. You'll get around faster in this space with a mask of speed, more elegantly with a mask of levitation; and you experience the whole space in a more subtle way when you have a mask of x-ray or of night vision.

The patterns of the plot as well as the space within which the plot develops, follow the logical lines dictated by this spatial grammar. All "metaphysical" powers that are beyond control are clearly defined in a non-spatial way. The bad god Makuta for example, negates even the most abstract spatial qualities when declaring that he appears as what cannot be *imagined*: "You cannot destroy me, as much as you cannot destroy the sea, the wind, the void… I am nothing". Though the Toas hasten to explain they have emerged from the water, Makuta insists that also they have "come out of nothing".

Compared to the old, organic Lego-space, space has here become more abstract and more "logical" than ever. But there is more to this space than simply its logic: the logic applied in this game has itself become spatial. The Bionicle-world still appears as a typical Lego product because it provides a well-structured, abstract space of an imagination that advances, uninspired by elements from the concrete world, solely through the power of intellect. New, however, is that here a spatial universe is created through a large number of abstract indications. These indications remain dynamic at every instant because they correspond to the rules of a game. This means that to "play" with Lego has a meaning different from the one it had before. True, children still reconstruct objects, build new ones and act out certain parts of a game. However, the kind of *empathy* or *imagination* required, is now much more *spatial* than it has been in traditional Lego. Children no longer create abstract-organic spaces with bricks into which objects can be inserted. On the contrary, they look at the Bionicles and are aware of their spatial capacities. In other words, the space they produce through the game is no longer the manifestation of a constructivist logic developed through the combination of some pieces, but *space is contained in these Legos*. (In this sense, the new Lego-space looks much more like a Greek *chôra*.)

All this accords very well with the fact that the Bionicle story is distributed on the internet (it is also available on DVD). To play with these Legos is absolutely uninteresting if one has no possibility following the cartoons that provide, so to speak, the space for these Legos. "Play" takes place, to a large extent, on the internet: it takes place in the corresponding Mata Nui online game as well as on the buzzpower site on which Bionicle fans discuss potential plotlines, construction projects, and philosophical questions related to the Bionicle civilization. In 2005, the buzzpower site gathered one of the largest brand name communities in the world. Here again, "Lego-space" stretches over an abstract sphere and playful imagination has to adapt to this fact.

In a way, the Bionicle-game is a play so perfect that Huizinga could have dreamt of it. In this world, the lightness of play is so absolute that it has become purely spatial. While conventional Lego-bricks can be stuck together in order to form a structure on their own, in the new Lego universe one sticks together abstract quantities of space in order to form a virtual play-space that produces space in the form of a spatial grammar. Is this the game for posthumans?

While in traditional Lego, space developed organically out of a para-logical activity, and in Playmobil it developed out of imitation, in the Bionicle-world space is "virtually" given like a grammar that is not applied to language but to space. We no longer move around, as did humanist Lego-engineers or practically minded Playmobil players, in the wide space of imagination, painstakingly taking care not to transcend the most basic rules of linguistic logic. Within the new Lego-space we are freer than ever. We no longer need to take for granted the organic structure of the mental space that develops out of logical patterns, that is, of those patterns that are supposed to exists "somewhere in the mind" and which make us believe that "play" is beneficial for the development of such mental, linguistic, structures. For these reasons, Bionicles might count among the most postmodern and posthuman machines that one can think of. In the 1980s Donna Haraway claimed that "our best machines are made of sunshine; they are all light and clean because they are nothing but signals, electromagnetic waves, a section of a spectrum" (Haraway 1994: 88-89). The best cyborgs, she concluded, are pure "ether", they are a "quintessence". Well, that's what Lego Bionicles actually are: basic powers that manifest themselves in space and determine this space.

More than anything else, the new Lego-space is a silent dream-space, which develops spatial structures out of itself. For this reason it represents the ideal space of a generation for whom "the virtual" has become a part of everyday life.

## Note

http://www.seriousplay.com

# 7. From Perspective to "All-Unity" or the Narrative of Virtual Cosmology

## Introduction

The term "All-Unity" is used as the official translation of the Russian philosophical term *vseyedinstvo*, which represents a "unity in multiplicity". Russian philosophers who were interested in All-Unity are, for example, pre-revolutionary "organicist" thinkers Vladimir Soloviov (1853-1900) and Lev Lopatin (1855-1922), but also more modern thinkers like Semën L. Frank (1877-1950) and Nicolai Berdyaev (1878-1948). I use the idea of "All-Unity" for an analysis of contemporary themes.

All-Unity is not an invention of Russian philosophers but has an essential place in Eastern as well as in Western philosophy. The ambition to grasp the world "as a whole" through a phenomenon so powerful that it is able to unify all diversity within it, is linked to one of the most primordial philosophical impulses or instincts. The idea of All-Unity subsists until today in the realm of posthumanism, for example in the contemporary vision of the earth as "one cyborg creature [...] including the procreation of other metamen throughout the galaxy" (Gray 2001: 10).

In India, truth is thought of in relation to "the unity of things", and such ideas of the whole universe being manifest in each atom are recurrent. Classical and modern Indian philosophy (Advaita Vedânda) sees Brahman (the Absolute) as a single reality, and systems like the one of the Yogâcâra conceive reality as undifferentiated.

In the West, Parmenides' "One Being" and Heraclitus' *logos* represent the starting points of philosophy. These ancient ideas of All-Unity, although indirectly and by first passing through Plato's dialectics, are present in Western "rationalist" philosophy to date. Among the most explicit attempts to grasp the idea of All-Unity are the writings of Russian philosophers of the nineteenth century. All-Unity became here a major philosophical concept, culminating in Vladimir Soloviev's concept of *vseyedinstvo* meant to be a cosmic process in the sense of the "soul of the world". Russian scientific elaborations such as Vladimir Vernadsky's "noosphere" (from Greek *noos*, mind) go in the same direction.[1]

While "All-Unity" can be found at the beginning of many philosophical reflections, it can also be found at many a reflection's end. What can be added, aspired or examined, once this All-Unity has been spelled out and officially given the status of an ultimate philosophical truth? Still two more things can be done: (1) All-Unity can be transformed into a more sophisticated dialectical, cosmological, monadological system; and (2) All-Unity can be defended against diverse attempts to formulate the world as nothing more than a random accumulation of single elements.

In Western philosophy both things have been done in various, often highly sophisticated ways. Spinoza, Bruno, Eckhart, and finally Hegel are the best known examples. The overall impression in these philosophies is that All-Unity is conceived of as simultaneously attractive and repulsive. In other words: it is *not* seen as an end in itself. Spinoza, for example, held that even though there is only one substance, this substance has infinite attributes. A large part of Western philosophy is indeed fuelled by a stimulating tension between descriptions of the world composed of clearly definable singularities on the one hand, and a unifying All-Unity on the other. In this sense, All-Unity as the expression of an ontological or existential self-contradictoriness, or even of an aporia simultaneously affirming the existence of single elements *and* their unity (an idea widely reflected by Idealism) has been philosophically fruitful. However, if the philosophy of All-Unity does nothing more than negate any difference it becomes mysticism. It becomes mysticism simply because it contradicts "reality".[2] As "mystic" is understood the attempt to think All-Unity as a self-sufficient intellectual phenomenon, carrying with it the "end of philosophy", meaning the dull repetition of identical intellectual models.

The last time the idea of All-Unity was put forth in a straightforward fashion was during Romanticism with its nostalgia for the unity of God, nature and man. In some respects, this discredited, for our age of science, further attempts to grasp any All-Unity. On the other hand, Hegel's Absolute Spirit announcing the "End of History", remains attractive even today (see Fukuyama 1992). Yet, the fact to consider a uniform unity as "real" and as the culmination point of philosophical thought still represents nothing more than pure mysticism.

One of the questions to be asked in the present chapter is if the current spreading of VR and of "cyberspace" cannot be linked to visions of an all-unifying end of history. Margareth Wertheim is convinced that "in a quite literal sense, cyberspace is outside the physical complex of matter-space-time that since the late seventeenth century has increasingly been held as not just the basis of reality, but as the totality of the real" (Werthheim 1998: 47). The question is thus: does VR represent the idea of a non-physical space enabling humans to grasp the world as a whole?

## 1. Perspective

It is interesting to examine a phenomenon whose connection with problems of All-Unity as much as with cyberspace has generally gone unnoticed: perspective. Modern science discovered and elaborated the definition of subjects, elements, substances, and the structures between them. Of course, all this was only possible on the firm ground of a fixed *perspective* from which subjects, elements, and so forth, could be perceived. This does not only concern the natural sciences but an entire *Weltanschauung*, including art, society, and religion.

In art and architecture, the invention of "perspective" has become most famous. The use of perspective in Renaissance painting was more than an artistic device creating the illusion of naturalist spatial depth. "Perspectivism" presents itself more like a dogmatic subjectivism attempting to reconstruct the world within a geometric system by relying on one single point of view. "Perspectivist rationalism" confines imagination to relatively narrow limits. It therefore runs the risk of failing to grasp reality since reality is neither geometrical, nor can its "whole" experience be covered by what is visible from one single point of view. In opposition to this, non-perspectival approaches strive towards All-Unity. In pre-seventeenth century Byzantine paintings for example, which were not yet influenced by linear perspective, the point of view from which an object is seen appears as moving and changing. Still, the aim of an art which ignores perspective is not simply to address, by moving around and constantly changing the perspective, a possibly high number of different mosaic glances, but rather to grasp the *essence* of reality itself.

Perspectival and non-perspectival paradigms are also present in approaches to society and religion. The aforementioned Russian philosophers of the nineteenth century insisted that Western-European philosophy had invented the idea of the "isolated individual" able to exist independently of a communitarian "Whole". This critique of "secular" society is closely linked to theological conceptions because, certainly, God is "all in all" (Cor. XV 28). From an Eastern-Orthodox point of view, in Western Christianity, God had become a *concept*, which means that it was no longer incorporated in the *inner drama of life* but became, in the words of Nicolai Berdyaev, "equivalent to an unstirring stone" (Berdyaev 1930: 50). Through the loss of the "tragic aspect within god" the inner drama and dynamic stirring related to religious experience, were replaced by a single, static, idolizing gaze dependent only on one single perspective.

For Berdyaev, this Western-Christian God is more "scientific" than his Eastern-Orthodox one. Of course, as so often in philosophical discussions about "Unity", the Western approach can rightfully insist that it has not lost All-Unity out of sight. While Berdyaev claims that his God is able to embrace All-Unity only because He embraces the "whole life" of human beings, Western Christianity can claim that it is just the more abstract approach to theology that is helpful in grasping the "whole world" within *one concept*.

In general, in modern Western civilization, the perspective vision of the world is supposed to signify a progress. The "unperspective" way of seeing the world that was current before the Renaissance is equated with a kind of weakened state of consciousness. Lack of perspective means to be unconscious of the space that one lives in and of one's own position within that space. On a social level it can be associated with an ancient, clan-like existence in which "the individual" as a social entity has not yet been discovered.

According to this model, perspective had to be installed as means of showing the way out of an All-Unity in which all cats are gray and that comes close to a kind of drunken mysticism. Once perspective leads us out of this "All-Unity", the whole is not necessarily lost: it can always be retrieved in the form of an abstract whole. What is certainly lost, however, is a certain dynamic of (social, visual, or theological) positions that is usually sparked off through the confrontation of one perspective with other peoples' perspectives as well as with the phenomenon of the whole.

In 1949, the German philosopher Jean Gebser (1905-1973) published a 600 pages long book called *Ursprung und Gegenwart* that was translated into English only in 1985 under the title *The Ever-Present Origin.* Gebser understands the antithesis of perspectival and unperspectival seeing as logocentric and believes that it will soon be overcome because at the end of the twentieth century man's concept of reality will undergo radical changes. Gebser's idea is that in Renaissance, "although man's horizon expanded, his world became increasingly narrow as his vision was sectorized by the blinders of the perspectival world view. The gradual movement toward clearer vision was accompanied by a proportionate narrowing of his visual sector. The deeper and farther we extend our view into space, the narrower is the sector of our visual pyramid" (23). However, the imprisonment of vision and consciousness through perspective will soon come to an end, as evidenced by Picasso's aperspective way of painting. Gebser finds that in a drawing from Picasso from 1926

> space and body have become *transparent*. In this sense the drawing is neither unperspectival, i.e., a two-dimensional rendering of a surface in which the body is imprisoned, nor is it perspectival, i.e., a three-dimensional visual sector cut out of reality that surrounds the figure with breathing space. The drawing is "aperspectival" in our sense of the term; time is no longer spatialized but integrated and concretized as a fourth dimension. By this means it renders the whole visible to insight, a whole which becomes visible only because the previously missing component, time, is expressed in an intensified and valid form as the present. It is no longer the moment… (24).

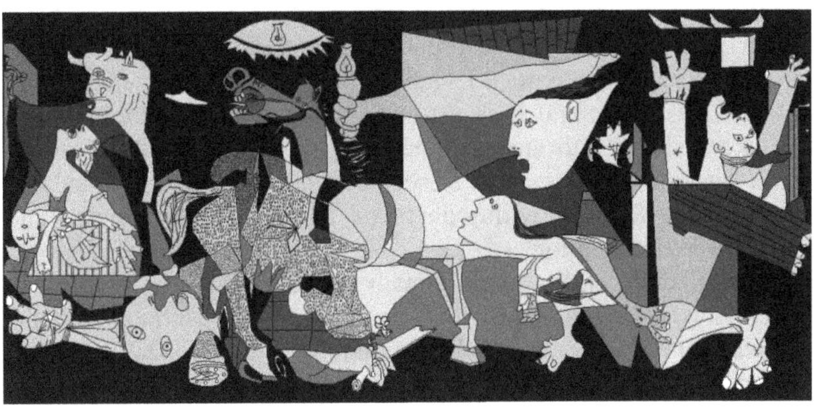

Fig. 17: Picasso: La Guernica © 2015 Estate of Pablo Picasso / Artists Rights Society (ARS), New York

In this drawing, like in Picasso's *Guernica*, spatiality is almost abolished (28), leaving only a "*pure present, the quintessence of time*". Some of Picasso's works "are almost devoid of any depth and any central point of illumination", and express the "eternal present" and not just a temporal moment.

Essentially, Gebser anticipates a "new reality" that will be more "intensive" as it is no longer ego-centric but determined by an "aperspectival" structure of consciousness that has overcome the perspective dichotomy of negation and affirmation. This consciousness is “a consciousness of the whole” in which “intensity and action, the effective and the effect co-exist” (7). It is an “integral reality” as an “intensive awareness of the world’s transparency, a perceiving of the world as truth” (5).

**2. Virtual Reality as Aperspectival Consciousness**

Gebser’s predictions are amazingly correct, except for the fact that the “new reality” has not been painted by Picasso or by some other artist experimenting with perspective. The new aperspectival consciousness of the whole is provided by VR. Here perspective (which still exists in simulation) is not simply negated but *overcome* precisely in the way imagined by Gebser, since all exterior points of view have been replaced with an absolutely “inner” one. Through this new, integral form of reality, man’s desire to return to social and spatial unity, a desire that has been so severely negated since Renaissance, seems to have been fulfilled.

While it is relatively easy to agree with the correspondence of VR with Gebser’s model, the consequences remain debatable. Liberals have much reason to remain relaxed, since, given the stimulation that VR provides in general it seems to be unlikely that its creation will provoke a slump into an unperspectival night. Aperspectival reality *could* function in the service of social, intellectual, and spiritual dynamism that Russian philosophers of the nineteenth century and Gebser were looking for.

Less liberal persons might remain skeptic because nothing really indicates with certitude that the invention of VR overlaps with the inauguration of an era in which “community”, “social experience”, or perhaps even “God”, will be rediscovered in a new, aperspectival, light. All these items *could* also be covered under that kind of mystical All-Unity that in the past has more than once brought thought to a standstill.

Still liberals can remain relaxed because they will understand the aforesaid rather as a proof for the fact that, in principle, nothing is new. All-Unity has once more reemerged with just as many reasons to be optimistic as there are reasons to be pessimistic. Everything depends on whether the All-Unity develops along the lines of a Hegelian monism or along the lines of a rather pluralistic empiricism in the sense of Bergson and William James; and, with the help of some minor regulations, why should the struggle between monism and pluralism not lead to positive results?

In the worst case the virtual fusion of perspectivism and unperspectivism will create a form of aperspectivism so peaceful that it *can* bring all personal reflection to a standstill.

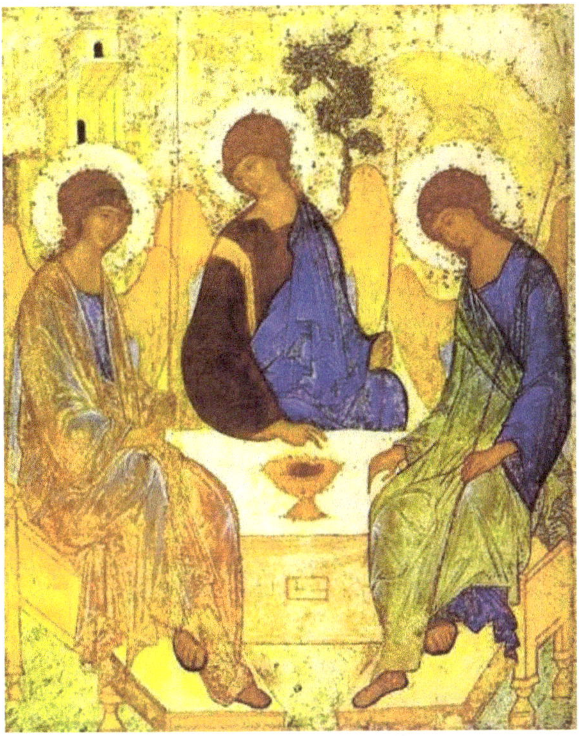

Fig. 18: Andrei Rublev, On the Holy Trinity (ca. 1410-1420), Tretjakov Gallery, Moscow.

We have to conclude that Gebser was mistaken. In the end, perspective thinking will not be overcome with the creation of an aperspectival world because this world is too close to abstraction. We need instead a courageous return to unperspectivism enabling the experience of tragic shifts from one perspective to the other. Gebser refused such a return because to him this represented (like icons and pre-Renaissance paintings) a concession to social primitivism and pre-civilizational paradigms of culture. However, being unduly afraid of the unperspectival night, did he not go too far by offering us a world entirely new and beaming with aperspective light? More modest approaches, like that of Bergson, seem to be more useful. Instead of a really new world in which perspective has been abolished, Bergson provided a "felt" *view* of the world perceived through (still perspectival) intuition.

Gebser's aperspectival world remains a utopia. It is seemingly impossible to change the fact that in reality the world is perspective as much as it is unperspective. Human experiences will always have to be made within a field of tension stretching between empiricism and intuition. Yet, looking at most recent technical developments, it seems indeed to be possible to create a world in which all "unsafe" and tragic experiences have been abolished.

According to Stephen Perrela, VR is the "*concrete* realization of Hegel's Absolute Spirit (my italics)" (Perella 1998: 237), and Michael Heim characterizes VR as a theological manifestation of Leibniz's monad (Heim 1993: 95) in which we experience no temporal unfolding, no dramatic shifts or delays, but only a kind of aperspectival presence. In principle, this strategy draws on the old "God as a concept" theory that avoids the "tragedy of life" in order to replace it with a stagnant form of reality as abstract as a concept. In this reality, changes of perspective are not permitted. Already once the Western European mind decided to avoid these changes by successfully gluing vision to one single point of view.

It goes without saying that such a "safe" attitude that counts on absolute abstraction on the one hand, but still enables concrete experience on the other, is particularly attractive in our present civilization. Through it a phenomenon like VR will come even closer to the phenomenon of the dream because also in dreams excitement and fun are embedded in such a realm of absolute peace. As a result, the dream experience adopts the character of a special form of reality. It cannot be a coincidence that the creation of VR often goes hand in hand with the development of a new cosmology available to laypersons through the media and popular books on science. Pierre Levy, in his optimistic evaluation of VR, likens VR to a "collective subjectivity in a cosmos" (Levy 1994: 169) while Paul Virilio is convinced that "virtual space" means to substitute the "real space" of the cosmos (2000: 95). Margareth Wertheim writes that "cyberspace creates a parallel world that in the very real sense is a new cosmos of the psyche [which is] not made up of atoms or particles, but is ontologically rooted in the ephemera of bits and bytes, not subject to the laws of physics and [...] not bound by the limitations of those laws" (Werthheim 1998: 58).

It is true that a reality that has been tested as a cosmological phenomenon is "safer" in the sense in which safety has been perceived in the Diesel "Safe Yourself" ad presented in Feature Scene I. The serenity provided by the awareness of being in harmony with a cosmos that is abstract though still real is dreamlike and, moreover, dispenses us from any responsibility towards concrete life ("it's the cosmos, you know") is indeed valuable. In a special issue from 2002 devoted to "The New Cosmology", the *Scientific American* presents diverse results of astrophysical research that laypersons may hesitate to associate with scientific learning. In these speculations on the nature of the cosmos, "being" and "nothingness" become intertwined, the word "energy" is used metaphorically rather than as a measurable quantity, and the meaning of the word "exact" becomes relative *par excellence* because "nothing is exact, not even nothingness" (31). In this issue entitled "The Once and Future Cosmos", a most remarkable hypothesis is pronounced with regard to "empty space" that is supposed to be filled with elementary particles able to "spontaneously pop out of nothingness and disappear again, if they do so for a time so short that one cannot measure them directly". Though the author admits that "such virtual particles, as they are called, may appear as far-fetched as angels sitting on the head of a pin" (11), his conclusion remains that "empty space is not empty at all" but that it must be filled with these "virtual particles". Even more, the entire universe "must be composed largely of an even more ethereal form of energy that inhabits empty space, including that which is in front of our noses" (32).

The reference to "virtual particles" shows that while theoreticians of VR borrow from astrophysics the technical metaphor of "cosmos", cosmologists borrow the metaphor of "the virtual" from theoreticians of VR in return. In fact, nothing could be more virtual. Space itself, because it begins embracing *everything* (from experiential life-space to space as a subject for astrophysical research), is defined as an ontological paradox: simultaneously empty and not empty, (perspectively) measurable and not measurable, living and dead, or most simply: virtual.

It is clear that in spaces as "safe" as this one, the most dangerous and potentially tragic experience of all human experiences had to be ruled out from the beginning: the possibility to meet another person. This does not mean that one would not meet other people in the virtual cosmos (Second Life, There, Active Worlds, Twinity or LambdaMOO have been created for the purpose of meeting pther people), but it is difficult to see how these people could still be recognized as "the other" in the sense of a Buberian "thou"[3] and not merely as objects. In 1967, the computer scientist Michael Polany could still complain about "the scientific outlook that appeared to have produced a mechanical conception of man" (Krauss 2002: 33). This statement perhaps best shows the extent to which technology has advanced since the 1960. The main problem today is not that the Other will be judged as too "mechanical", but rather that a mechanically all-unified character of reality does not necessarily permit the perception of the other as the other.

Cyberspace allows a shared reality with another person to a point that his/her reality is mine in the sense that it permits me, as says Wertheim, "to experiment and play with others" (Werthheim: 58). However, in reality this is not true sharing. "To share reality" essentially means to look at the same things, or the same symbols from different perspectives. Even more, it is the very constellation of two persons looking at the same object from two different perspectives *that creates space* as a social phenomenon. At the moment there is no tragic shift from one perspective to the other, the Other is lost along with the potential space that could have been created. If there *is* no perspective, I cannot adopt the perspective of the Other.

In Japanese Noh-plays the quality known as "detached viewing" describes a sophisticated self-other relationship through which experience is shared between the performer and each member of the audience. "Detached viewing" (the fact that the spectator is prepared to leave her own perspective of the event and to view it with the supra-perspectival eye of the others), is seen as an achievement of dramatic art, as a part of the dramatic experience of the Noh-play itself (Komparu 1983: 18-20).[4] The important point is that spatial consciousness is here created "tragically" through a *loss* of perspective which, for that reason first of all had to exist. Then could be adopted another, all-uniting perspective.

The "detached viewing" is reminiscent of Gebser's aperspectival seeing, but in reality it is different. It is not the attribute of a synthetically created reality but the result of real experience. All-Unity that has been obtained in this way, that is, through a tragic shift from one individual perspective to a larger one, represents real, mature understanding. Once this shift has been obtained, there is no return to naïve perspectivism because: once the cake is eaten you cannot have it. This, however, is probably a less popular thing to claim in the realm of virtual aesthetics.

## Notes

1. Vladimir Vernadsky believed that man had become such an important geological agent that what he had earlier called the biosphere had now been replaced by the noosphere. In his earlier work on the biosphere Vernadsky tried to break with the romantic vision of earth sciences relevant since the time of Humboldt. By formulating the principles of the noosphere ("sphere of reason"), Vernadsky created a kind of anti-ecology able to conceive of even biological givens as man-made. In a way of speaking, in Vernadsky's theory, man is not a part of the ecosystem; rather the ecosystem is a part of man. See Vernadsky 1945 and also Botz-Bornstein 2008 Chapter 5. Noosphere is also used by Pierre Teilhard de Chardin in his *Cosmogenesis* (1922).
2. A curious case is the Christian Church, which understood any attempts to see the world as an All-Unity as Pan-Theism. The only All-Unity it would accept was God who created a world composed of singularities. In some way, the Church wanted to monopolize "all-unifying" mysticism and not permit its use outside definitions of God.
3. In his book *Ich und Du* (1962-64), Buber attempts to redefine the value of a personal 'Thou' as an alternative to an alienated, modern environment in which the "Other" is mainly experienced as a numerical accumulation of information.
4. See my Chapter on Noh-plays and Russian icons in Botz-Bornstein 2009.

## Feature Scene VII

## In Praise of Blandness: Some Thoughts on Japanese Television

When zapping through the international channels of a hotel television we can immediately tell when we have reached the *Japanese* news. Almost no newscast will pass without the display of silent pictures of building facades or ordinary streets overlaid with a report of the crime that has happened *here*. The problem is that the *here* looks like everywhere else, which makes the entire coverage spooky. An accident has happened or somebody has been murdered: the camera takes endless shots of the street segments and the walls where the event took place though there are absolutely no traces to be seen.

In this entirely normal looking house took place a group suicide. The flying curtains make us shudder (did the victims leave the widows open before…?). Another popular morbid element is the empty hospital bed in which the victim *could* be seen if the television had been able to film her.

Next comes the almost daily corruption scandal: with unwearing routine the news producers first provide a shot of the company's name plate at the entrance after which the camera will pan towards the office windows through which we can guess the shadowy shapes of persons or – most of the time – *nothing*.

Hundreds of similar looking places are shown in this way per year. As a matter of fact, who would actually like to *see* what had really happened? Which saturated consumer society would like to witness its crimes in real or almost real time? These gray, claustrophobic shots of concrete and asphalt that deny any point of view are not supposed to establish a scenic place of an event. This is not fiction but a *newscast*: we are not asked to *imagine* anything. The "event" must rather be found in these impersonal shots in the form of an absent code that cannot be deciphered but which can perhaps be felt while staring at these bland pictures. The crime presented is not supposed to appear as a narrative, it is not even a fact (which could best be reproduced by evoking a scenic real place) but appears through an abstract space linked to some bits of information.

The other element that lets us immediately recognize that we are on *Japanese* television is the omnipresence of cooking shows. Japanese watch on average 3.5 hours television daily and food shows are on almost every channel. A Japanese will probably not spend a single day without watching at least one food show. These programs – which are rather food-assisted talk shows – come as game or variety shows and are hilarious mixtures of serious information about recipes, diets, food history and geography, and absolute nonsense. In almost all shows the food is used as an element of competition. It is prepared by following often complex plots and the highlight of every cooking show is the tasting of the product. Here it comes, we have seen it a thousand times: the actress tastes, for some seconds her face displays a *critical* though still overall *appreciating* expression which will, after exactly five seconds, give way to the outcry: "oishiiii!" Women might jump up a little from their seats while men are usually more restrained. One can consider this as a ritual. Still I am surprised that so far nobody seems to have been worried about the most obvious fact: that you cannot taste food on television. Of all senses, those that cannot be transmitted by television waves are *smells* and *tastes*. What are we actually supposed to think while we are watching the actress tasting the food? Are we supposed to re-experience the taste through empathy? One can empathize with people when they have feelings like happiness; but how can one empathize with a person's taste that one does not even know?

Again we are confronted with an interesting blandness. The taste conveyed in food shows is a taste that is neither real nor imagined but *virtual* because it is "there" simply in the way it is enacted; it is there not through an "as if" but as a reality that is apparently self-sufficient. As mentioned in Chapter 1, François Jullien has called the aesthetic quality of "insipidity" (which he finds especially in traditional Chinese paintings) a "beyond" which does not lead the spectator into another, metaphysical world, but which appears as a "virtual" quality (Jullien 1991: 115ff). For Jullien this insipidity provides a "special type of intuition of existence" which is extremely rich on an experiential level. For the Chinese this was particularly important in connection with food as shows a passage quoted by Jullien. The passage is from Tu Sikong who provided an analysis of the "beyond taste" (味外味, *wei wai wei*) in the ninth century:

> South of Jianling [that is, among the non-Chinese barbarians] the following thing is true for everything that serves us as food: what is acid like vinegar does certainly not lack acidity but there is nothing more than the acidity to it; what is salty does certainly not lack saltiness but there is nothing more than the saltiness to it. If, however the Chinese stop eating [these things] as soon as they are no longer hungry it is because they are aware that a certain perfection whose cause resides in what is beyond acidity and saltiness is lacking. The people from [South of] Jiangling, on the other hand, are used to this [saltiness and acidity] and do not make such distinctions. (Jullien 1985: 136)

The virtual is always richer than both reality and imagined non-reality (it is a taste beyond taste) because the "nothing" through which it is conveyed contains *infinite* possibilities. The real taste is that which is tasteless (味無味, *wei wu wei*, 128). This aesthetic insipidity is not meant to lead us towards some hidden truth that needs to be revealed, but it rather unfolds itself as an "*all there is*" without locking us in between the rough and immediate limits drawn by our own perception. In a way, it represents a reality in itself, which is not real but virtual.

Ironically we might say that this is exactly what we are confronted with in Japanese television. The blandness of the news images or of the taste in the food shows is not due to a *lack of reality* but is part of its underlying concept. It produces a presence that does not need to be either actual or hidden but which is simply there as if it produced itself. This is the particular blandness of VR.

# 8. What Would Nietzsche have Said about Virtual Reality? Dionysus and Cyberpunk

In 1844, the year Nietzsche was born, Samuel F.B. Morse went to the American Congress to request an extension of the only existing telegraph line from Baltimore to New York. Some years later, hundreds of messages per day would be sent along several lines in the United States. The "Victorian Internet" (Standage 1998) soon extended to Europe where, in 1852, an instant message was sent from London to Paris. During Queen Victoria's reign, "a worldwide communications network whose cables spanned continents and oceans (...) revolutionized business practice, gave rise to new forms of crime, and inundated its users with a deluge of information (...) A technological subculture with its own customs and vocabulary was establishing itself" (Standage: viii).

Nietzsche could observe the rise of a globalizing system of communication during his lifetime; but what could he have anticipated about the Internet or about an apparently futuristic concept such as VR as a virtual landscape made up of all information in the world? What could he have thought of a culture of simulation that has begun to conceptualize our thinking and, therefore, also our relationship with the real? The present chapter considers Nietzsche's potential reservations with the virtual taking into account his views on history and modernity by interpreting them within a contemporary context of economic and cultural globalization. Nietzsche's thoughts on the virtual are conceptually connected to his ideas about the tragic on one hand and to dialectics on the other. Most importantly, Nietzsche counters optimistic techno evangelism by putting forward the original Greek concept of the tragic. Most recently, the urbanist Mike Davis has called the "gilded dreamworlds" that are overtaking the planet in the form of Disneyfied suburbs "narcissistic withdrawals from the tragedies" of real life (Davis 2007: xvi). The tragic should be understood in this sense. A re-evaluation of the Nietzschean idea of the tragic helps to formulate a criticism of those virtual stances that permeate everyday life in the contemporary world. Nietzsche anticipated the work of Heidegger, who held that the advance of simultaneity in technicized civilization suggests that "time as history has vanished from the lives of all peoples" (Heidegger 1956: 31). The above reflections on "autism" have shown how true this is. However, the present chapter will show that a distinction needs to be made between different manifestations of VR, some of which Nietzsche might have disliked and some he might have supported. Nietzsche, who has has repeatedly been proclaimed as a proto-posthumanist thinker, can certainly not be classified as a technophone. But it is also safe to assume that he would not be particularly impressed with the current widespread posthumanist techno-euphoria.

## 1. The Tragic, the Dramatic, the Virtual

We have come across the tragic in the context of Chapter 6, showing how Russian philosophers criticized the reduction of God to a concept. As a concept, God is no longer incorporated in the *inner drama of life* and the "tragic aspect within god" is lost (Berdyaev 1930: 50). Nietzsche's philosophy is a critique of modern Western culture and its moral values, political values (democracy and egalitarianism), philosophical values (Platonism and all forms of metaphysical dualism), and religious (Christian) values. Nietzsche suggests new values transcending the nihilism that has so far governed European history under the influence of Christianity. Within this context, the notion of the tragic becomes predominant. No other philosopher has defined the tragic in more subtle terms than Nietzsche who, in fact, stated that "tragedy suggests that nobility is possible, that courage is admirable, and that even defeat can be glorious" (Kaufmann 1968: 349-50).

While in his early work Nietzsche tended to defend drama as compatible with the tragic, he later designed an anti-dialectical concept of the tragic that is opposed to the dramatic and is important in art while coming closer to an existential notion of play. The tragic is different from the dramatic, which is pompous and full of pathos and often involved in dialectical calculations. Nietzsche insists that the tragic artist is not a (dramatic) pessimist, but rather a playful manipulator of tragic events. His concept of the Dionysian as the aesthetic and existential element of drunkenness puts forward the tragic as a positive power:

> Saying Yes to life even in its strangest and hardest problems, the will to life rejoicing over its own inexhaustibility even in the very sacrifice of its highest types – that is what I called Dionysian, that is what I guessed to be the bridge to the psychology of the tragic poet. (Nietzsche 1966–77: Ger. 160/ Eng. 80)

At first sight, a dissociation of the tragic from the dramatic is difficult, which becomes clear when reading Philip Bagby's analysis of historical science in the twentieth century:

> In recent decades some historians have adopted what they call a "tragic" view of history, by which they mean the assumption, not only that the good need not triumph at the end, but that it can never be fully realized because of the inherent limitations of human powers and human nature. This has been a useful corrective to the overweening optimism of the liberal historians, to their tendency to see everything in terms of the predestined victory of Reason and Democracy, Progress and its age-old battle with Reaction. But such a tragic view is still a moral view, it still interprets history in terms of good and evil. (Bagby 1959: 2)

However, tragedy is more than a drama with a bad ending. As long as history is interpreted in terms of good and evil, it is made to follow the model of drama, but not that of tragedy which reaches beyond good and evil as well as beyond optimism and pessimism. In this sense, the tragic is most clearly opposed to moralistic, progressive, dialectical Hegelian historical systems which view history as a dramatic – though optimistic – event. Francis Fukuyama, the dean of all contemporary Hegelian "End of History" visionaries, insists that Hegel's idea of History is "implicit in our use of words like "primitive" or "advanced", "traditional" or "modern", when referring to different types of human societies" (Fukuyama 1992: xii). Based on these understandings, Fukuyama describes a "coherent development of human societies from simple tribal ones based on slavery and subsistence agriculture, through various theocracies, monarchies, and feudal aristocracies, up through modern liberal democracy and technologically driven capitalism" (ibid.). While Fukuyama's dialectical world theatre presents a drama with a "good" ending, Nietzsche suggests a world which is modern without following any Hegelian scheme of civilizational perfection. He views the "tragic" as a quality able to consider "reality" in the way that it is, while simultaneously suggesting to us "that life and the world are beautiful in spite of all the suffering, cruelty, and terrors of existence" (Kaufmann 1968: 347).

The contemporary economically and technologically developed world – even more than the world described by Bagby – has brought about the apparent loss of the tragic in culture and fostered the kinds of dialectics that Nietzsche disliked. First, civilization in industrialized countries has managed to exclude most of the tragic events that were still common in the lives of those born only a generation earlier, as illustrated by a description by Richard Sennett:

> Our parents and grandparents were filled with anxiety in the 1940s, having endured the wreckage of the Great Depression and facing the looming prospect of war. What's particular about uncertainty today is that it exists without any looming historical disaster; instead it is woven into the everyday practices of a vigorous capitalism. (Sennett 1998: 31)

War became a "cold war", that is, a potential war creating uncertainty but not the feeling of tragedy. Further, the loss of the tragic becomes manifest in VR where reality is not defined as an existential, ever-changing phenomenon but appears as an extended, stable quantity in which no tragic losses will bar the way to an eternal, virtual life. It is clear that the role VR plays in society is more complex than the preceding statement suggests; varieties of more or less tragic uses of VR exist and will be presented below. However, first I want to make clear what I mean by the absence of the tragic in VR, which can best be illustrated by looking at computer games. To make the point clearest, I will look here first at a more "traditional" version of computer games. Massive multiplayer online games (MMO) firmly installed in global communications networks, and which can involve large numbers of people and are interconnected with non-game reality, will be considered afterwards. Traditionally, computer games are games that are "played": and play as it has been used in philosophy and in game scholarship over decades must be free, fun and safe (that is, consequence free). Games can be dramatic, but they will not be tragic in the sense of a mental participation or of a "real" suffering sparked off through enactment. This quality goes together with the "virtual" tendency to eternalize or accumulate, within the same "absolute present", a maximum of elements coming from the past, present, and future. Nothing gets lost. "Play-time" is thus opposed to the structure of tragic time as it is lived in real life and where events have real consequences.

In this sense, those computer games are anti-tragic phenomena *par excellence* because even death is not real. The virtual, as it is striving towards "immortality and transcendence" (Graham 2002: 159), attempts to stop the mortal coil of real life and to "ascend into a brilliant celestial realm". Cyberspace, as said Graham, "becomes effectively a portal into another world" (170). Walter Kaufmann's judgment of the tragic as being able to make us "feel that suffering is no insuperable objection to life, that even the worst misfortunes are compatible with the greatest beauty" (Kaufmann 1968: 347) alludes to dynamic gaiety based on the reunifications of opposite extremes. Also, Sartre's existentialist views are a good illustration of "tragic reality". All our choices are free, but once the choice has been made there are no opportunities to clean the slate after the fact. This makes life tragic and, in principle, the have-your-cake-and-eat-it-too ideology of online existences in the style of Second Life attempts to elude this consistency be it only because consequences can be negotiated. Jasper Juul, who insists very much on the "half-real" character of the next generation of computer games, has called those games "activities with negotiable consequences" (Juul 2003). The "hyperreal" can easily look like a Nietzschean play of surfaces brought about by a paralytic fascination with exteriority. The mode of signification used in VR is one in which "signs are divorced from their referents in the object world, becoming organized into a 'hyperreal' of screen surfaces" (Poster 2001: 133) in which all referentials have been liquidated.

This is the negative conception of "the virtual" as the empty play of commutation and convergence in which elements seem to refer to each other but to nothing essential. Since today no part of culture is exempt from VR, an often bizarre interlinking of "real" life and the virtual has led many people to the conclusion that "First Life" suffers from a similar loss of the tragic. Illustrations of the "coldest" form of modernity very often evoke images of a digitalized world in which reality as a whole is lost because it has been subsumed under a reality that is virtual, or, as Michael Benedikt wrote 20 years ago, that "life is not really lived anywhere but arranged for the viewing" (1991: 10). Andrew Keen describes "gated communities where all the people have identical views and the whole conversation is mirrored in a way that is reassuringly familiar" as a "dangerous form of digital narcissism" (Keen 2007: 55). The "autism" topic is invited back into the discussion. "CoolTown", which is for Jeff Rice a locality concentrating in itself all devices of "cold techno-coolness", is described as a place "where the physical world and the virtual world meet, where technology works for you" (Rice 2007: 125). This is a structured world with a collective mind where "the collaborative intelligence of tens of millions of people" forms a "networked you" (Keen 2007: 28). It goes without saying that in this world real power remains "beyond the reach of citizens' control [as it has been displaced] into the exterritoriality of electronic networks" (Bauman 2000: 40).

## 2. Nietzsche and the Virtual

How would Nietzsche react to this? Gilles Deleuze has pointed out that "according to Nietzsche it has never been understood that the tragic = the joyful" (Deleuze [1962] 1982: 36). In spite of Nietzsche's tragic Dionysian ambitions, for some people his philosophy that propagates a sort of superhuman world cut off from all "all-too-human" values represents a precursory movement of VR. Deleuzian philosophers have attempted to use the notion of the virtual, as it has been developed by Deleuze in *Difference and Repetition*, as a concept that has affinities with "Nietzsche's configuration of the Dionysian" (Cox 2005: 505). This makes sense to some extent, but is problematic in general. Deleuze distinguishes between the actual (in the sense of empirical objects) and the virtual as a flux of not yet stabilized forces (Deleuze 1994: 260) that remain irreducible: "The virtual is opposed not to the real but to the actual" (208). According to Deleuze, whenever we think of reality "we must avoid giving the elements and relations which form a structure of an actuality which they do not have" (ibid.). One can indeed be tempted to interpret this concept of the virtual as Dionysian but it will be shown below that such observations are difficult to support once they are reflected against more systematic philosophical formulations of reality. The other motive that leads to associations of Nietzsche's philosophy with VR is the philosopher's ambition to view the world in its totality, be it through the Will to Power or through Dionysian forces. Artificial reality as the realm of a posthuman world "in which humanity, having displaced the gods, achieves heights of wisdom and selfaggrandizement" (Graham 2002: 155) seems to concur with a technopaganism that some people find in Nietzsche. The god Dionysus breaks the *principuum individuationis* and swallows up all individual rationality. The result is the formation of something like a general, collective form of reason reminiscent of the Internet.

It is thus not surprising that Kroker and Weinstein designate Nietzsche as the patron saint of the hyper-texted body whose concept of the "Will to Power" creates a "World Wide Webbed Body" present as a Dionysian outflow of virtual achievement similar to Keen's "networked you". In their article "Nietzsche Gets a Modem", Kroker and Weinstein write:

> Refusing to be remaindered as flesh dumped by the virtual class, the hyper-texted body bends virtuality to its own purposes. Here, the will to virtuality ceases to be one-dimensional, becoming a doubled process, grisly yet creative, the hyper-texted body swallows its modem. (Kroker and Weinstein 1994: 3)

However, Nietzsche's Will to Power, just like Schopenhauer's concept of the Will, need to be seen in utmost proximity with the Dionysian musical symbol of the will, and it is difficult to understand how this can result in something as abstract as VR. It remains difficult even when we define the virtual prudently as the "not yet actualized", as does Deleuze. Schopenhauer saw the will as "released and satisfied willing (joy) and even more as an impending will (sorrow), always as emotion, passion [*Affekt*], an agitated state of mind" (Schopenhauer 1978–1982, 349/250). Similarly, Nietzsche's "Will", as it is opposed to judgments that are made merely in terms of ideas, remains immediately linked to concrete and real life. It is true that the Dionysian character can become dissociated from reality, but this will not be due to an act of fatalistic resignation but rather to a disgust caused by an intensive contact with life:

> The ecstasy of the Dionysiac state, which destroys the usual barriers and limits of existence, contains, for as long as it lasts, a lethargic element in which all personal experiences from the past are submerged. This gulf of oblivion thus separates the worlds of everyday life and Dionysiac experience from one another. (Nietzsche 1976a: 81/94)

The Dionysian man is like Hamlet who has grasped an essential truth and thus becomes incapable of action. He is disgusted by society because he knows life too well. The only way to prevent incapacity of action is to link the Dionysian to the Apollonian. It is not desirable to have knowledge alone, but knowledge needs to be veiled by a dream-like illusion in order to become bearable. The soothing illusion is provided by Apollo. Apollo is the god of all creative and imaginative forces and also the god of prophecy. Where Dionysus grants an immediate insight into the tragic realities of life, Apollo provides beautiful appearances and artistic fantasies that humans find necessary in order to endure the Dionysian realities. For Nietzsche, Apollo and Dionysus are not opposed to each other. They are not "extremes to be regulated into some kind of golden mean" (Lenson 1987: 22), but they complement each other as they both strive to resolve the contradiction of existence.

While Dionysus is drunkenness, Apollo is dream. While Dionysus is suffering, Apollo is the element which overcomes the suffering of the individual by the radiant glorification of eternity. Dionysus is shattering while Apollo is suggestive. Within Nietzsche's mythological system, the Apollonian dream world of the stage action is married to the Dionysian "real" world of the satyr-chorus: what is born is the tragedy as a reflection of real life.

Neither Dionysus nor Apollo suggests a flight from reality into an abstract virtuality. Both are advocates of reality even though they attain the stage of reality only through a paradox: the Dionysian man manages to stay close to reality only through the dreamlike element of the Apollonian. "Reality" is only what is produced by a combination of both a well-measured and wise representation of savage truth, which is different from any calculated and bombastic effect of dramatic presentations of historical reality or of dialectical philosophies about its overcoming.

Most probably Nietzsche would have had no sympathies towards VR as a dystopian cyberpunk vision of reality that is not "real" though constantly searching for a Dionysian form of pleasure within a reality that has been reduced to images. There are many reasons to state that VR, which had initially raised dreams of a new critical system or of a new Surrealism able to revise disparities and to raise modernity on a more humane level, has ended up as a self-conscious, self-sufficient World Wide Webbed Body bearing the same symptoms as the reality which spawned it. If this is VR, Nietzsche could only have been against it because for him it is the tragic consciousness of the drunken gambler and not the self-righteous enjoyment of the cold technocrat that creates the Dionysian spirit. Nietzsche puts forward "reality" as a transcendent interplay of the Apollonian and the Dionysian. He might, however, have had sympathies towards another, more interactive form of VR in which a Dionysian quantity constantly challenges too static forms of the Apollonian, preventing it from becoming an official world. This version of VR will be explained below.

In general, Nietzsche "abhorred excessive and uncritical transcendentalism" (Graham 2002: 173), just as he disliked the concept of art as a self-contained and self-enclosed sphere of activity and experience detached from the rest of life. Kroker and Weinstein's vision of a postmodern Will to Power smoothly flowing into a Will to Virtuality has dramatic and untragic undertones of resignation that can be found neither in the idea of the Dionysian nor in that of the Apollonian. Even worse, the "Will to Virtuality" comes closer to Fukuyama's concept of history that has come to an end. Fukuyama uses Nietzsche's philosophy in order to back up his Hegelian project when writing that "[Nietzsche's] last man had no desire to be recognized as greater than the others, and without such desire no excellence or achievement was possible. The last man ceased to be human" (Fukuyama 1992: xxii).

When the end of history is reached, all struggle, danger, risk, and daring are neutralized within a serene ambiance of historical accomplishment.

Nietzsche, on the other hand, does not attribute the Will to Virtuality, but wants the Dionysian to remain a drunken and instinctive insight into life's tragic reality. There are no suggestions of a serene escape from reality that Fukuyama believes to find in Nietzsche. Though it is right that Nietzsche remains anti-Aristotelian in general and privileges "suffering over action and the aesthetic over the moral" (Witt 2007: 26), it is entirely contrary to his intentions to equate his Dionysian philosophy with that of Schopenhauerian resignation and inactivity. Nietzsche believed that it "is Dionysus's task to make us graceful, to teach us to dance, to give us the instinct of play" (Deleuze [1962] 1982: 18). The Dionysian element fractures and delays the flow of cold, "official" civilization. Nietzsche believed that "the satyr himself, the imaginary natural being, is related to the cultural person in the same way that Dionysian music is related to civilization" (Nietzsche 1976a: 80/92).

**3. The Apollonian and the Virtual**

Since Dionysian culture is unsuitable for equations with VR, does the virtual have more affinities with the Apollonian? The Apollonian stands for dream, which suggests the existence of an "unreal" world. However, the Apollonian dream functions only like a screen that will remain empty as long as it does not receive Dionysian projections of the will. Once again it is important to point out that the unification of the Dionysian and the Apollonian does not follow a dialectical process though it is often represented as such (cf. Pizzato 2007: 186). Any dialectics neutralizes the Dionysian power of the tragic. Hamlet was no master of dialectical reflection but he had a spontaneous insight. Apollonian aesthetics stabilizes this insight, but this has nothing to do with dialectics. Also, Deleuze affirms that "in general, dialectics is not a tragic vision of the world but, on the contrary, the death of tragedy, the replacement of the tragic vision by a theoretical conception" (Deleuze 1982: 18). The unification of the Dionysian and the Apollonian becomes an "original enjoyment of the world's eye", a "double art" that we hear only in tragedy (Nietzsche 1976b: 207). There is no suggestion of an all-embracing view of the world in the sense of VR achieved through the work of dialectics. Nietzsche wants objectivity and uninterested contemplation and not scientific resignation. Both Dionysus and Apollo speak artistic languages; the former that of a drunken visionary and the latter that of aesthetic measurement and stylization. None of them likes the cold distance that a scientific vision of the world establishes between the subject and the living world and none of them can be associated with VR.

Joel Wainwright, in his article "Nietzsche Contra the Real Word", speaks of Nietzsche's "pyrophilosophy" that he opposes to geophilosophy's conventional notions of the world as a measurable phenomenon. He concludes that Nietzsche's world is "neither 'the real world', nor imminent materialism, but world – burning, becoming, Dionysian. Within the apparent world, one seeks not being, nor one fire, but instead a pyrophilosophy of local fires through which the world endures" (Wainwright 2010: 26). This shows how much the hot/cold aspect, once it is approached in terms of space, reflects also the tension between the local and the global. Local identity can only live through global culture or, more precisely, just because reality is composed of Dionysian localities, it needs the cooling effect of the Apollonian. This bears no link with a "virtualizating" detachment from reality, but leads to the production of a tragic reality dependent on the cool rhetoric of the antidialectical juxtaposition of both the Apollonian and the Dionysian.

For this very reason the Dionysian–Apollonian presentation of reality never becomes an all-embracing, authoritative discourse; the Nietzschean reality is based on a measured knowledge of the self that is always conscious of its own tragic status. Megalomaniac selfdramatization, on the other hand, is "demonic" and derives from the "pre-Apollonian era of the Titans":

> Apollo, as the ethical divinity, demands moderation from his followers and self-knowledge. And so alongside the aesthetic necessity of beauty run the demands "Know thyself" and "Nothing in excess". Arrogance and excess are considered essentially hostile daemons of the non-Apollonian period, the age of the titans. (1976a: 63/61)

Cold flows of dramatization occur in the music of Wagner whom Nietzsche perceives as the decadent representative of one who has not understood the imperatives of the new tragedy. Hegel's (or Fukuyama's) dialectics would be another example for such a cold dramatization of culture.

## 4. The Virtual and the Socratic

The contrary of Dionysian–Apollonian tragedy is for Nietzsche the Socratic or Schopenhauerian intellectualization of life, Euripides' anti-tragic reformulation of art and theatre, and Wagner's operas. It all started with Socrates: "Dionysus had already been chased off the tragic stage by a daemonic power speaking out from Euripides. But Euripides was, to some extent, only a mask. The divinity which spoke out of him was not Dionysus, and not Apollo, but an entirely new-born daemon called Socrates" (1976a: Ger. 110/Engl. 145). Rational, Socratic thought excludes mystery and ambiguity, believing that in order to be beautiful, everything must first be intelligible. Often this thought is no more than a snobbish rationalization of reality. This is why, for Nietzsche, Socrates is "the first genius of decadence. He opposes the idea to life, he judges himself in terms of the idea" (Deleuze [1962] 1982: 13-14).

Euripides has integrated this decadence into his plays and into aesthetics: "It was Euripides's disposition to dislike whatever was 'ambiguous and subterranean' and to excise every powerful Dionysiac element from tragedy and to rebuild it, purified and new, upon the foundation of non-Dionysiac art, morality and outlook" (Danto 1965: 57). However, "Euripides did not succeed in basing his drama solely on Apollonian principles [but] his un-Dionysian tendencies much rather led him astray into an inartistic naturalism" (Nietzsche 1976a: 112/149).

In many instances the Socratic agenda overlaps with the project that we today call "modernity", a project that was "a sworn enemy of contingency, variety, ambiguity, waywardness and idiosyncrasy, having declared on all such 'anomalies' a holy war of attrition" (Bauman 2000: 25). To "separate true knowledge from appearance and error seems to the Socratic man to be the noblest, even the single truly human vocation…" (Nietzsche 1976a: 129/180). Today, the Socratic, anti-tragic reality wears the face of globalization, the search for fun, as well as theatrical discourses of Disneyfication; and the World Wide Webbed Body, as an all-embracing imitative and anti-tragic second world, does certainly go hand-in-hand with this discourse.

The scientific spirit of Socrates that speaks through Euripides changes the constellation of all elements that are supposed to define reality. What matters now is no longer the cooperative opposition of Dionysus and Apollo but rather the self-righteous opposition of cold Socratic culture to "hot" Dionysianism. This is, as Nietzsche explains, how a "new comedy" became possible as well as the "middle-class mediocrity, on which Euripides built all his political hopes (...). Up to that point, in tragedy the semi-god and in comedy the intoxicated satyr or semi-human had determined the nature of the language" (104/134).

Nietzsche's shift from Socrates to Euripides expresses more or less what Sherry Turkle has formulated as computer culture moving from a culture of calculation to a culture of simulation (Turkle 1995: 19).

The parallel can also be easily reproduced within the framework of Wainwright's "pyrophilosophy" for which hot localities are "neutralized" by cold globalization or a sort of McWorld. Here, the concept of a Dionysian–Apollonian tragic middle-ground is lost. Nietzsche clearly defines the consequences, suggesting that the "bourgeois mediocrity" of a cold, state-sponsored cultural system advances to the status of unquestionable reality. The system of the "new comedy" promotes naturalism as much as optimism and bans all tragic Dionysian presentations. More precisely, it painstakingly distinguishes between "reality" and "appearance", the former being scientific and accepted and the latter being rejected for its scientific incorrectness. In this system there is little space for the notion of "artistic reality" or for that of "local reality" just as there is little space for myths; but there is plenty of space for imitation. Music, for example, will be "criminally turned into a mimetic demonstration of appearances, a battle or storm at sea, and in the process is totally robbed of all its power to create myths" (Nietzsche 1976a: 142/203). All this happens through Socrates' art-killing tendency.

Nietzsche saw the opera as the latest product of the Socratic European culture; a dramatic and imitative reproduction of reality excelling in the character of pleasurable play with form invented not by the artist but by the technically talented layman who "succeeded with alarming speed in stripping music of its Dionysian world meaning and stamping on it a formally playful and entertaining character" (158/232). Nietzsche's analysis of the spirit of the opera indeed shows amazing parallels with that of computer games as a caricature of dramatic, but anti-tragic, reality: "Thus what the features of opera express is not at all the elegiac pain caused by eternal loss but rather the cheerfulness of eternal re-discovery [*die Heiterkeit des ewigen Wiederfindens*]" (157/231). Nietzsche wanted to combat the ascetic ideal underlying this Socratic culture by advancing not only the Dionysian idea of the tragic but also the equally Dionysian one of innocence and games. Games are answerable to the idea of art as a form of play that has been emptied of its subjective components and which corresponds most correctly to Nietzsche's aesthetic sentiments: "The only subjective artist we know is the bad artist and the prime demand we make of every kind and level of art is the conquest of subjectivity, release and redemption from the I" (66/66). According to Hans-Georg Gadamer, play is not "the freedom of a subjectivity engaged at play, but the mode of being of the work of art itself" (Gadamer [1975] 1989: 101). The project of VR as it is conceived in computer games, on the other hand, can too easily appear as a typical manifestation of the "death of the tragic through reason".

It becomes clear that, from an anti-Platonic, Nietzschean point of view, nobody else but the theoretical, Socratic man could have invented VR as a place for fun, games, and control. Of course, this is only true for the dystopian side of VR that we will call Socratic. A confusion of Socratic dialectics with Nietzschean tragedy will necessarily lead to entirely wrong interpretations of Nietzsche's possible relationships with contemporary phenomena, a confusion that has been the focus of Allan Bloom's interpretation of a part of American Nietzsche scholarship. Bloom points out that though "Nietzsche sought with his value philosophy to restore the harsh conflicts for which men were willing to die, to restore the tragic sense of life at a moment when nature had been domesticated and men become tame", his "value philosophy was used in America for exactly the opposite purpose – to promote conflict-resolution, bargaining, harmony" (Bloom 1987: 228).

Twenty years later, Bloom's points can be clarified by reflecting Nietzsche's philosophy against the current culture of VR. The Socratic Virtual is compulsively fixated on technology by viewing it as a source of salvation from reality and turns its users into passive consumers by marrying them to a technological determinism that does not give them power, but makes them "virtually powerless". This is at least one way of seeing computer games; another way will be explored in the conclusion of this book. Here, the world appears as flattened through electronic representation and the self can become unstable, fragmented, and decentered. Individualism cannot subsist when all individuals melt into a single mass. The result is the kind of "electronic wanderer wired to the world but separated from much that matters in human life" (Slouka 1995: 132). Computer technology has been developed in order to improve global communication, but in many cases it has led to the isolation of individuals in their homes. This means that the individual "Will to Power" (through information) has created a comprehensive network of power by which the individual is subsequently swallowed until it retreats into fortified technologized private worlds.

Nietzsche found not only that the Socratic principle turns the world into a technologically mediated representation; he also found that the Dionysian element, as long as it is not compromised by the Apollonian, will break the *principuum individuationis* and swallow up all individual rationality, creating "another world" reminiscent of a private VR that is disconnected from all social life. The solution to the paradox is that it should not be solved, but maintained in a tragic fashion: the Dionysian man stays close to reality only through the dream-like element of the Apollonian refusing to accept the "death of the tragic through reason". While Dionysus is suffering, Apollo is the element which overcomes the suffering of the individual by the radiant glorification of eternity. Again, this is not dialectical as both the Dionysian and the Apollonian are supposed to subsist in the process.

There is indeed a version of VR that can be characterized as "Dionysian–Apollonian": VR is separate from the real yet it is also part of it and this paradox needs to be affirmed. Here is the answer: critical cyberculture studies should not give in to excessive and uncritical transcendentalism, nor should they see VR as a purely operational phenomenon. According to Ken Hillis, "optical technologies such as VR clearly have utilitarian applications; however, in no way do these applications preclude VR from being positioned within "the social imaginary as a transcendence device" (1999: xx). This means that not only is real life often like VR, but VR is often like real life. One of the reasons is that technology is "always already infected by social, political, theoretical, and ethical assumptions" (58). Terrorist groups recruit members on Second Life. Second Life communities and online relations are determined by cultural mores valid in the real world. We even care about those virtual worlds in ethical terms, as philosophers working on computer ethics have shown (Spence 2012; Sicart 2009). This means that on the one hand, computer games are "posthuman" because the hardware or the avatar is merely a "prosthetic telepresence" (Rune 2012) and not a real human being. On the other hand, gaming sets up social and economic worlds in which "real" banks, computer organizations, shops, and universities can have branches. Companies specialize in the production of in-game gold that can be sold on e-Bay and some "players" employed by those companies receive real money. Hundreds of Web sites sell "WoW Gold" and provide "Gold Farming" or "Gold Mining." Games like WoW and EverQuest are "extensions of physical economies into our own ideological imaginaries, much like movies and television before them" (Golumbia 2009: 196).

It is necessary to distinguish, like Hillis, between VR and "virtual environments". If we chose the latter term, it becomes impossible to reduce the reality of those games to images. This means that in virtual existence there remains an awareness of corporeal existence linked to the real world. VR is thus not a disconnected realm but is integrated into a life that can appears as an event as tragic (though also as playful) as life itself. According to Hickey-Moody and Wood, Second Life communities can foster diversity and act as alternatives to the capitalist economy (807–809). Consequently, Philip Rosedale, Founder and Chief Executive Officer of Linden Lab, even suggests that participation in Second Life does not lead to self-virtualization, but rather to self-actualization: "There is a very strong sense that you are in a way becoming more of yourself" (US Government Printing Office 2008: 67). Research by Turkle has shown that the redefinition of the self as a "multiple, distributed system" (1995: 14) is not necessarily negative as long as it does not enter an 'autistic' circuit of virtual self-sufficiency.

As long as the computer is used as an evocative object, it can function as a new location for our fantasies. Even psychologically challenged individuals can engage in constructive role playing in Second Life (188). As mentioned, autistic children can benefit from playing certain video games. In 2000, "some disgruntled employees in the Philippines wrote a virus program that disrupted governments and economies across the globe. With the Internet, Goliath is having fits with David" (Poster 2002: 16). Another example of this is "Wikileaks for Transparency", which published an entire repository of classified material that is embarrassing for world leaders. The boundaries between the real and the virtual are eroding which is – tragic. But this is the only chance we have to derive positive qualities from VR. The undialectical coexistence of Dionysian suffering combined with Apollonian glorification of eternity must oppose purely technical, Socratic forms of VR.

# Conclusion

This book finishes with a somewhat promising distinction between Dionysian-Apollonian and Socratic forms or understandings of VR, hoping that the latter will not take over. It remains to be verified whether this optimism is justified. VR has been presented as a realm not real but which cannot be dismissed as unreal either. VR is not just an alternative reality, but its existence influences the relationships between subjects as well as the relationships between subjects and objects. As a result, reality itself can no longer be seen as a stable platform. The "human" becomes similarly unstable under the impact of VR, not only because it is prone to all sorts of combinations and hybridizations, but also because VR has an impact on the perception of consciousness and the body. This book has dealt with the interference of computer representations with individual imagination; with shifts in embodied experience through VR; and, to borrow a phrase from Katherine Hayles , with "the penetration of computational processes (...) into the construction of reality itself" (2006: 161). It has been shown that there is no reason to oppose this per se. Rather, what is required is the correct management of a paradox already anticipated by Nietzsche, which was the topic of the last chapter. At the bottom of all those analyses lurks Braidotti's question: "How can we stop the posthuman from becoming inhuman(e)?" (Braidotti: 187).

Looking into the future, it appears that not only will virtual environments or so-called social worlds like Second Life play an increasingly important role, but so will more formally oriented computer games. A VR compatible with Dionysian–Apollonian principles is indeed feasible. While social worlds have merely a few rules of conduct and are not created for game play, computer games employ formal patterns proper to analog games such as explicit goals and a certain game mechanics like character levels. Those games clearly function like games though their social functions differ very much from those of conventional games. During the last decade, computer games have not only economically overtaken traditional media like film or television in many respects but have also become a driving force in creating new social networks and new forms of social interaction. The growing attention computer games receive from several academic fields is to a large extent due to the fact that they no longer represent a self-enclosed second reality. Like virtual environments, Massive Multiplayer Online Games (MMOs) or Massively Multiplayer Online Role-Playing Games (MMORPGs) can involve large numbers of people situated around the globe cooperating and interacting in unprecedented ways. Above that, compared with traditional games, they often develop through complex narratives. This means that in those games an interactive global structure perpetuates itself in the form of an open narrative. We reencounter several topics here that have been addressed in the present book.

The combination of the video games' media structure with ludic formal patterns produces a strange reality effect. Some scholars have found that computer games occupy a halfway place between traditional representational media and traditional rule based games (Juul 2005). Even in formal games like FPS (First Person Shooter) games, play and work become fused as "many of the programs we call video games today much more nearly resemble something like work" (Golumbia 2009: 179).

Paradoxically, the Socratic-reasonable wins here over the image: there is "too much work" involved, to the point that Golumbia criticizes those games not for overengaging young people into too much play but for replacing play with work. This "play" is not stimulative and imaginative (196–197) as players can even "buy" themselves into games by purchasing higher level characters with real money instead of going through the process of ingame upgrading.

In any case, gameplay is no longer a geographically or psychologically separate sphere of activity but interrelated with many other forms of experience. This is why Johan Huizinga's metaphor of the "magic circle" has become a hotly debated topic in contemporary game studies. Huizinga's intention in his classical study defining games (*Homo Ludens*, 1955) was to articulate a spatial boundary between games and the real world. Today, many researchers find that the notion of play has been revised to the point that the game's space can no longer be seen as confined by such a magic circle (Larsen 2012; Taylor 2006, 2007). The criticism hitting Huizinga might be unjustified because Huizinga saw the boundary of these "temporary worlds within the ordinary world" (Huizinga: 10) as metaphorical. What matters is that inside the circle we find "a temporary, a limited perfection" (ibid.). It is possible to see non-game activities *as games*, which means that the circle is not drawn in a physical fashion. In this sense, the magic circle concept already projects a great deal of the fusion of game and non-game activities that we observe today. Culture or even war (Huizinga: 210) contain ritualistic elements traceable to games. Huizinga is thus in agreement with the existence of relative boundaries: his strategy is not to confine games to a physically existing playground, but play is essentially interrelated with other forms of experience (see also Juul 2008 and Dibbell 2006, 59-60 on this). The magic circle is not absolute but it has degrees.

No matter how we decide to evaluate Huizinga's position within this discourse, computer games show that through VR, the distinct division between reality as a serious and useful undertaking, and play as its contrary, is not a stable one. Or, as Calleja says, "play is an intractable manifestation of reality" (Calleja 2012: 81). Huizinga's idea of play is thus more pragmatic than has often been assumed. It is not that far removed from Thomas Malaby's definition of games as "social artifacts that are always in the process of becoming [and] grounded in human practice and as fundamentally processual" (Malaby 2007: 96).

The reproach that games turn users into passive consumers by marrying them to a determinism, a reproach that has been clinging to the gaming activity ever since, becomes more ambiguous. Traditionally, games have suffered from the same criticism that mass art had to confront. Playing a game seems to be more passive than, for example, reading a book. The players "don't do anything" but are simply hedonistically consuming the game. Playing is not a "real" activity because games are – "just games". However, the player is also *actively* playing. She might be found passive and even autistic with regard to the extra-ludic world, but *in* the game she is socially engaged, open towards others, imaginative... Especially MMORPGs demand "intimate and profound engagement from individual users" (Golumbia 196). What sounds like a sophism becomes crucial in contemporary gaming activities as the ludic and the non-ludic, the real and the non-real become more and more merged. In the future, this fusion of games with reality, plus the more and more pronounced interactive character of computer games might turn out to be one more powerful force shifting VR away from the technical, Socratic VR. In order to win a game, the player "must battle the adversaries they find in that world, scrounge for resources, and interact with the gameworld inhabitants through conversation ..." writes Grant Tavinor (2009). This paradox, which lets the computer game simultaneously appear as a fictional form (see Atkins 2003) and as a social activity comes close to the unification of the Apollonian and Dionysian that has been discussed in the last chapter. To this must be added the fact that some games are rather like toys because they can be transformed by the players and used for different ends. Will Wright, the creator of the open-ended city-building game *SimCity* points out that what attracts people to this game is that "it forces you to determine the goals. So when you start SimCity, one of the most interesting things that happens is that you have to decide, 'What do I want to make'?" (in Henthorne 2003: 65).

Finally, games are not only played, but also replayed. The play and replay possibilities offer possibilities of open narratives. Since the same subject can be approached from different narrative angles, the interactor's choices produce an aperspectival world evoking Gebser's deconstruction of the logocentric antithesis of perspectival and unperspectival seeing. Tavinor speaks of the "immense depth and replay value of such open-world games: whereas a linear first-person shooter may be finished in ten or so hours, open-world games can support hundreds of hours of gameplay" (Tavinor 2009).

Of course one should not be naïve and believe that this is true for all games. In FPS games, complex narratives are missing. Golumbia confirms that "few people play computer games for their narrative richness or for their resemblance to the complex human events at the representation of which novels, films, and even television have always been adept" (Golumbia: 186). The typically *human* engagement with narratives in literature appears rather like a *posthuman* sequence of events. However, conservative and moralistic motives based on the apparent opposition between technological development and human nature à la Fukuyama are overcome in a Nietzschean way, without embracing transhumanist developments of a new digital species as a world with fantastic new potential.

# Bibliography


Aarseth, Espen. 1997. *Cybertext*. Baltimore: Johns Hopkins University Press.

Abbot, Porter. 2002. *The Cambridge Introduction to Narrative*. Cambridge: Cambridge University Press.

Allison, Anne. 2004. 'Cuteness as Japan's Millennial Product' in J. Tobin (ed.), *Pikachu's Global Adventure: The Rise and Fall of Pokémon*. Durham: Duke University Press, 34–52.

Appadurai, Arjun. 1990. 'Disjuncture and Difference in the Global Cultural Economy' in Mike Featherstone: *Nationalism, Globalization and Modernity*, London: Sage, 295–310.

Areopagite. 1980. *The Divine Names and Mystical Theology*. Milwaukee: Marquette University Press.

Astruc, Alexandre. 1968. 'The Birth of a new Avant-Garde: La Caméra-Stylo' in Peter Graham, ed., *The New Wave*. London: Secker and Warburg, 17–23.

Atkin, Barry. 2003. *More Than a Game: The Computer Game as Fictional Form*. Manchester: Manchester University Press.

Augier, Natalie. 2006. 'The Cute Factor' in *New York Times* Jan. 3.

Aunger, Robert. 2000. *Darwinizing Culture: The Status of Memetics as a Science*. Oxford: Oxford University Press.

Ayfre, Amédé. 1969. *Le Cinéma et sa vérité*. Paris: Cerf.

Bachelard, Gaston. 1942. *L'Eau et les rêves*. Paris: Corti.

Bagby, Philip. 1959. *Culture and History: Prolegomena to the Comparative Study of Civilizations*. Berkeley and Los Angeles: University of California Press.

Baillie, Harold & T. Casey (eds.). 2005. *Is Human Nature Obsolete? Genetics, Bioengineering, and the Future of the Human Condition*. Cambridge MA: MIT Press.

Baillie, Harold. 2005. 'Aristotle and Genetic Engineering: The Uncertainty of Excellence' in Baillie & Casey, 209–232.

Ballard, J. G. 1984. 'Interview' by Lynn Barber. Reprinted in Re/Search 8-9, 157.

Barber, Benjamin R. 1995. *Jihad vs. McWorld*. New York: Times Books.

Baron, N. S. 1998. 'Letters by Phone or Speech by Other Means: The Linguistics of Email' in *Language and Communication* 18, 133–170.

Barthes, Roland. 1957. 'La nouvelle Citroën' in *Mythologies*. *Œuvres complètes* I. Paris: Seuil, 140–42. Engl.: *Mythologies*, trans. A. Lavers. New York: Farrar, Strauss and Giroux, 1972, 91–93.

Bartneck, C., T. Suzuki et al. 2007. 'People's Culture and Prior Experiences with Aibo Towards Robots' in *AI Society – The Journal of Human-Centered Systems* 21: 1-2, 217–230.

Bary Theodore et. al. 1964. *Sources of Japanese Tradition*. New York: Columbia University Press.

Baudrillard, Jean. 1986. *Amérique*. Paris: Grasset.

———. 1993 [1976]. *Symbolic Exchange and Death*. London: Sage.

Bauman, Zygmunt. 2000. *Liquid Modernity*. Cambridge: Polity Press.

———. 2007. *Liquid Times: Living in an Age of Uncertainty*. Cambridge: Polity Press.

Bavelier, D. C., C. S. Green, D. H. Han, P. F. Renshaw, M. M. Merzenich, and D. A. Gentile. 2011. 'Brains on Video Games' in *Nature Review of Neuroscience* 12: 12, 763–68.

Bazin, André. 1961. *Qu'est-ce que le cinéma? I, II, III*. Paris: Cerf.

Benedikt, Michael. 1991. *Cyberspace: First Steps*. Cambridge, MA: MIT Press.

Benjamin, Andrew. 1991. *Art, Mimesis and the Avant-Garde*. London: Routledge.

Benjamin, Walter. 1982. 'Paris, die Hauptstadt de XIX Jahrhunderts' in *Gesammelte Werke* ed. by R. Tiedemann & H. Schweppenhäuser, Bd. V, 1. Frankfurt: Suhrkamp.

———. 1982b. 'Passagenwerk' in *Gesammelte Werke*, Bd. I. Frankfurt: Suhrkamp.

Berdyaev, Nicolai A. 1930. 'Iz etiudov o ya beme: etiud 1. Uchenie ob ungrunde i svobodie' (Studies Concerning Jacob Böhme Etude I: The Teaching about the Ungrund and Freedom) in *Put'* 20, 47–79.

Bergson, Henri. 1888. *Essais sur les données immédiates de la conscience*. Paris: Presses univesitaires françaises.

———. 1907. *L'Evolution créatrice*. Paris: Alcan. Engl.: *Creative Evolution* (trans. A. Mitchell). New York: The Modern Library, 1944.

———. 1939. *Matière et mémoire*. Paris: PUF.

———. 1940. *Le Rire*. Paris: Presses univesitaires françaises.

Bettelheim, Bruno. 1967. *The Empty Castle: Infantile Autism and the Birth of the Self*. New York: Free Press.

Binswanger, Ludwig. 1957. *Le Cas Suzanne Urban. Etude sur la schizophrénie*. Paris: Desclée de Brouwer.

Bjorkman, Stig, et al. 1970. *Bergman om Bergman*. Stockholm: Norstedt.

Bloom, Allan. 1987. *The Closing of the American Mind*. New York: Simon & Schuster.

Bobrinskoy, Boris. 2001. 'L'Icône: Objet d'art ou de culte?' in Saint Jean Damascène: *L'Icône: Objet d'art ou objet de culte?* Paris: Cerf.

Bornoff, Nicolas. 2002. 'Sex and Consumerism: The Japanese State of the Art' in Lloyd, Fran (ed.) *Consuming Bodies: Sex and Contemporary Japanese Art*. London: Reaktion Books.

Bostrom, Nick. 2005. 'A History of Transhumanist Thought' in *Journal of Evolution and Technology* 14: 1, 1–25. Also available at http://www.nickbostrom.com/ papers/ history.pdf

Botz-Bornstein, Thorsten. 2002. 'Khora or Idyll: The Space of the Dream' in *The Philosophical Forum* 33:2, 173–194.

———. 2004. *Place and Dream: Japan and the Virtual*. Amsterdam, New York: Rodopi.

———. 2007. *Films and Dreams Tarkovsky, Bergman, Sokurov, Kubrick, Wong Kar-wai*. Lanham: Lexington-Rowman & Littlefield.

———. 2007b. 'Dreams in Buddhism and Western Aesthetics: Some Thoughts on Play, Style, and Space' in *Asian Philosophy* 17:1, 65–81.

———. 2008. *Space in Russia and Japan: A Comparative Philosophical Study*. Lanham: Lexington-Rowman & Littlefield.

———. 2009. *Aesthetics and Politics of Space in Russia and Japan: A Comparative Philosophical Study*. Lanham: Lexington-Rowman & Littlefield.

———. 2011. *The Cool-Kawaii: Afro-Japanese Aesthetics and New World Modernity*. Lanham: Lexington-Rowman & Littlefield.

Bourdieu, Pierre. 1984. *Distinction: A Social Critique of the Judgement of Taste*. London: Routledge and Kegan Paul.
Bouterwek, Friedrich. 1799. *Idee einer Apodiktik*, 2 vols. Halle: Renger.
———. 1800. *Anfangsgründe der spekulativen Philosophie: Versuch eines Lehrbuchs.* Göttingen: Dietrich, [Brussels: Culture et Civilisation, 1968].
———. 1802. *Epochen der Vernunft nach der Idee der Apodiktik: Eine gemeinnützige Anmerkung zum Quodlibet der neuesten Philosophie*. Brussels: Culture et Civilisation, 1968.
———. 1804 [1976]. *Geschichte der spanischen Poesie und Beredsamkeit*. Hildesheim, New York: Olms.
———. 1805 [1976]. *Ästhetik.* Hildesheim, New York: Olms.
Braidotti, Rosi. 2013. *The Posthuman*. Cambridge: Polity Press.
Braudel Fernand. 1969. *Ecrits sur l'histoire.* Paris: Flammarion. Engl.: 'On the History of Civilizations: The Past Explains the Presence' in *On History.* Chicago University Press, 1980.
Breton, Philippe and Serge Proulx. 1991. *L'Explosion de la communication.* Paris: Découverte.
Breton, Philippe. 1992. *L'Utopie de la communication*. Paris: Découverte.
Broch, Hermann. 1975. 'Notes on the Problem of Kitsch' in Dorfles, 49–76.
Brook, Peter. 1968. *The Empty Space*. New York: Touchstone.
Brower, Robert & Earl Miner. 1962. *Japanese Court Poetry*. London: Cresset.
Buber, Martin. 1962-64. *Ich und Du* (Werke, Vol. 1). München: Kösel.
Buchloh, Benjamin. 2001. 'Andy Warhol's One-Dimensional Arts: 1956-1966' in A. Michelson (ed.) *Andy Warhol*. Cambridge MA: MIT Press, 1–46.
Buruma, Ian and Avishai Margalit. 2004. *Occidentalism: The West in the Eyes of its Enemies*. New York: Penguin.
Buruma, Ian. 1984. *Behind the Mask*. New York: Pantheon Books.
Butler, Rex. 2007. 'Two Warhols' in Andy Warhol [catalogue]. South Brisbane: Queensland Art Gallery, 60–69.
Caldwell, John. 1992. 'Jeff Koons: The Way we Live Now' in Jeff Koons. San Francisco: The San Francisco Museum of Modern Art, 9–14.
Calinescu, Matei. 1987. *Five Faces of Modernity*. Durham: Duke University Press.
Calleja, Gordon. 2012. 'Erasing the Magic Circle' in Sageng, John R., Hallvard Fossheim and Tarjei M. Larsen (eds.). *The Philosophy of Computer Games.* Dordrecht: Springer, 77–93.
Callus, Ivan & Stefan Herbrechter. 2015 (forthcoming). *Critical Posthumanism: An Introduction.* Amsterdam & New York: Rodopi.
Celent, Germano. 1998. 'Mariko Mori: Eternal Present' in Mariko Mori: Dream Temple. Milano: Fondazione Prada.
Chalmers, David. 2005. 'The Matrix as Metaphysics' in Grau (ed.), 132–176.
Clark, Andy. 2005. 'The Twisted Matrix: Dream, Simulation, or Hybrid?' in Grau (ed.), 177–197.
Clarke, Bruce. 2008. *Posthuman Metamorphosis: Narrative and Systems*. New York: Fordham University Press.
Clore, Gerald L. & Andrew Ortony. 1988. 'The Semantics of the Affective Lexicon' in Vernon Hamilton, Gordon H Brower, Nico H Frijda (eds.) *Cognitive Perspectives on Emotion and Motivation.* Dordrecht: Kluwer, 365–379.
Cox, Christoph. 2005. 'Nietzsche, Dionysus, and the Ontology of Music' in Keith Ansell Pearson (ed.), *A Companion to Nietzsche*. Oxford: Blackwell, 495–513
Danto, Arthur. 1965. *Nietzsche as a Philosopher.* New York: Macmillian.

Davis, Mike & Bertrand Monk (eds.). 2007. *Dreamworlds of Neoliberalism: Evil Paradises*. New York: New Press, 495–513.

Deleuze, Gilles & Félix Guattari. 1975. *Kafka. Pour une littérature mineure*. Paris: Minuit. Engl.: Kafka: *Toward a Minor Literature* (trans. D. Polan). Minneapolis : Minnesota University Press, 1986.

Deleuze, Gilles. 1966. *Le Bergsonisme*. Paris: PUF. Engl.: *Bergsonism* (trans. H. Tomlinson and B. Habberjam). New York: Zone Books, 1988.

———. 1980. *Capitalisme et schizophrénie vol. 1: mille plateaux*. Paris: PUF. Eng.: *Capitalism and Schizophrenia: A Thousand Plateaus* (trans. B. Massumi). Minneapolis : Minnesota University Press, 1987.

———. 1972. *Capitalisme et schizophrénie vol. 2: L'Anti-Œdipe*. Paris: Minuit. Eng.: *Capitalism and Schizophrenia: Anti-Œdipus* (trans. R. Hurley, M. Seem and H. R. Lane). London and New York: Continuum, 2004.

———. 1982 [1962]. *Nietzsche and Philosophy*. New York: Columbia University Press.

———. 1994. *Difference and Repetition*. New York: Columbia University Press.

Descartes, René. 1985. *Meditations on First Philosophy*. Cambridge: Cambridge University Press.

Dibbell, Julian. 2006. *Play Money: Or, how I Quit my Day Job and Made Millions Trading Virtual Loot*. New York: Basic Books.

Doi, Takeo. 1973. *The Anatomy of Dependence*. New York, London, Tokyo: Kodansha.

Dorfles, Gillo. 1975. *Kitsch: The World of Bad Taste*. New York: Bell.

Drancy, Jonathan. 1985. *Introduction to Contemporary Epistemology*. Oxford: Blackwell.

Elias, Norbert. 1969. *Über den Prozess der Zivilisation* Bd. I. München & Bern: Francke.

———. 1998. 'The Kitsch Style and the Age of Kitsch' in J. Goudsblom & S. Mennel (eds.), *The Norbert Elias Reader*. Oxford: Blackwell, 26–35.

Ellul, Jacques. 1991. *L'Explosion de la communication*. Paris: Découverte.

Espagne, Michel. 2004. *En deça du Rhin: L'Allemagne des philosophes français au XIXe siècle*. Paris: Cerf.

———. 1988. 'Friedrich Bouterweks "Kritische Geschichte der Philosophie". Ein Pariser Manuskript' in *Archiv für Geschichte der Philosophie* 70:3, 280–304.

Esposito, Scott. 2013. 'An Interview with Ottilie Mulzet' in *Music and Literature* 2, 108–127.

Falzon, Chris. 2006. 'Philosophy and the Matrix' in Diocaretz & Herbrechter (eds.), *The Matrix in Theory*. Amsterdam & New York: Rodopi, 97–113.

Fédida, Pierre. 1961. 'Autoérotisme et autisme: Conditions d'efficacité d'un paradigme en psychopathologie', in *Revue Internationale de Psychopathologie* 1990: 2.

Fink, Eugen. 1960. *Spiel als Weltsymbol*. Stuttgart: Kohlhammer.

Fogarsi, George. 1997. 'All that is Solidu Melts into Kitty' in *CTheory: Theory, Technology and Culture* 20:3, Article 55.

Foucault, Michel. 1961. *Folie et déraison*. Paris: Plon. Engl.: *Madness and Civilization: A History of Insanity in the Age of Reason* (trans. R. Howard). New York: Vintage, 1965.

Fox Keller, Evelyn. 2000. *The Century of the Gene*. Cambridge MA: Harvard University Press.

Fukuyama, Francis: 1992. *The End of History and the Last Man*. New York: Free Press.

———. 2002. *Our Posthuman Future: Consequences of the Biotechnology Revolution*. New York: Farrar, Straus & Giroux.

Gadamer, Hans-Georg. 1975. *Truth and Method*. New York: Continuum.

Gaudin, Thierry. 1984. *Les Pouvoirs du rêve*. Paris: CRCT.

Gebser, Jean. 1985. *The Ever-Present Origin*. Athens, London: University of Ohio Press.

Gelbart, William M. 1998. 'Databases in Genomic Research' in *Science* 282, 659–661.

Giesz, Ludwig. 1975. 'Phenomenology of Kitsch' in Dorfles, 156–174.

Gilson, Marc. 1998. 'A Brief History of Japanese Robophilie' in *Leonardo* 31: 15, 1998, 367–369.

Goethe, Johan Wolfgang. 1963a [1829]. 'Analyse und Synthese' *Hamburger Ausgabe* Vol. 13 (Naturwissenschaftliche Schriften). Hamburg: Wegener.

———. 1963b. *Maximen und Reflexionen*. München: Deutscher Taschenbuch Verlag. Engl.: *The Maxims and Reflections of Goethe* (trans. B. Saunders). New York: Macmillan, 1906. Available on Project Gutenberg: http://www.gutenberg.org/files /33670/33670-h/33670-h.htm

———. 1817. 'Morphologie' in *Naturwissenschaftliche Schriften* (Vol. 13). München: Beck. Engl.: *Morphology*. Available on zeno.org: http://www.zeno.org/Literatur/M/Goethe,+Johann+Wolfgang/Naturwissenschaftliche+Schriften/Morphologie

———. 1999. *Sämtliche Werke* (Frankfurter Ausgabe) Band 22: *Ästhetische Schriften 1824-1832. Über Kunst und Altertum*.

Goldschmidt, Victor. 1982. *Temps physique et temps tragique chez Aristote*. Paris: Vrin.

Golumbia, David. 2009. 'Games without Play' in *New Literary History* 40: 1, 179–204.

Gomarasca, Alessandro. 2001. *Poupées et robots: La culture pop japonaise*. Paris: Autrement.

Gombrich, Ernst. 1960. *Art and Illusion: A Study in the Psychology of Pictorial Representation*. London: Phaidon.

Graham, Elaine L. 2002. *Representations of the Post/Human: Monsters, Aliens, and Others in Popular Culture*. New Brunswick: Rutgers.

Granger, Gilles-Gaston. 1995. *Le Probable, le possible et le virtuel. Essai sur le rôle du non-actuel dans la pensée objective*. Paris: Odile Jacob.

———. 1988. *Essai d'une philosophie de style*. Paris: Odile Jacob.

Grau, Christopher (ed.). 2005. *Philosophers Explore the Matrix*. Oxford: Oxford University Press.

Gray, Chris Hables. 2001. *Cyborg Citizen: Politics in the Posthuman Age*. New York: Routledge.

Greenberg, Clement. 1986-93 [1961]. 'Avantgarde and Kitsch' in *Collected Essays and Criticism* Vol. 1. Chicago: Chicago University Press, 5–22.

Guattari, Félix. 1979. *L'Inconscient machinique*. Paris: Recherches.

Habermas, Jürgen. 2003. *The Future of Human Nature*. Oxford: Polity Press.

Halberstam, Edith & Ira Livingston. 1995. *Posthuman Bodies*. Bloomington: Indiana University Press.

Haraway, Donna. 1994. 'The Cyborg Manifesto: Science, Technology, and Socialist Feminism in the 1980s' [first published in 1985] in Steven Seidman, *The*

*Postmodern Turn: New Perspectives on Social Theory*. Cambridge: Cambridge University Press, 82–115.
Harootunian, Harry and Tetsuo Najita. 1988. 'Japanese Revolt against the West: Political and Cultural Criticism in the Twentieth Century' in Peter Duus (ed.) *The Cambridge History of Japan*. Cambridge, MA: Cambridge University Press, 711–774.
Hayles, N. Katherine. 1999. *How We Became Posthuman: Virtual Bodies in Cybernetics, Literature, and Informatics*. Chicago: Chicago University Press.
———. 2006. 'Unfinished Work: From Cyborg to Cognisphere' in *Theory Culture Society* 23, 159–168.
Hegel, Georg Wilhelm Friedrich. 1986. 'Bouterweks Anfangsgründe der der spekulativen Philosophie' in *Jenaer Schriften, Werke* Vol. 2. Frankfurt: Suhrkamp.
Heidegger, Martin. 1956. *An Introduction to Metaphysics*. New York: Anchor.
Heim, Michael. 1993. *The Metaphysics of Virtual Reality*. New York: Oxford University Press.
———. 1998. *Virtual Realism*. New York: Oxford University Press.
Heine, Steven. 1991. *A Dream Within a Dream*. New York: Lang.
Henthorne, Tom. 2003. 'Cyber-utopias: The Politics and Ideology of Computer Games' in *Studies in Popular Culture* 25: 3, 63–76.
Herbrechter, Stefan & Myriam Diocaretz (eds.). 2006. *The Matrix in Theory*. Amsterdam & New York: Rodopi.
Herbrechter, Stefan. 2013. *Posthumanism: A Critical Analysis*. London: A&C Black.
Hickey-Moody, Anna and Denise Wood. 2008. 'Virtually Sustainable: Deleuze and Desiring Differentiation in Second Life' in *Continuum: Journal of Media & Cultural Studies* 22:6, 805–816.
Hillis, Ken. 1999. *Digital Sensations: Space, Identity, and Embodiment in Virtual Reality*. Minneapolis: University of Minnesota Press.
Hjorth, Larissa. 2005. 'Odors of Mobility: Mobile Phones and Japanese Cute Culture in the Asia Pacific' in *Journal of Intercultural Studies* 26:1-2, 39–55.
Hochmann, Jacques. 1994. 'Cordélia ou le silence des sirènes: Une relecture de l'autisme infantile de Kanner' in Roger Perron & Denis Ribas (ed.): *Autismes de l'enfance*. Paris: PUF, 29–54.
Huizinga, Johan. 1970. *Homo Ludens*. London: Temple Smith.
Hunter, Graeme K. 2000. *Vital Forces: The Discovery of the Molecular Basis of Life*. London: Academic Press.
Huntington, Samuel. 1996. *The Clash of Civilizations and the Remaking of World Order*. London: Simon & Schuster.
Husserl, Edmund. 1954. *Die Krise der europäischen Wissenschaften*. Haag: Nijhoff.
Huxley, Aldous. 1946. *Brave New World*. New York: Modern Library.
Hyman, Timothy. 1976. '*Solaris*' in *Film Quarterly* 29:3, 54–58.
Illies, Florian. 2000. *Generation Golf*. Berlin: Argon.
Irving, William (ed.). 2002. *The Matrix and Philosophy Vol. 1*. London: Open Court.
———. (ed.). 2005. *The Matrix and Philosophy Vol. 2*. London: Open Court.
Itoh, Teiji (with T. Ikko and S. Tsune). 1993. *Wabi, Sabi, Suki: The Essence of Japanese Beauty*. Hiroshima: Mazda Motor Corp.
Izutsu, Toshiko & Toyo. 1981. *The Theory of Beauty in the Classical Aesthetics of Japan*. Haag: Nijnhoff.
Jacob, François. 1998. *Of Flies, Mice, and Men*. Cambridge MA: Harvard University Press.

James, William. 1985. *The Varieties of Religious Experience*. Cambridge MA: Harvard University Press.

Jameson, Frederic. 1986. 'Third-World Literature in the Era of Multinational Capitalism' in *Social Text* 15, 65–88.

Jankélévitch, Vladimir. 1959. *Henri Bergson*. Paris: PUF.

Jullien, François. 1985. *La Valeur allusive: des catégories originales de l'interprétation*. Paris: Ecole française d'Extrême Orient.

———. 1991. *Eloge de la fadeur: A partir de la pensée et de l'esthétique de la Chine*. Paris: Livre Poche.

Jung, Carl-Gustav. 1946. *Über psychische Energetik und das Wesen der Träume*. Zürich: Rascher.

Juul, Jesper. 2003. 'The Game, the Player, the World: Looking for a Heart of Gameness' in M. Copier and J. Raessens (eds.), *Level Up: Digital Games. Research Conference Proceedings*, Utrecht: Utrecht University, 30–45. http://www.jesperjuul.net/text/gameplayerworld/

Juul, Jesper. 2005. *Half Real: Videogames between Real Rules and Fictional Worlds.* Cambridge, MA: MIT Press.

Juul, Jesper. 2008. 'The Magic Circle and the Puzzle Piece' in S. Günzel, M. Liebe and D. Mersch (eds.), *Conference Proceedings of the Philosophy of Computer Games 2008*. Potsdam: Potsdam University Press.

Kang, Sangjung. 2005. 'The Imaginary Geography of a Nation and Denationalized Narrative' in Richard Calichman (ed.): *Contemporary Japanese Thought*. New York: Columbia University Press, 84–100.

Kant, Immanuel. 1929. Preface to the 2nd edition to the *Critique of Pure Reason*. Engl. transl. by Norman Kemp Smith; London & Basingstoke: Macmillian.

———. 1908. *Kritik der Urteilskraft* [Critique of Judgment]. Berlin: Reimer. Engl.: *Critique of Judgment* (trans. W. S. Pluhar). Indianapolis: Hackett, 1987.

Kaplan, Frédéric. 2004. 'Who is Afraid of the Humanoid? Investigating Cultural Differences in the Acceptance of Robots' in *International Journal of Humanoid Robotics* 1:3, 465–480.

Kass, Leon. 2001. 'Preventing a Brave New World: Why We Should Ban Cloning Now' in *The New Republic*, May 21, 30–39.

Kaufmann, Walter. 1968. *Tragedy and Philosophy*. Princeton: Princeton University Press.

Keen, Andrew. 2007. *The Cult of the Amateur: How Today's Internet is Killing our Culture*. New York: Doubleday.

Keene, Donald. 1988. *The Pleasures of Japanese Literature*. New York: Columbia University Press.

Kimmerle, Heinz & Henk Oosterling (eds.). 2000. *Sensus communis in Multi- and Intercultural Perspective*: *On the Possibility of Common Judgments in Arts and Politics*. Würzburg: Königshausen & Neumann.

Kinsella, Sharon. 1995. 'Cuties in Japan' in Lise Skov & Brian Moeran (eds.), *Women, Media and Consumption in Japan*. Honolulu: Hawaii University Press, 220–254. Article available on Sharon Kinsella's research website.

Klevjer, Rune. 2012. 'Enter the Avatar: The Phenomenology of Prosthetic Telepresence in Computer Games' in Sageng, John R., Hallvard Fossheim and Tarjei M. Larsen (eds.). *The Philosophy of Computer Games*. Dordrecht: Springer, 17–38.

Koelwel, Eduard. 1937. 'Kitsch und Schwäb' in *Mutterprache* 52, 58–60.

Komparu, Kunio. 1983. *The Noh Theatre: Principles and Perspectives*. New York & Tokyo: Weatherhill.

Koons, Jeff. 1992a. *Jeff Koons*. San Francisco: The San Francisco Museum of Modern Art.

Koons, Jeff. 1992b. *The Jeff Koons Handbook*. New York: Rizzoli.

Kracauer, Siegfried. 1973. *Theorie des Films*. Frankfurt: Suhrkamp.

Krauss, Lawrence M. 2002. 'Cosmological Gravity' in *Scientific American* (issue: 'The Once and Future Cosmos') 12:2.

Kroker, Arthur & Michael Weinstein. 1994. 'The Hyper-Texted Body, Or Nietzsche Gets a Modem' in *CTheory*: *An International Journal of Theory, Technology and Culture,* November 24.

La Mettrie, Julien Offray de. 1865. *L'Homme machine*. Paris: Henry.

Laurel, Brenda. 1991. 'Virtual Reality Design: A Personal View' in S.K. Helsel & J. Roth (eds.): *Virtual Reality: Theory, Practice and Promise* Westport & London: Meckler, 95–99.

Lawrence, Matt. 2004. *Like a Splinter in Your Mind: The Philosophy behind the Matrix Trilogy*. Oxford: Blackwell.

Leboyer, Marion. 1985. *Autisme infantile: Faits et modèles*. Paris: PUF.

Lem, Stanislav. 1978. *Solaris*. New York: Harcourt, Brace & Company.

Lenson, David. 1987. *The Birth of Tragedy*. Boston: Twayne.

Levy, Pierre. 1994. *L'Intelligence collective: pour une anthropologie du cyberspace*. Paris: La Découverte.

Lewinter, Roger. 1972. 'Pans de mur jaune' in *Nouvelle Revue de Psychanalyse* 5 ('L'espace du rêve').

Lugg, Catherine A. 1999. *Kitsch: From Education to Public Policy*. New York and London: Falmer Press.

Lutzka, Sven. 2006. 'Simulacra, Simulation and *The Matrix*' in Herbrechter & Diocaretz, 114–130.

Lyotard, Jean-François. 1984. *The Postmodern Condition: A Report on Knowledge*. Minneapolis: Minnesota University Press.

———. 1991. *The Inhuman*. Standford: Stanford University Press.

Maine de Biran, Pierre-François. 1922. *Influence de l'habitude sur la faculté de penser*, in *Œuvres* Vol. II. Paris: Alcan. Engl.: *The Influence of Habit on the Faculty of Thinking*. Baltimore: Williams and Wilkins, 1930.

Malaby, Thomas M. 2007. 'Beyond Play: A New Approach to Games' in *Games and Culture* 2, 95–113.

Martin, Jean-Clet. 1996. *L'Image virtuelle: Essai sur la construction du monde*. Paris: Kimé.

Mazurek, M., P. Shattuck, M. Wagner, and B. Cooper. 2011. 'Prevalence and Correlates of Screen-Based Media Use Among Youths with Autism Spectrum Disorders' in *Journal of Autism and Developmental Disorders* 42: 8, 1757–1767. http://www.springerlink.com/content/984812t131480547. Last accessed 2/1/2015.

McVeigh, Brian. 2000. *Wearing Ideology: State, Schooling and Self-Presentation in Japan*. New York: Berg.

Meltzer, Donald. 1984. *Dream-Life. A Reexamination of the Psycho-analytical Theory and Technique*. Strach Tag: Clunie Press.

Michelis, Panayotis A. 1964. *An Aesthetic Approach to Byzantine Art*. London: Batsford.

Miller, Roy Andrew. 1982. *Japan's Modern Myth*. New York: Weatherhill.

Moravec, Hans. 1992. *Une Vie après la vie*. Paris: Odile Jacob.

Mori, Mariko. 1998. *Dream Temple*. Fondazione Prada, Milano.

Morris-Suzuki. Tessa. 1995. 'The Invention and Reinvention of Japanese Culture' in *The Journal of Asian Studies* 54: 3, 759–780.

Münsterberg, Hugo. 1964. *The Ceramic Art of Japan: A Handbook for Collectors*. North Clarendon: Tuttle.

Napier, Susan. 1998. 'Vampires, Psychic Girls, Plying Women and Sailor Scouts: Four Faces of the Young Female in Japanese Popular Culture' in D. P. Martinez (ed.): The World of Japanese Popular Culture: Gender, Shifting Boundaries and Global Cultures. Cambridge University Press, 91–109.

Newitz, Annalee. 1995. 'Magical Girls and Atomic Bomb Sperm: Japanese Animation in America' in *Film Quarterly,* December, 1–15.

Nietzsche, Friedrich. 1976a. *Die Geburt der Tragödie*. Stuttgart: Kröner. Engl.: *The Birth of Tragedy*, trans. Ian C. Johnston. New York: Plain Label Books 1956.

———. 1976b. *Gedanken zur Geburt der Tragödie*. Stuttgart: Kröner.

———. 1966-77. *Götzendämmerung* [in *KSA* 6]. München: Deutscher Taschenbuchverlag. Engl.: *Twilight of the Idols*. Oxford: Oxford University Press, 1998.

Nishida, Kitaro. 1970. *Fundamental Problems of Philosophy. The World of Action and the Dialectical World.* Tokyo: Sophia University Press.

Nitschke, Günter. 1995. 'From Ambiguity to Transparency: Unperspective, Perspective and Perspective Paradigms of Space' in *Supplement of Louisiana Revy* 35:3.

Ohashi, Ryôsuke. 1999. 'Phänomenologie der Noh-Maske' in *Japan im interkulturellen Dialog.* München: Iudicium.

Ohmae, Kenichi. 2000. *The Invisible Continent*. New York: Harper Business.

Okakura, Kakuzô. 1905. *Ideals of the East*. New York: Dutton.

Panofsky, Erwin. 1991. *Perspective as Symbolic Form*. New York: Zone Book.

Pearson, Keith Ansell. 1999. *Germinal Life: The Difference and Repetition of Deleuze*. London: Routledge.

Peat, David. 1990. *Einstein's Moon: Bell's Theorem and the Curious Quest for Quantum Reality.* Chicago: Contemporary Book.

Pepperell, Robert. 2003. *The Post-Human Condition: Consciousness Beyond the Brain.* Bristol and Portland OR: Intellect.

Perella, Stephen. 1998. 'Hypersurfaces: Social Fluxus' in John Beckmann, *The Virtual Dimension.* Princeton: Princeton Architectural Press, 286–291.

Piaget, Jean. 1978. *La Formation du symbole chez l'enfant*. Neuchâtel, Paris: Delachaux & Niestlé.

Pizzato, Mark. 2007. 'Nietzschean Neurotheater: Apollonian and Dionysian Spirits in the Brain Matters of *Our Town*' in May Ann Frese Witt (ed.), *Nietzsche and the Rebirth of the Tragic*. Madison: Farleigh Dickinson University Press.

Poster, Mark. 2001. *What's the Matter with the Internet?* Minneapolis: Minnesota University Press.

Poster, Mark. 2002. 'High-Tech Frankenstein, or Heidegger Meets Stelarc' in J. Zylinska (ed.) *Cyborg Experiments: The Extensions of the Body in the Media Age*. London: Continuum, 15–32.

Raku, Kichizaemon XV. 2000. 'Raku Tea Bowls: The Essence of the Form. The Evolution of Wabi' in *Raku Museum*. Kyoto: Raku Museum.

Relph, Edward. 1976. *Space and Spacelessness*. London: Pion.

Rice, Jeff. 2007. *The Rhetoric of Cool: Composition Studies and New Media*. Carbondale: Southern Illinois University Press.

Richie, Donald. 1992. *Lateral View: Essays on Culture and Style in Contemporary Japan*. Berkeley: Stone Bridge.

———. 2003. *The Image Factory: Fads and Fashions in Japan*. London: Reaktion Books.

Roach, Mary. 1999. 'Cute Inc.' in *Wired* 7:12. http://www. wired.com/wired/archive/ 7.12/cute.html

Robertson, Roland. 1992. *Globalization: Social Theory and Global Culture*. London: Sage.

Rodin, Auguste. 1911. *L'Art*. Paris: Grasset.

Roeper, Thomas. 1988. 'Formal and Substantive Features of Language Acquisition: Reflections on the Subset Principle and Parametric Variation' in S. Schiffer & S. Steele (eds.): *Cognition and Representation*. Westview: Boulder, 161–182.

Roman, Eric. 1975. 'Will, Hope, and the Noumenon' in *The Journal of Philosophy* 72:3, 59–77.

Rorty, Richard. 1989. *Contingency, Irony and Solidarity*. New York: Cambridge University Press.

Rosenblum, Robert. 1992. 'Notes on Jeff Koons' in R. Rosenblum (ed.), *The Jeff Koons Handbook*. New York: Rizzoli.

Rutter, Michael. 1978. 'Diagnostic et définition' in M. Rutter & E. Schopler (eds.) *L'Autisme: Une réevaluation des concepts et du traitement*. Paris: PUF.

Ryan, Marie-Laure. 2001. *Narrative as Virtual Reality: Immersion and Interactivity in Literature and Electronic Media*. Baltimore: John Hopkins Press.

Sagoff, Mark. 2005. 'Nature and Human Nature' in Bailly & Casey, 67–98.

Said, Edward. 1978. *Orientalism*. New York: George Borchardt.

Sakai, Naoki. 1997. *Translation and Subjectivity. On "Japan" and Cultural Nationalism*. Minneapolis: University of Minnesota Press.

Sato, Kumiko. 2004. 'How Information Technology Has (Not) Changed Feminism and Japanism: Cyberpunk in the Japanese Context' in *Comparative Literature Studies* 41:3, 335–355.

Schelling, F. W. J. 1982. *Texte zur Philosophie der Kunst*. Stuttgart: Reclam. Engl.: *Philosophy of Art*. Minnesota: University of Minneapolis Press.

———. 1967 [1798]. 'Ideen zu einer Philosophie der Natur als Einleitung in das Studium dieser Wissenschaften' in *Schriften von 1794-1798*. Darmstadt: Wissenschaftliche Buchgesellschaft. Engl.: *Ideas for a Philosophy of Nature*. Cambridge: Cambridge University Press, 1988.

Schneider, Eckhard. 2001. 'Surface and Reflection' in E. Schneider (ed.) Jeff Koons. Köln: König.

Schopenhauer, Arthur. 1948-1961. *Über die vierfache Wurzel des Satzes vom zureichenden Grunde* in *Sämtliche Werke* Bd. 7. Wiesbaden: Brockhaus. Engl.: *On the Fourfold Root of the Principle of Sufficient Reason*. La Salle: Open Court. 1974.

Schopenhauer, Arthur. 1978-1982. *Die Welt als Wille und Vorstellung I* (in *Sämtliche Werke* ed. by W. Löhneysen, Vol. 1). Darmstadt: Cotta-Insel. Engl.: *The World as Will and Representation*. New York: Dover, 1969.

Schrödinger, Erwin. 1956. *What is Life and Other Essays*. New York: Doubleday.

Sennett, Richard. 1998. *The Corrosion of Character: The Personal Consequences of Work in the New Capitalism*. New York & London: Norton.

Sfez, Lucien. 1990. *Critique de la communication*. Paris: Seuil.

Shigematsu, Setsu. 1999. 'Dimensions of Desire: Sex, Fantasy, and Fetish in Japanese Comics' in in John A. Lent (ed.). *Themes and Issues in Asian Cartooning:*

*Cute, Cheap, Mad, and Sexy*. Bowling Green: Bowling Green State University Popular Press, 127–163.

Shiokawa, Kanako. 1999. 'Cute but Deadly: Women and Violence in Japanese Comics' in John A. Lent (ed.). *Themes and Issues in Asian Cartooning: Cute, Cheap, Mad, and Sexy*. Bowling Green: Bowling Green State University Popular Press, 93–126.

Sicart, Miguel. 2009. *The Ethics of Computer Games*. Cambridge, MA: MIT Press.

Simon, Bart. 2003. 'Introduction: Toward a Critique of Posthuman Futures' in *Cultural Critique* 53 (special issue 'Critical Posthumanism'), 1–9.

Slouka, Mark. 1995. *War of the Worlds*. New York: Basic Books.

Smith, Donald L. 1974. 'Ribbing Engrish: Innovative Borrowing in Japanese' in *American Speech* 49:3/4, 185–196.

Springer, Claudia. 1996. *Electronic Eros: Bodies and Desires in the Post-industrial Age*. Austin: University of Texas Press.

Standage, Tom. 1998. *The Victorian Internet*. New York: Walker.

Stelarc. 1991. 'Prosthetics, Robotics and Remote Existence: Postrevolutionary Strategies' in *Leonardo* 1991, 24:5, 591–595.

Stock, Gregory. 1993. *Metaman: The Merging of Humans and Machines into a Global Superorganism*. New York: Simon & Schuster.

Strugatsky, Boris & Arkady. 1978. *Roadside Picnic*. London: Victor Gollancz.

Talbot Rice, David & Tamara. 1974. *Icons and Their History*. Woodstock: Overlook Press.

Tarkovsky, Andrei. 1986. *Sculpting in Time*. London: The Bodley Head.

Tavinor, Grant. 2009. 'Videogames, Interactivity, and Art' in *Aesthetics Online* http://www.aesthetics-online.org/articles/index.php?articles_id=44

Taylor, T.L. 2006. *Play between Worlds: Exploring Online Game Culture*. Cambridge, MA: MIT Press.

Taylor, T.L. 2007. 'Pushing the Borders: Player Participation and Game Culture' in J. Karaganis (ed.), *Structures of Participation in Digital Culture*. New York: SSRC, 112–130.

Thacker, Eugene. 2004: *Biomedia*. Minneapolis: Minnesota University Press.

Turkle, Sherry. 1995. *Life on the Screen*. New York: Simon & Shuster.

US Government Printing Office. 2008. 'Online Virtual Worlds: Applications and Avatars in a User-Generated Medium. Hearing before the Subcommittee on Telecommunications and the Internet of the Committee on Energy and Commerce House of Representatives', April 1, Serial No. 110-102 (online).

Van Renterghem, Marion. 2015. 'L'antisémitisme impulsif de cinq gars sans problème' in *Le Monde* Feb. 19 http://lemonde.fr/religions/article/2015/02/19/l-antisemitisme-impulsif-de-cinq-gars-sans-probleme_4579692_1653130.html?xtmc= l_antisemitisme_impulsif_de_cinq_ gars_sans_probleme&xtcr=1

Vernadsky, Vladimir. 1945. 'The Biosphere and the Noosphere' in *Scientific American* 33:1, 1–12.

Virilio, Paul. 1997. *Open Sky*. London: Verso.

———. 2000. *La Bombe informatique*. Paris: Galilée.

Volli, Ugo. 1975. 'Pornography and Pornokitsch' in Dorfles, 224–250.

Wainwright, Joel. 2010. 'Nietzsche Contra the Real World' in *ACME: An International E-Journal for Critical Geographies*, 9:1, 21–33.

Waldman, Michael, Sean Nicholson, and Nodir Adilov. 2006. 'Does Television Cause Autism?' *NBER* Working Paper nr. 12632. http://www.nber.org/papers/w12632. Last accessed 2/1/2015.

Wallerstein, Immanuel. 1974-1989. *The Modern World System* (3 Vol.). New York: Academic Press.

———. 1991. *Geopolitics and Geoculture: Essays on the Changing World System*. Cambridge: Cambridge University Press.

———. 1990. 'Culture as the Ideological Battleground of the Modern Word-System', in M. Featherstone (ed.): *Global Culture: Nationalism, Globalization and Modernity*. London: Sage, 31–55.

Warwick, Kevin. 2005. 'The Matrix – Our Future?' in Grau.

Weber, Alfred. 1997 [1946]. *Abschied von der bisherigen Geschichte: Überwindung des Nihilismus? Werke* Vol. 3. Marburg: Metropolis. Engl.: *Farewell to European History or the Conquest of Nihilism.* Westport: Greenwood Press.

Weismann, August. 1892. *Das Keimplasma: eine Theorie der Vererbung*. Jena: Fischer.

Weizenbaum, Joseph. 1976. *Computer Power and Human Reason.* Harmondsworth: Penguin.

Wertheim, Margareth. 1998. 'The Medieval Return of Cyberspace' in John Beckmann, *The Virtual Dimension.* Princeton: Princeton Architectural Press, 46–61.

Whittier Treat, John. 1996. 'Yoshimoto Banana writes home: The Shôjo in Japanese Popular Culture' in J. Whittier Treat (ed.) Contemporary Japan and Popular Culture. Honolulu: Hawaii University Press, 275–308.

Windelband, Wilhelm. 1957. *Lehrbuch der Geschichte der Philosophie*. Tübingen: Mohr. Engl.: *A History of Philosophy*. New York, Harper, 1901.

Winner, Langdon. 2005. 'Resistance is Futile: The Posthuman Condition and its Advocates' in Baillie & Casey, 385–412.

Witt, May Ann Frese. 2007. 'Introduction' to Witt (ed.), *Nietzsche and the Rebirth of the Tragic*. Madison: Farleigh Dickinson University Press.

Wolfe, Cary. 2010. *What is Posthumanism?* Minnesota: University of Massachusets Press.

Wolmark, Jenny. 2002. 'Staying with the Body: Narratives of the Posthuman in Contemporary Science Fiction' in V. Hollinger & J. Gordon, *Edging into the Future: Science Fiction and Contemporary Cultural Transformation*. Philadelphia: University of Pennsylvania Press, 75–89.

Wuthnow, Robert. 1984. *Cultural Analysis: The Work of Peter L. Berger, Mary Douglas, Michel Foucault, and Jürgen Habermas.* London & Boston: Routledge and Kegan Paul.

Yeffeth, Glenn (ed.). 2003. *Taking the Red Pill: Science, Philosophy and Religion in The Matrix.* Dallas: BenBella Books.

Žižek, Slavoj. 1999. 'The Thing from Inner Space: On Tarkovsky' in *Angelaki: Journal of the Theoretical Humanities* 4:2, 221–231.

# Index

www.ingramcontent.com/pod-product-compliance
Lightning Source LLC
LaVergne TN
LVHW020635300926
849161LV00004B/717
*9789042021099*